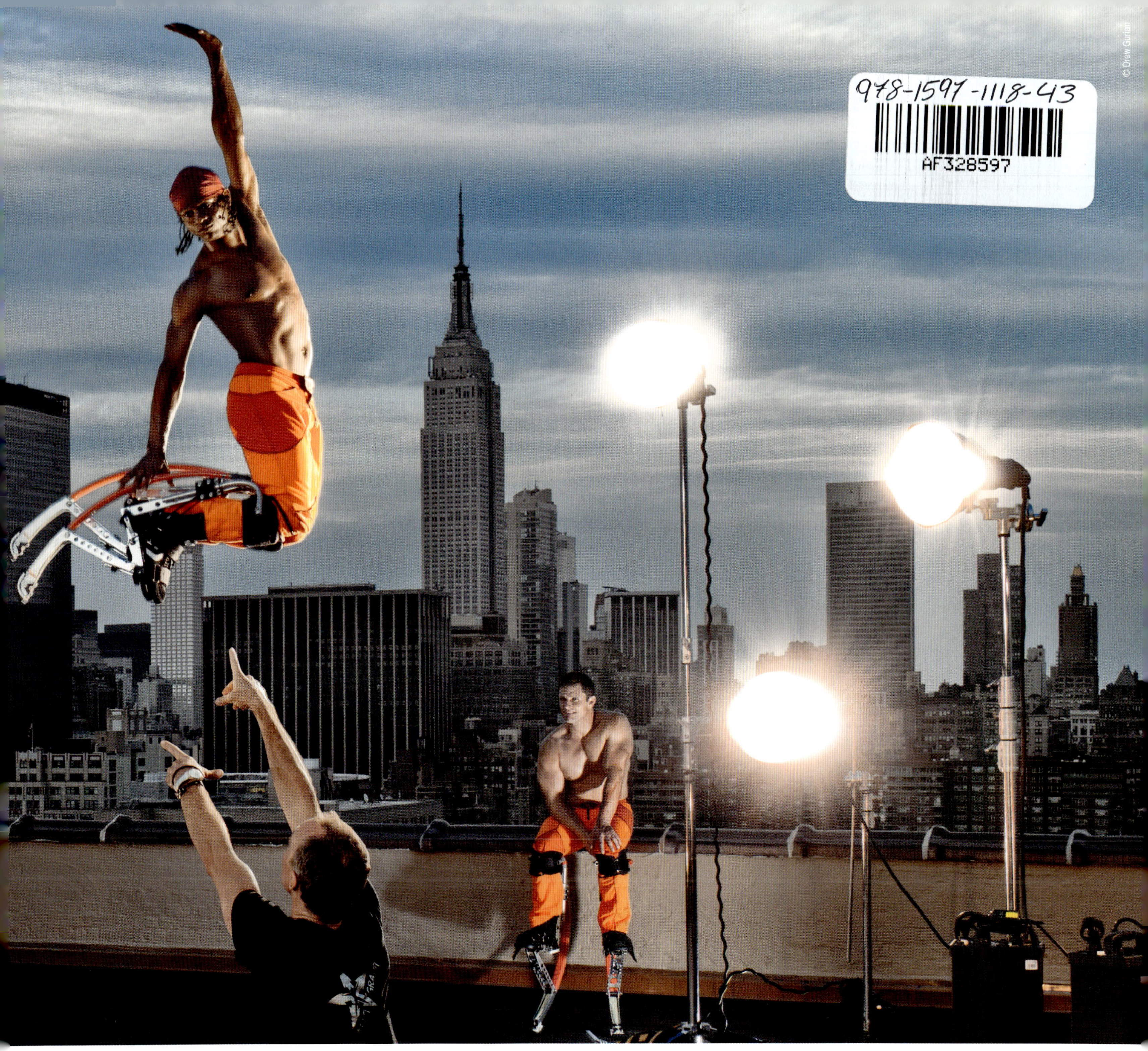

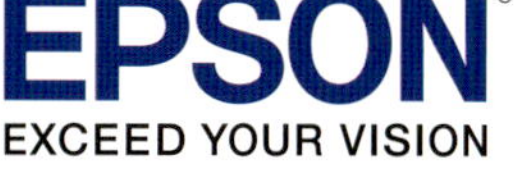

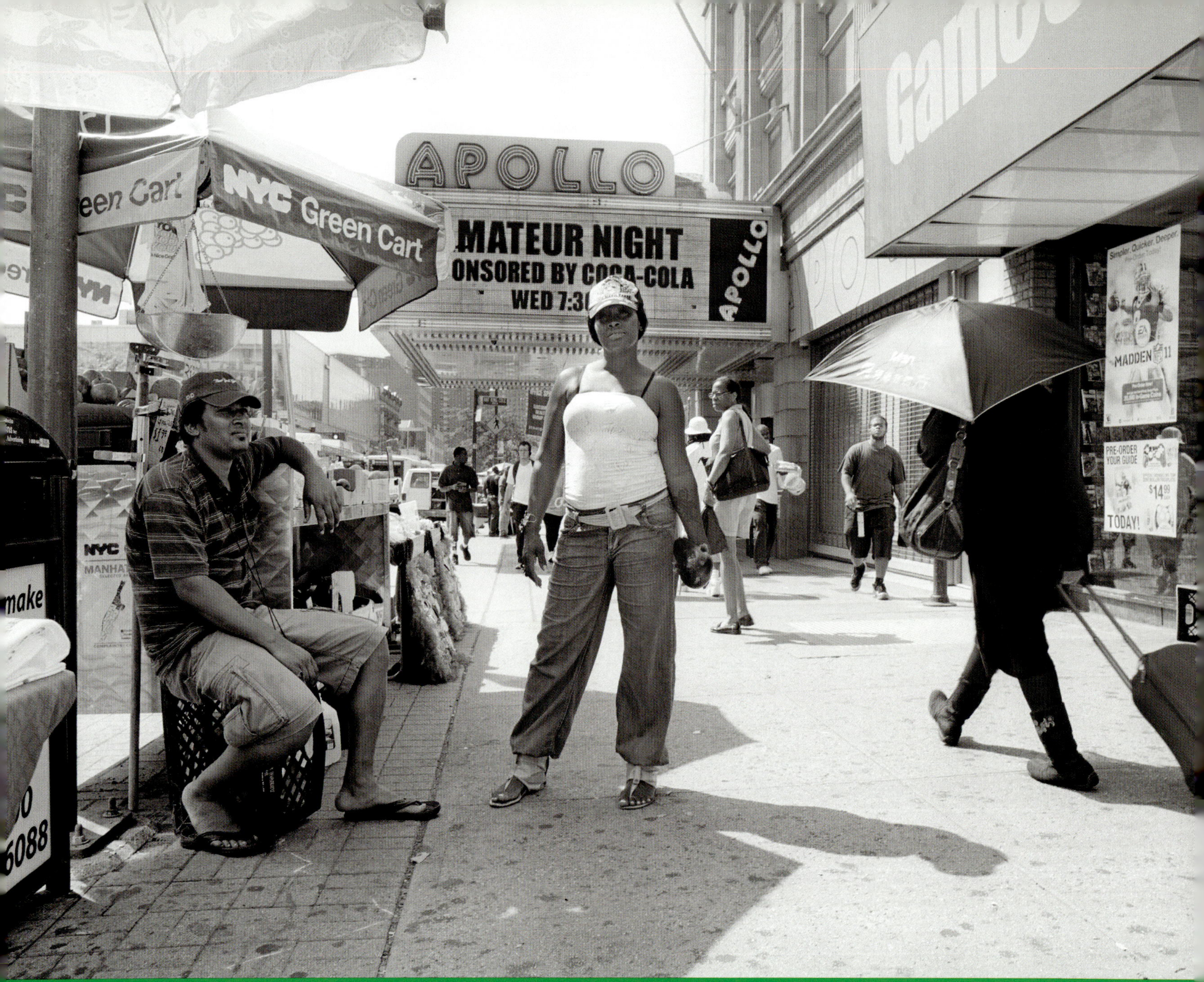

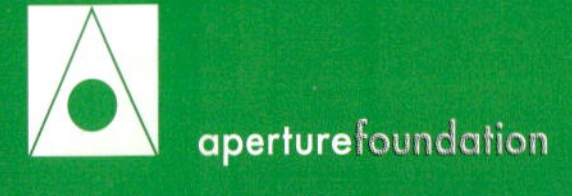
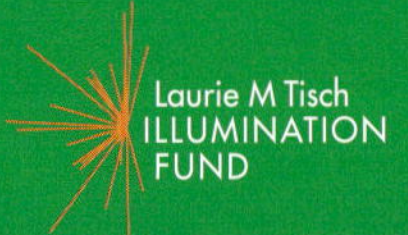

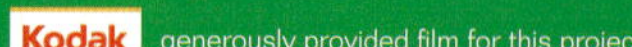

Photographed using Kodak Tri-X 320

West 125th Street

From a Project by LaToya Ruby Frazier for the NYC Green Cart Photography Commission

"I learned that the workers at a Green Cart are not always the owners, that they encounter fierce competition for business with other nearby vendors, and that there are constant worries about health department code violations and fears of harassment from the New York City Police. It's funny how vendors are visible outside on the street, working sunrise to sunset and sometimes twenty-four hours a day, but somehow they remain invisible."

—LaToya Ruby Frazier

The NYC Green Cart Photography Commission

in partnership with the Laurie M. Tisch Illumination Fund and the New York City Department of Health and Mental Hygiene

Learn more by visiting www.aperture.org/greencart.

aperture

Winter 2011 / Issue no. 205

FRONT COVER: Nick Waplington,
Outpost of Givat Hahish, 2009.

© Nick Waplington

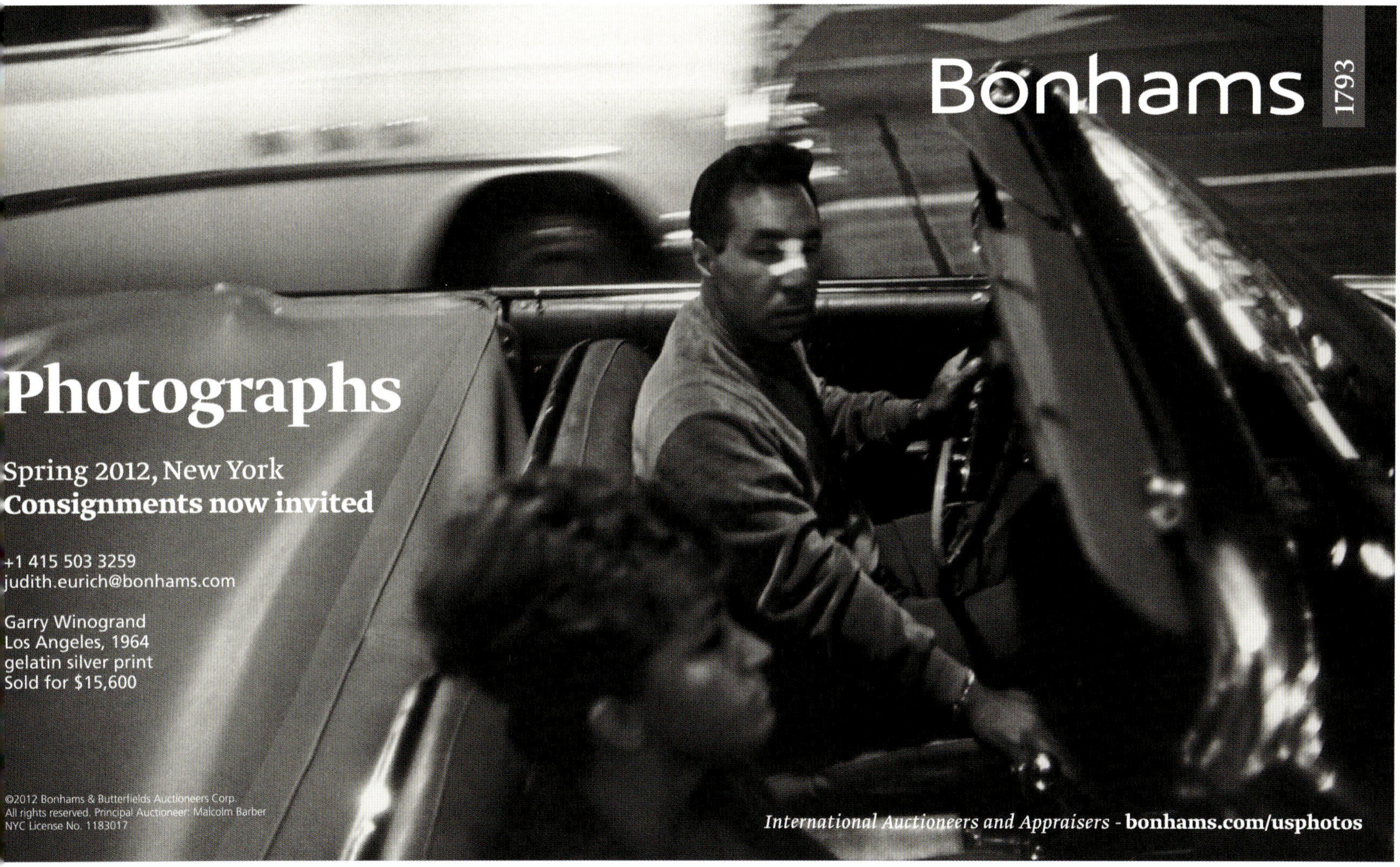

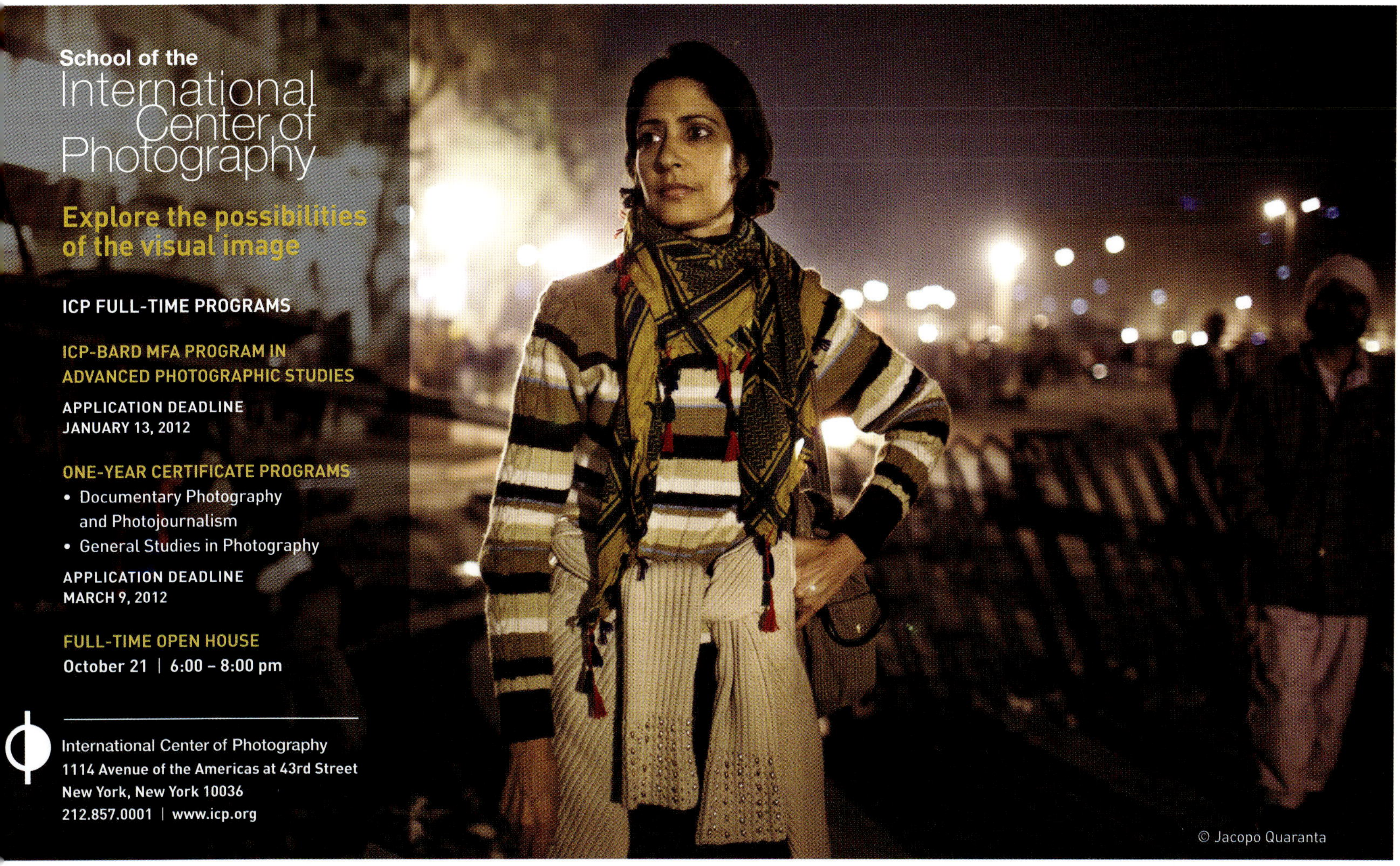

NOTE

Renowned for creating photographs that compress the architectural jumble of the American landscape into tight, sometimes ironic, compositions, Stephen Shore has long been absorbed with questions of structure. With his essay "Form and Pressure" in this issue, Shore examines the dependent relationships among preconception, content, and formal iteration, not only in terms of his own photographs but also as these notions apply to other fields, from painting to theater to science. He describes a photograph's frame as the "image's proscenium," noting that "the frame of the picture forms a line that all the visual elements of the picture relate to."

The conceit of the frame as proscenium may be applied to much of the diverse work in this issue. David Goldblatt and writer Ivan Vladislavić are interviewed here by Johannesburg-based editor and critic Bronwyn Law-Viljoen. Goldblatt, who has documented the fraught social landscape of his native South Africa from the apartheid era to the present, has recently collaborated with Vladislavić on a narrative composed of photographs and a novel—widening the image's proscenium. In these pages, the two artists discuss their working process, precedents for mixing written story and image, and the goal of creating what Vladislavić calls "the uncomfortable fit" between the two.

Vince Aletti considers the work of Bill Cunningham, who in his regular "On the Street" column in the *New York Times* has persistently documented the sartorial flair of New Yorkers for decades. The subject of director Richard Press's recent film *Bill Cunningham New York*, this intriguing, maverick artist appears to view the city's street life as an unfolding theater—and keeps his attention focused sharply on the performers' costumes.

Swedish photographer Julia Peirone's recent series of portraits, published here for the first time, engage the age-old tradition of depicting girls in that liminal space between childhood and adulthood. Peirone's concern is her teenage subjects' complex, disarming, and sometimes hilarious repertoire of gestures, which she addresses in the manner of classic, elegant portraiture.

Sam Falls plays with the notion of photographic form itself, as he merges photography with other media, including painting and video. For Falls, all modes—including publication and exhibition—are of potential use to his copious, intelligent, expressionistically abstracted work. As Lesley Martin writes here, Falls's images "create a joyously undifferentiated shuffle of the seriously theoretical, the unironically pop, and the unapologetically gorgeous."

Longtime *Aperture* contributor Charles Bowden confers with saints and sinners alike—from Augustine and Teresa to seasoned killers working out of Ciudad Juárez—in his search for moral footing in the world. His lyrical text in these pages interacts with photographs by Gregory Crewdson, Julio César Aguilar Fuentes, Luis Mazariegos, and David Wojnarowicz, to make an impassioned call for connection and conscience.

Our features begin with images and notes from Nick Waplington's ongoing project about settlers in Judea and Samaria, also known as the West Bank. Waplington, who has spent extended periods investigating the area since 2008, turns his incisive lens on families and individuals living in this violently contested region and recounts the stories of how they came to be here.

Also in these pages, we inaugurate a new column, "Crowd Sourced," with John Saponara's *Picture Black Friday*—a citizen-journalist project on the mystifying American tradition of the post-Thanksgiving shopping frenzy. And this issue's "Backstory" is a moving personal note to Mary Ellen Mark from Lourdes Sanchez, a woman who was photographed by Mark twenty-five years ago. Finally, in "Mind's Eye," writer Neil LaBute considers Ruth Orkin's classic 1951 photograph *An American Girl in Italy*.

—The Editors

EDITOR-IN-CHIEF Melissa Harris

ART DIRECTOR Yolanda Cuomo

SENIOR EDITOR Diana C. Stoll

DESIGNER Kristi Norgaard

MANAGING EDITOR Michael Famighetti

EDITORIAL AND CIRCULATION COORDINATOR: Paula Kupfer

PRODUCTION MANAGER Matthew Harvey

WORK SCHOLARS Terri Beckles, Andrea Chlad, Javaher Nooryani, Monica Siwiec

....

CONTRIBUTING EDITORS
Vince Aletti, Robert Atwan, Elizabeth H. Berger, Elisabeth Biondi, Fernando Castro, Pieranna Cavalchini, David Frankel, Alice Rose George, Vicki Goldberg, Nan Goldin, David Griffin, Mark Haworth-Booth, John Howell, Alfredo Jaar, Burton Joseph, Thomas Keenan, Sally Mann, Mary Ellen Mark, Carlo McCormick, Susan Meiselas, Richard Misrach, Pablo Ortiz Monasterio, Susan Morgan, Martin Parr, Marianne Petit, Francine Prose, Eugene Richards, Fred Ritchin, Mark Sealy, Clarissa Sligh, Abigail Solomon-Godeau, Carol Squiers, David Levi Strauss, Mariko Takeuchi, Anne Wilkes Tucker, Deborah Willis, Sylvia Wolf, Gu Zheng

PUBLISHER
Dana Triwush
magazine@aperture.org

....

ADVERTISING REPRESENTATIVE
Bill Besch
631-665-0467
bbesch1@verizon.net

....

APERTURE FOUNDATION EXECUTIVE DIRECTOR
Chris Boot

....

Aperture Foundation, Inc., a non-profit organization dedicated to promoting photography in all its forms, publishes *Aperture* at 547 West 27th Street, 4th Floor, New York, NY 10001. To subscribe, visit www.aperture.org; if in the U.S. or Canada, call 866-457-4603.

Visit the Aperture website at www.aperture.org; email letters to the editor at magazine@aperture.org

....

APERTURE FOUNDATION BOARD OF TRUSTEES
Robert Anthoine, Antonia Paepcke DuBrul, Annette Y. Friedland, Barry H. Garfinkel, Celso Gonzalez-Falla, John H. Gutfreund, Cathy Kaplan, Susana Torruella Leval, Joel Meyerowitz, Todd Oldham, Frederick M. R. Smith, Anne Stark, Alan Siegel, D. Severn Taylor, Willard Taylor, Matthew S. Tierney, Rhett L. Turner, Tommaso Zanzotto

....

Michael E. Hoffman, Publisher and Executive Director (1964–2001)

Minor White, Editor (1952–1971)

CONTRIBUTORS

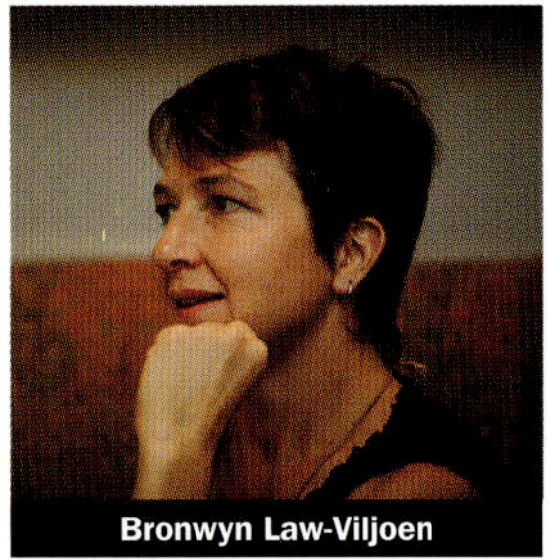
Bronwyn Law-Viljoen

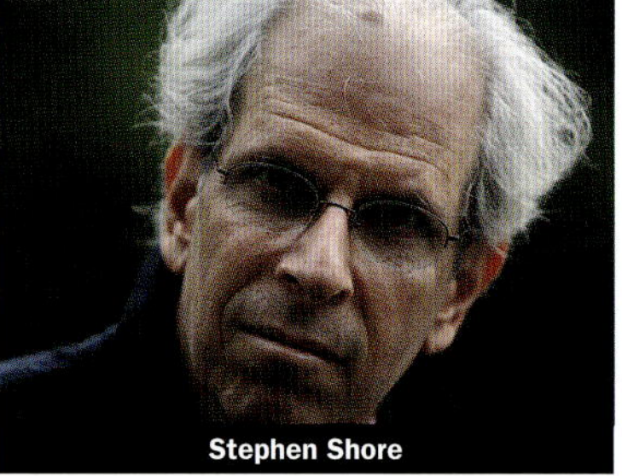
Stephen Shore

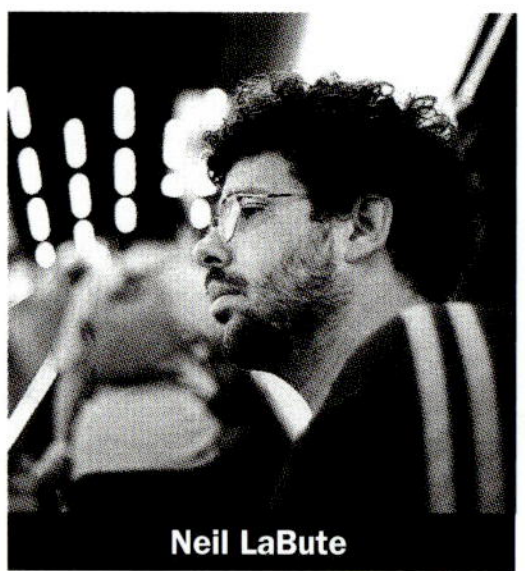
Neil LaBute

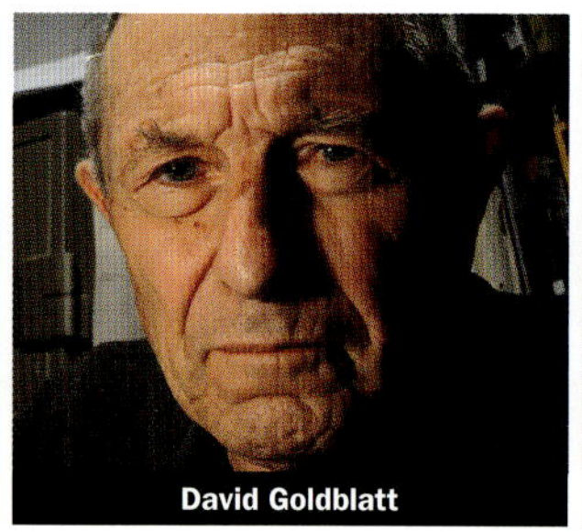
David Goldblatt

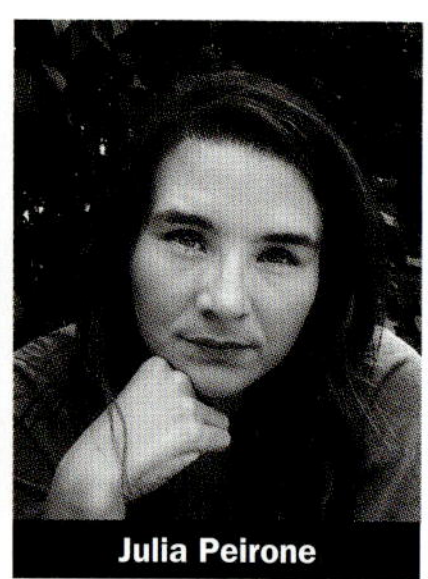
Julia Peirone

VINCE ALETTI reviews photography exhibitions for the "Goings on About Town" section of the *New Yorker* and photography books for *Photograph*. One of the curators of the International Center of Photography's 2009 "Year of Fashion," including the exhibitions *Avedon Fashion: 1944–2000* and *Weird Beauty: Fashion Photography Now*, he returned to ICP for the 2011 exhibition *Harper's Bazaar: A Decade in Style*. He was one of the jurors for the 2011 World Press Photo Awards as well as the new World Pride Photo competition in Amsterdam.

CHARLES BOWDEN lives in Las Cruces, New Mexico. His most recent publication is *Murder City: Ciudad Juárez and the Global Economy's New Killing Fields* (Nation Books, 2010), and he is currently at work on a book titled *Café Blood: Songs from No Man's Land*.

BILL CUNNINGHAM has been photographing the streets of New York City for the *New York Times* since the early 1970s. In 2008 he was awarded the Ordre des Arts et des Lettres by the French Ministry of Culture.

SAM FALLS, originally from San Diego, currently resides in Brooklyn, New York. He has had multiple solo shows and has published many books; the latest is *Paint Paper Palms* (Dashwood Books, 2011).

DAVID GOLDBLATT's recent exhibitions include *Fale le Fale* at the Market Photo Workshop and *TJ: Some Things Old, Some Things New* and *Some Much the Same* at Goodman Gallery (both in Johannesburg); his work was featured at the 2011 Venice Biennale. He is the 2010 Lucie Award Lifetime Achievement Honoree.

NEIL LaBUTE is a writer/director for theater, film, and television. On occasion he writes short stories and nonfiction.

BRONWYN LAW-VILJOEN is the editor and co-director of Fourthwall Books, editor of *Art South Africa* magazine, and senior lecturer in creative writing at the University of the Witwatersrand. She edited photographer Pierre Crocquet de Rosemond's book *Pinky Promise* (Fourthwall and Hatje Cantz, 2011) and is co-curating the related exhibition.

MARY ELLEN MARK's recent exhibitions include *Falkland Road, Indian Circus, and Ward 81* at the Blue Sky Gallery in Portland, Oregon; and *Twins* at the Galleri Magnus Åklundh in Sweden. She is the recipient of numerous awards, including the 2006 Photo Vision Award and the Cornell Capa Award from the International Center of Photography in 2001. Her latest book is *Seen Behind the Scene* (Phaidon, 2008).

LESLEY A. MARTIN is the Publisher of Aperture's books program.

JULIA PEIRONE's work was recently featured in solo shows at Sweden's Galleri Magnus Åklundh and Copenhagen's Peter Lav Gallery. She will have a solo exhibition at Crystal Contemporary Art Gallery, Stockholm, in 2012.

LOURDES SANCHEZ is a mother of three children; she and her family are based in Miami. She was photographed by Mary Ellen Mark in 1986, at the age of six.

JOHN SAPONARA earned a BFA in photography from the School of Visual Arts in New York and subsequently worked for five years as the manager of Joel Meyerowitz's archive. Saponara is currently collaborating on a new digital-photography company, SmoochNYC. He initiated the *Picture Black Friday* project in 2009.

STEPHEN SHORE has had solo exhibitions at the Museum of Modern Art, the Metropolitan Museum of Art, and the International Center of Photography, all in New York; the Art Institute of Chicago; and the Jeu de Paume in Paris. The most recent book of his photographs is *The Hudson Valley* (Blind Spot, 2011). His book *The Nature of Photographs* (Phaidon, 2007) is about the formal attributes of photography. Since 1982 he has been the director of the Photography Program at Bard College, where he is the Susan Weber Professor in the Arts.

IVAN VLADISLAVIĆ is the author of the novels *The Folly* (Serif, 1993), *The Restless Supermarket* (David Philip, 2001), and *The Exploded View* (Random House, 2004); his 2010 book *Double Negative* was initially published as a collaborative project with David Goldblatt's *TJ*. Vladislavić's work has won many awards, including the *Sunday Times* Fiction Prize and the Alan Paton Award for nonfiction.

Over the past twenty years, British artist **NICK WAPLINGTON** has exhibited globally and published several photographic books, including *Double Dactyl* (Trolley, 2008), a project that was also exhibited at the Whitechapel Art Gallery, London. At present he is working on a sculpture project with Jewish and Palestinian residents of the West Bank. Waplington lives in New York.

TO SUBSCRIBE

Aperture (ISSN 0003-6420) is published quarterly, in spring, summer, fall, and winter, at 547 West 27th Street, 4th Floor, New York, New York, 10001. In the United States: a one-year subscription (four issues) is $40; a two-year subscription (eight issues) is $66. In Canada: a one-year subscription is $65. All other international subscriptions are $70 per year. Visit www.aperture.org to subscribe. Single copies may be purchased at $18.50 for most issues. Periodicals postage is paid at New York and additional offices. Postmaster: Send address changes to *Aperture*, P.O. Box 3000, Denville, NJ 07834. Address queries regarding subscriptions, renewals, or gifts to: *Aperture* Subscription Service, 1-866-457-4603 (U.S. and Canada) or email custsvc_aperture@fulcoinc.com. Newsstand distribution in the U.S. handled by Curtis Circulation Company, 1-201-634-7400. For international distribution, contact Central Books.

Editorial contributions must be accompanied by return postage and will be handled with reasonable care; however, the publisher assumes no responsibility for return or safety of unsolicited artwork, photographs, book maquettes, or manuscripts. When photographs or art submissions are requested by the publisher, any value for which *Aperture* could be liable must be agreed upon in writing in advance of delivery. If no agreement in writing is in effect, *Aperture* will not accept responsibility for the care or safety of material in its possession.

The Aperture Foundation's nonprofit status provides it with the independence and integrity fundamental to its efforts to publish, without compromise, the most significant work in photography. Individuals who wish to help maintain this vital force in photography may become Benefactors ($2,500), Patrons ($1,000), Sponsors ($500), Fellows ($250), Associates ($150), and Friends ($75). Gifts are tax-deductible to the full extent of the law. They also may join Aperture's Patron Membership Program at the following levels: Art Circle ($1,000), Art Net ($2,500), and Art Council ($5,000). For more information about this membership program, please visit www.aperture.org/patron or contact the Development department at 1-212-946-7108.

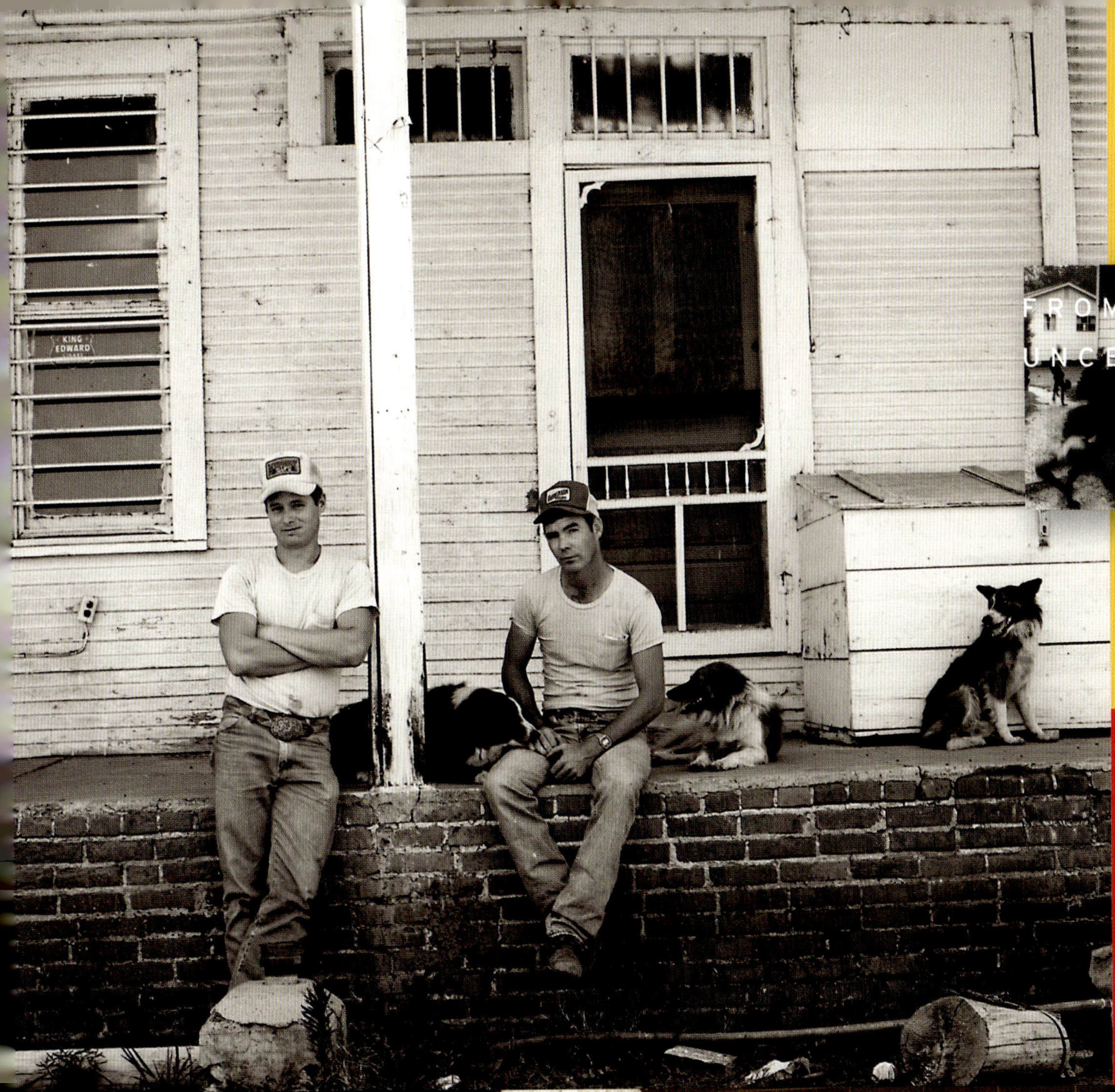

From Uncertain to Blue

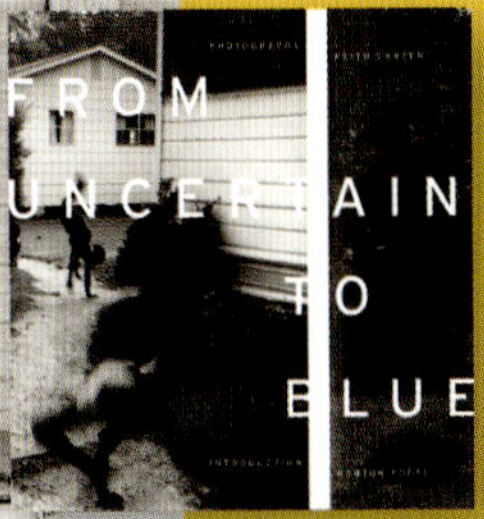

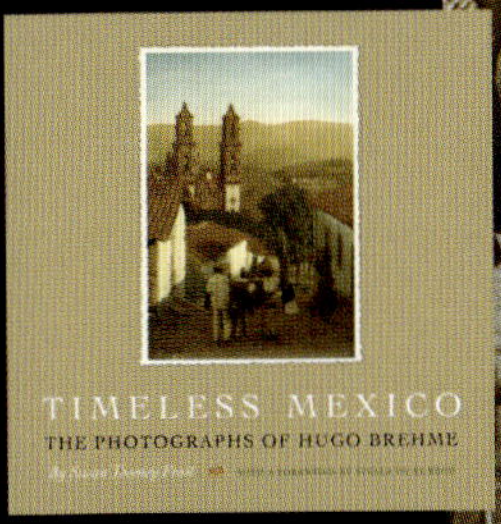

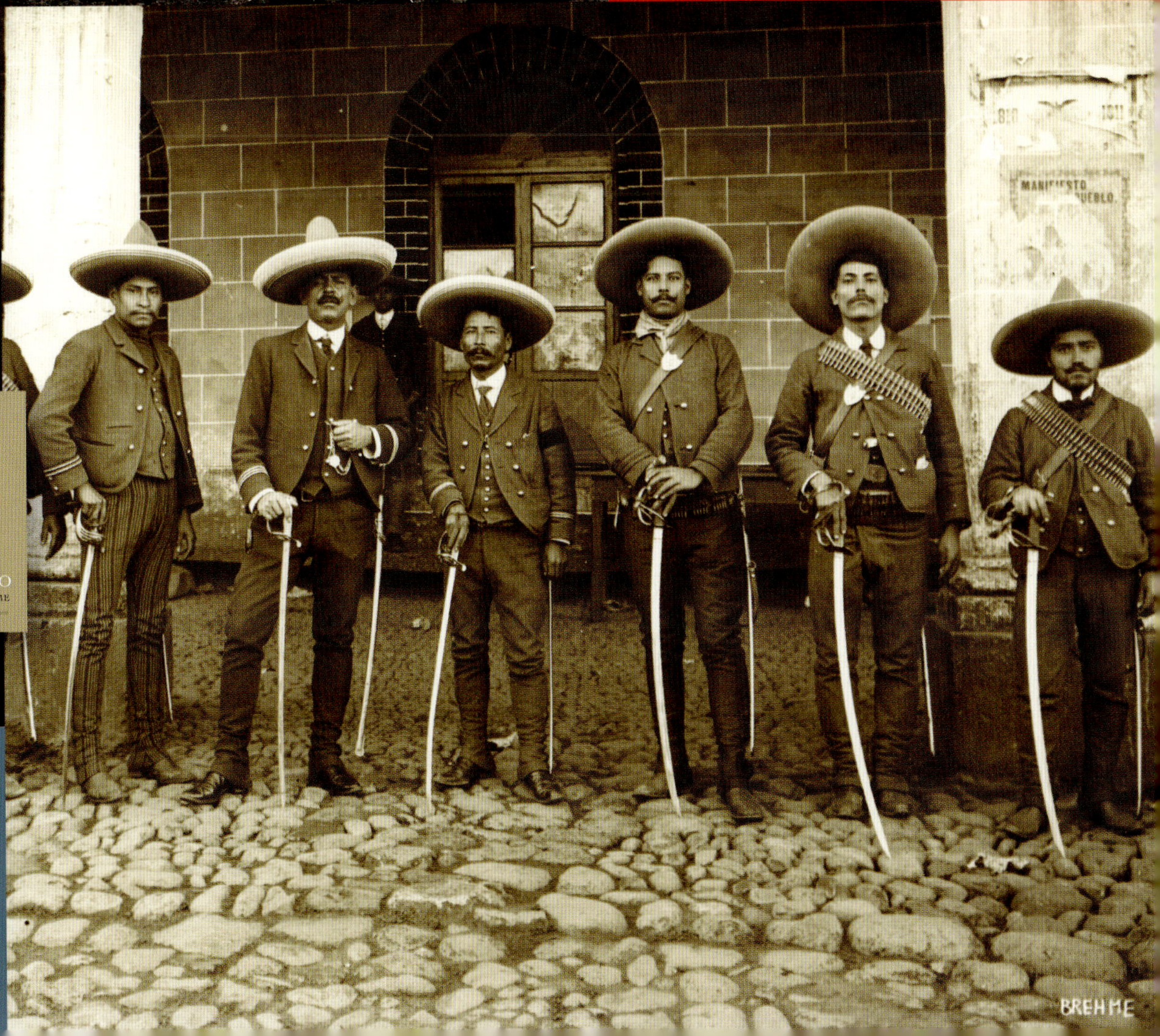

TARYN SIMON

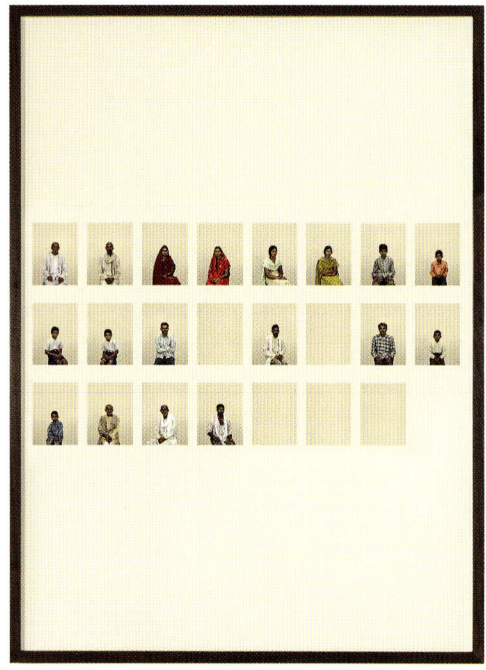

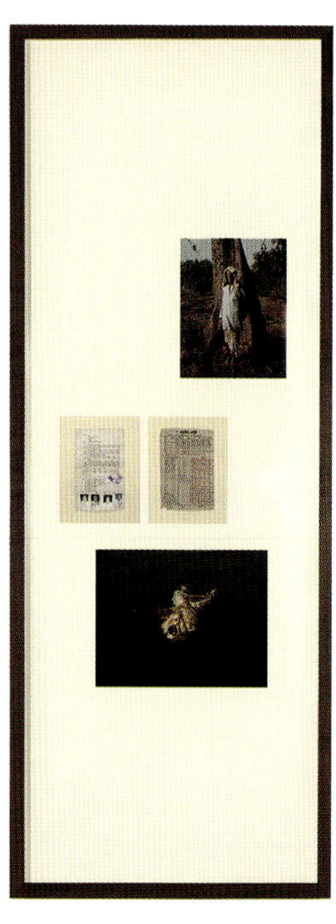

and accompanied by an 864-page monograph published by MACK—Simon adopts a heightened, evidentiary version of Evans's "straight" documentary style, and at the same time entirely undermines it (in the manner of Agee) by blatantly overemphasizing the strictures, structures, and open-endedness of the systems within which such "evidence," in the form of both text and image, operates.

The project delves into eighteen bloodlines around the world and their related stories—albinos in Tanzania; victims of genocide in Bosnia; descendents of an Igorot tribesman exhibited at the 1904 St. Louis World's Fair (showcasing America's acquisition of the Philippines); a family selected by China's State Council Information Office to "represent China"; a family in India, alive but officially declared dead as part of a land-grab by distant relatives; and so on. Each bloodline is presented as a chapter in the form of a triptych: a grid of portraits on the left, a series of captions and texts in the middle, and on the right a collection of what Geoffrey Batchen refers to in his accompanying essay as "supplementary images."

The portraits follow a complex and precise order that delineates the given bloodlines. They are shot in the manner of conventional identity photographs—bare backgrounds, expressionless, straight-on—the images' "objectivity" so weighted that apart from the basic physical features and fashions of each subject, individual identity is practically erased; these are still-lifes more than portraits. In fact, the most striking images in each grid are those that are empty, the blank wall testifying to the absence of members of each bloodline due to disappearance, imprisonment, disease, fear of kidnapping, missing visas, refusal to participate, or in the case of many women, the lack of their family's permission to be photographed due to "social and religious reasons."

Of course, this information is not proffered by the photographic grids alone. The texts in the central panels of Simon's triptychs

The notion that the pursuit to encapsulate and convey objective "truth" via documentation—in particular through text, image, or a combination of the two—is inevitably contrived and doomed to failure is certainly not a new one. In 1936 James Agee and Walker Evans received an assignment from *Fortune* magazine to investigate conditions among sharecropping communities in the American South by reporting on the life of one family. The project (famously rejected by *Fortune* but published in book form five years later as *Let Us Now Praise Famous Men: Three Tenant Families*) led Agee to question the honesty of journalism altogether, castigating its false neutrality and its underlying brutality as a context. "It seems to me curious, not to say obscene and thoroughly terrifying," he writes in the book's preamble, "that it could occur to an association of human beings . . . to pry intimately into the lives of an undefended . . . ignorant and helpless rural family, for the purpose of parading [their] nakedness, disadvantage and humiliation . . . in the name of science, of 'honest journalism' (whatever that paradox may mean)."

In the foreword to her 2003 project *The Innocents*, Taryn Simon echoes Agee's concerns regarding the manipulability of documentation, as well his fear of the imposing nature of context. "Photography's ability to blur truth and fiction is one of its most compelling qualities," she says. "But when misused . . . this ambiguity can have severe, even lethal consequences. . . . Photography's ambiguity, beautiful in one context, can be devastating in another." In her most recent body of work, *A Living Man Declared Dead and Other Chapters: I–XVIII*—on view at London's Tate Modern

identify each subject by name, age, location, and so on, and tell the stories of each bloodline. These are presented in an authoritative and seemingly neutral tone—that of "non-fiction," of "respectable journalism"—a familiar voice that we have been conditioned to trust but that nevertheless, as Agee pointed out long ago, is by no means impartial or entirely trustworthy.

It is in the third panels, the "supplementary images," where the bloodlines' stories take full form. In Chapter I this consists of a location-portrait of one of the living men declared dead; two legal documents—one officially certifying life (through photographs and fingerprints), the other, death (through government letterhead); and an image of an anonymous corpse floating in the Ganges. In Chapter XV (the Chinese state's "representative" family) it contains a cityscape—the China Central Television Tower looming over the Beijing skyline—and a photograph of a gift bag given to Simon by the Chinese government. Such images, ephemera collected while investigating these stories, are coolly photographed but borrow more from Evans's documentary style than from the document. Hinting at both ambiguity and ephemerality—of lineage, identity, truth, fact, and evidence—these endnotes imbue the work with visual accessibility and narrative, and simultaneously reveal the quiet yet commanding role that authorship plays throughout.

In a 1997 interview, the writer David Foster Wallace—famed for using endnotes that practically overrun his primary texts—stated: "It seems to me that reality is fractured right now. . . . The difficulty in writing about that reality is that text is very linear and very unified, and I am constantly on the lookout for ways to fracture the text that aren't totally disorienting. . . . There's got to

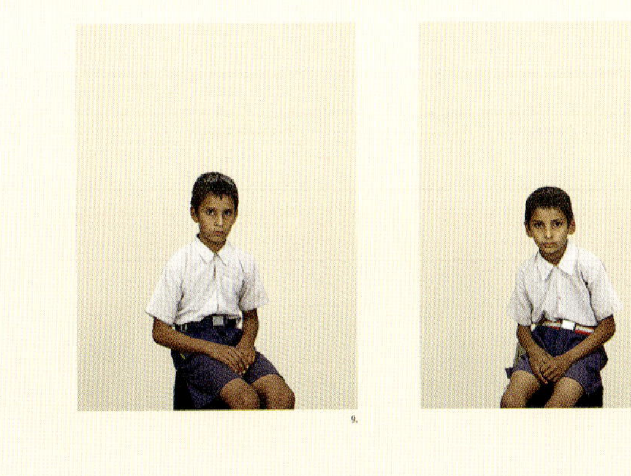

be some interplay between how difficult you make it for the reader, and how seductive it is for the reader if they are willing to do it. The endnotes [. . . are] a useful compromise." Simon's *A Living Man Declared Dead and Other Chapters* engages with similarly fractured realities, and explores how notions of history, truth, and identity are (mis)represented and (mis)understood within such realities. By contrasting her wholly "evidentiary" images and texts with surreptitiously powerful photographic endnotes, she undermines the ambiguity of the photographic medium and at the same time harnesses it to convey meaning, narrative, and purpose from the edges of the subject at hand.◉

—Aaron Schuman

Taryn Simon's A Living Man Declared Dead and Other Chapters: I–XVIII *was presented at Tate Modern, London, May 25–November 6, 2011. The series is also on view at Berlin's Neue Nationalgalerie, September 21, 2011–January 1, 2012; it will have its American premiere at the Museum of Modern Art, New York (exhibition curated by Roxana Marcoci), opening May 22, 2012.*

Aaron Schuman is an American photographer, writer, editor and curator. He is also a senior lecturer at University of Brighton and the Arts University College at Bournemouth, and is the founder and editor of the online photography journal *SeeSaw Magazine*.

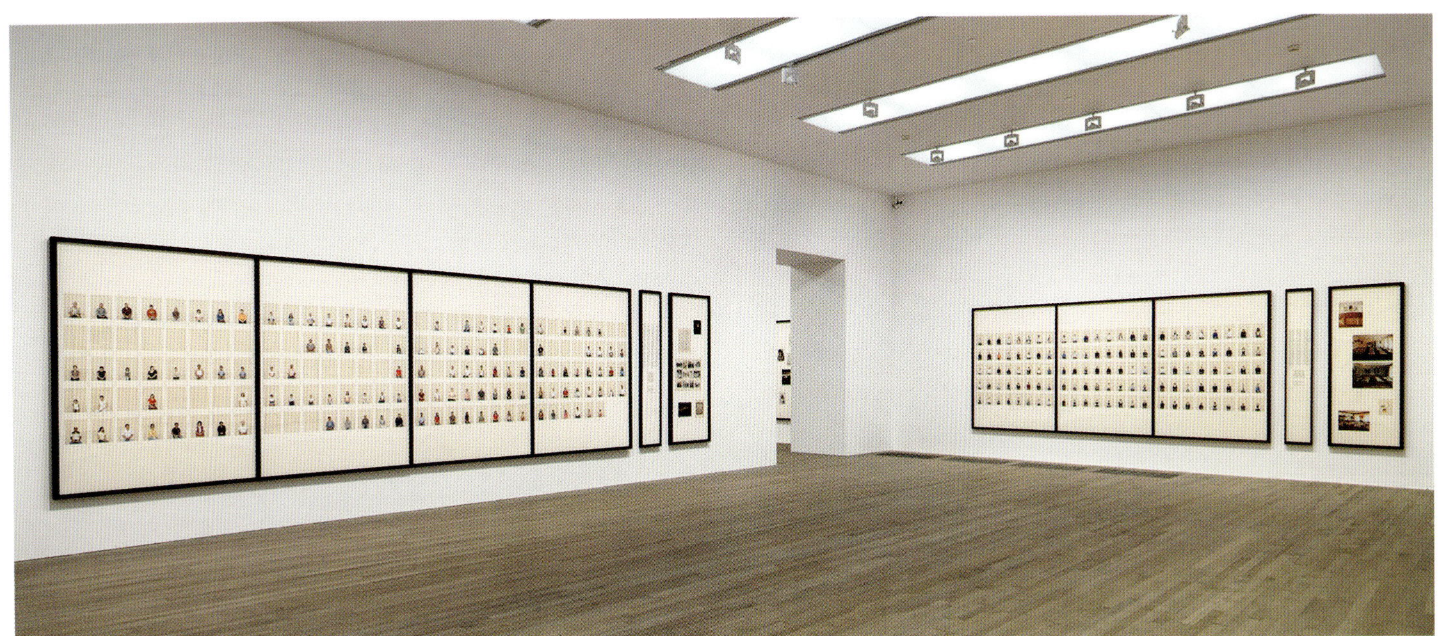

CONTEMPORARY SOUTH AFRICAN PHOTOGRAPHY

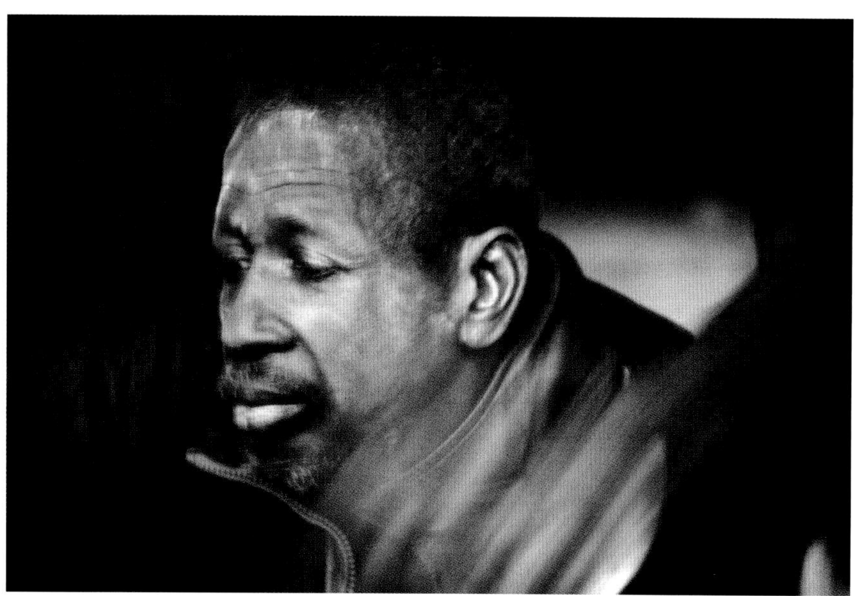

Contemporary photographic practice in South Africa seems to bear the weight of the world on its shoulders. Entrenched in a history of ethnographic colonial classification, photojournalistic reportage of atrocities under apartheid, and recently sophisticated documentary work, the field of image making is unavoidably politicized—its objective, to show and to tell. This history is not necessarily exclusive to South Africa, however, and in the exhibition *Figures and Fictions: Contemporary South African Photography*, at London's Victoria and Albert Museum, curator Tamar Garb attempts to unburden the seventeen projects on display from the pathologies of indigenous figurations of particularly charged local sites.

Along the exhibition's aubergine walls, established names such as Zwelethu Mthethwa and Jo Ractliffe converse with a newer generation of practitioners, Roelof Petrus Van Wyk and the brothers Hasan and Husain Essop. This collection of work has been produced over the past decade, in what might be called the post-post-apartheid period—a moment suspended, as Garb puts it, "between what has been and what is imagined to be coming." It is a kind of unbearable lightness (not to be confused with superficiality) that allows for a return from the depth of field to the speculation and subjectivity of a new photographic politics—a politics of shadows and surfaces.

One group of works, located at the heart of the exhibition, put this surface tension to work, challenging the holy cows of identity politics and representation. Set amid the leafy-green idyll of suburban Johannesburg dwellings, Mikhael Subotzky's large-scale *Wendy*

Santu Mofokeng, *Ishmael after Washing with Holy Ash at Motouleng Cave*, 2004. From the series *Chasing Shadows*, 2000–2006.

House images (from his 2008 series *Security*) layer a benign mise-en-scène onto a brooding paranoia—signaled by the leitmotifs of security structures and guards. His keen aesthetic unsettles the dramatic scruples of the social-documentary grids within which his work operates.

A wall cuts through the exhibition space, separating Subotzky's series from the work of Sabelo Mlangeni, reproducing an ironically fragile but very real urban border that must be traversed every day between suburbs and townships. Drawing on and updating the mobile yet fiercely accurate stylings of Ernest Cole, Mlangeni's *Men Only* (2008–9) offers the backstory of those same security guards and other itinerant laborers populating hostels set up by the apartheid government for mineworkers migrating from the former rural Bantustans. In jarring contrast, Mlangeni's *Country Girls* (2009) presents the fashions and the private and public lives of black gay men in the province of Mpumalanga. The closeness of Mlangeni's surveillance results in an imaging of insecurity: his portrayals are complicit with his subjects. No less telling, the juxtapositions and crossovers of the two series results in a double-vision that ultimately destabilizes the coherence and veracity promised by the "visual platforms" designated by this show.

It is not an "antidocument" but rather a blindsiding of the nature of the document itself that completes this particular prism of the exhibition. Santu Mofokeng's deeply personal, haunting *Chasing Shadows* (2000–2006) casts the ritual healing ceremony of his HIV-positive brother, Ishmael, into the Motouleng caves in South Africa's Eastern Free State, with exquisite gelatine-silver prints. This spiritual shading of a devastating sociopolitical crisis is suspended in a haze of almost invisible ash lingering along the surface of the image—the image *Ishmael after Washing with Holy Ash at Motouleng Cave* (2004) obscures the gaze of the sitter as well as our own. With eyes wide shut, Mofokeng's tender portrait restores a refreshing limitation on the possibilities of photographic representation. It is configured, it is fictive, it is a surface under pressure.⊙

—Clare Butcher

Figures and Fictions: Contemporary South African Photography *was presented at the Victoria and Albert Museum, London, April 8–July 31, 2011.*

Clare Butcher is a curator and fellow researcher with the Centre for Curating the Archive at the University of Cape Town, South Africa.

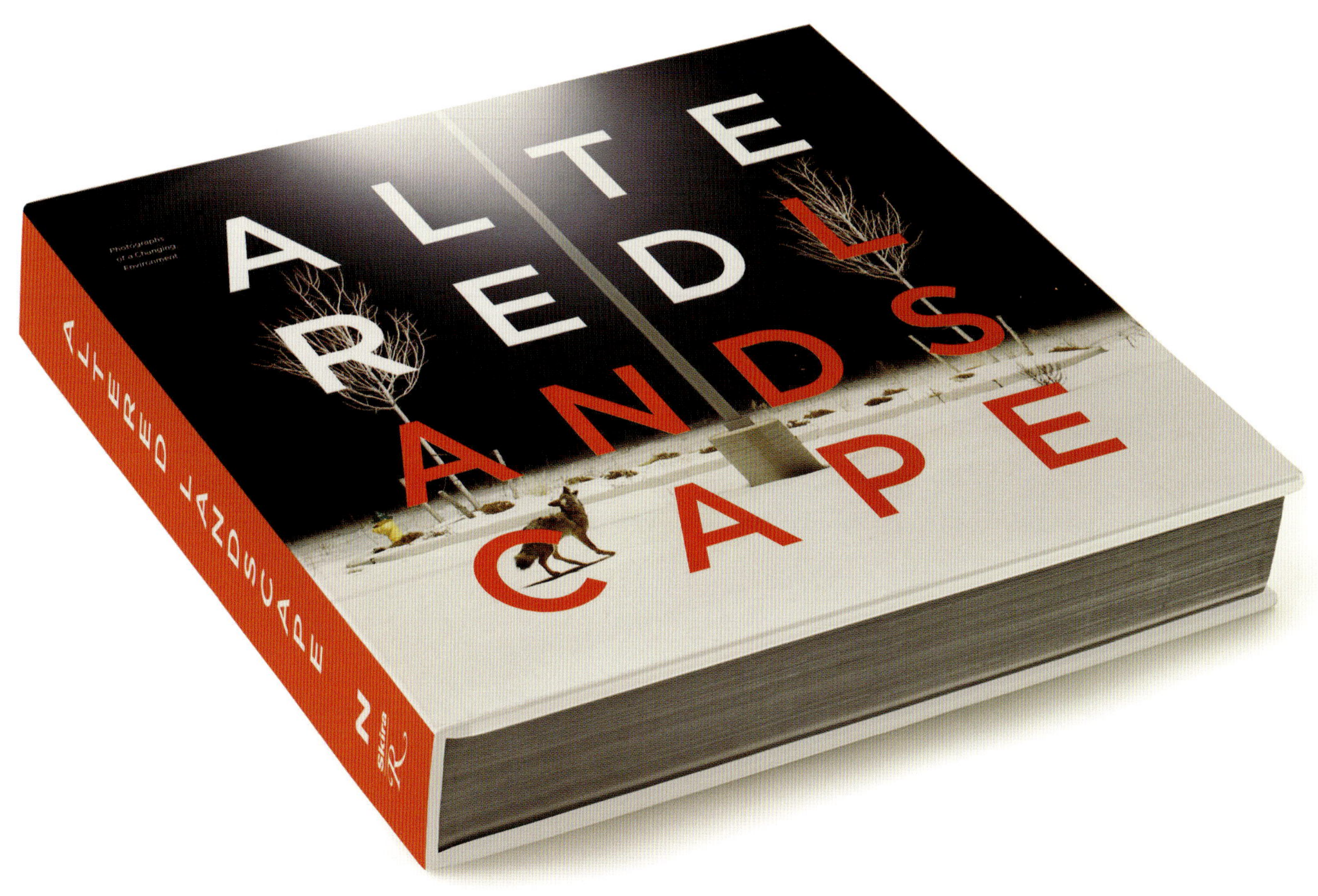

A comprehensive, deluxe volume of essays and photographs from the signature collection of the Nevada Museum of Art, showcasing recent and emerging trends in the field of landscape photography.

This book accompanies a major exhibition presented at the Museum September 24, 2011 to January 8, 2012.

288 pages, 150 color & black/white photographs

Available now at
nevadaart.org/shop/store

Published by
Skira Rizzoli New York

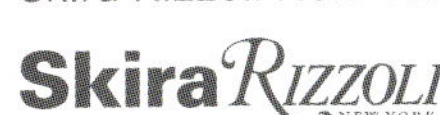

ANSEL ADAMS
ROBERT ADAMS
STUART ALLEN
LEWIS BALTZ
SUBHANKAR BANERJEE
OLIVO BARBIERI
VIRGINIA BEAHAN
BERND AND HILLA BECHER
OLAF OTTO BECKER
PETER BIALOBRZESKI
BARBARA BOSWORTH
MARILYN BRIDGES
DREX BROOKS
JEFF BROUWS
LAURIE BROWN
DEAN BURTON
EDWARD BURTYNSKY
FANDRA CHANG
WILLIAM CHRISTENBERRY
STÉPHANE COUTURIER
DAWN-STARR CROWTHER
ROBERT DAWSON
PETER DE LORY

JEAN DE POMEREU
JOE DEAL
JOHN DIVOLA
WILLIAM EGGLESTON
MITCH EPSTEIN
TERRY EVANS
TERRY FALKE
J. BENNETT FITTS
GEOFFREY FRICKER
LEE FRIEDLANDER
FRANK GOHLKE
PETER GOIN
ANDY GOLDSWORTHY
EMMET GOWIN
WANDA HAMMERBECK
TIMOTHY HEARSUM
RODERIK HENDERSON
TODD HIDO
AVI HOLTZMAN
CHRISTIAN HOUGE
LEN JENSHEL
EIRIK JOHNSON
STEPHEN JONASSEN

CHRIS JORDAN
SANT KHALSA
MARK KLETT
SHAI KREMER
DARIUS KUZMICKAS
MICHAEL LIGHT
GREG MAC GREGOR
DAVID MAISEL
MASLEN & MEHRA
LAURA MCPHEE
RICHARD MISRACH
REINHART MLINERITSCH
KARIN APOLLONIA MÜLLER
JOAN MYERS
PATRICK NAGATANI
PIPO NGUYEN-DUY
OTOBONG NKANGA
ANNE NOBLE
CATHERINE OPIE
TED ORLAND
ERIC PADDOCK
TREVOR PAGLEN
RONDAL PARTRIDGE

JOHN PFAHL
LISA M. ROBINSON
EDWARD RUSCHA
MARK RUWEDEL
VICTORIA SAMBUNARIS
JIM SANBORN
TOSHIO SHIBATA
AMY STEIN
SHARON STEWART
KIM STRINGFELLOW
MARTIN STUPICH
JAMES TURRELL
MICHELLE VAN PARYS
ROBERT VOIT
WOLFGANG VOLZ
CATHERINE WAGNER
WIM WENDERS
HENRY WESSEL
EDWARD WESTON
MICHAEL WOLF
YANG YONGLIANG
AMIR ZAKI
R. M. ZOMORRODINIA

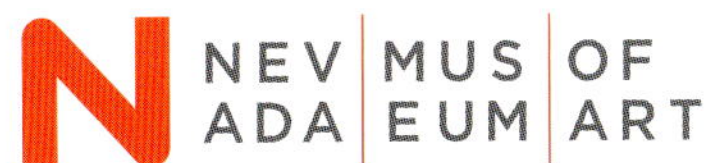

NEV MUS OF
ADA EUM ART

Donald W. Reynolds Center for the Visual Arts
E. L. Wiegand Gallery

160 W. Liberty Street, Reno, Nevada
775.329.3333 | nevadaart.org

Major Sponsor Carol Franc Buck Foundation **Sponsors** National Endowment for the Arts, Andy Warhol Foundation for the Visual Arts **Generous Supporters** Wilhelm and Elke Hoppe Living Trust, The Robert Mapplethorpe Foundation, Atlantis Casino Resort and Spa, Daniel Greenberg & Susan Steinhauser, Stremmel Gallery, Maureen Mullarkey, Kathie Bartlett **Additional Support** Cultural Services of the French Embassy, New York, The Institute of Museum and Library Services (IMLS), Western States Arts Federation (WESTAF) with the Nevada Arts Council, National Endowment for the Arts

REVERSAL

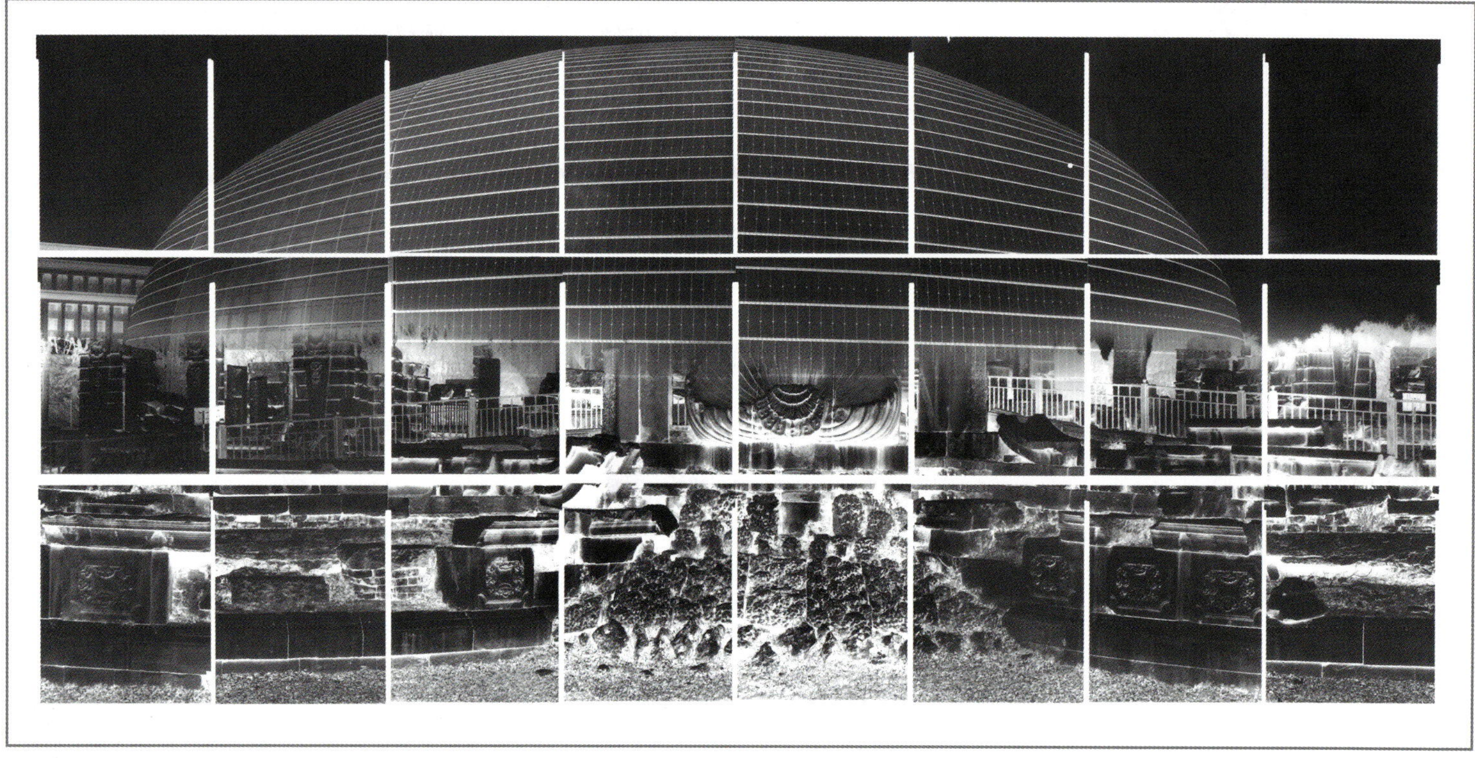

This series applied Cheng's original artistic skills: shot by 8X10 camera; the silver salt paper replacing traditional
paper replacing traditional
direct exposure filming; multi-point shooting as well as the negative mosaic image.
This is the sole piece of artistic work of him in this style, is thus unreplicable.
It makes Cheng the path founder in China's history of photography.

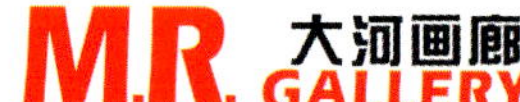

M.R. Gallery,798 Art District,No.2 Jiuxianqiao Lu,Chaoyang District, BeiJing
TEL: +86 10 59789058   mr@mrgallery.com.cn   www.mrgallery.com.cn

Announcing the

2011 Tierney Fellows

Kristoffer Axén

Nicholas Calcott

Luo Dan

Ishaan Dixit

Gabrielle Goliath

Emily Kinni

Bryan Krueger

Carlos Licon

Mack Michael Magagane

Bruno Ruiz

Rubi Rose Siblo-Landsman

Roberto Tondopó

Aubrey Tseleng

Terttu Uibopuu

Past Fellows

Thomas Bangsted • Rachel Barrett • Canon Bernaldez • Lea Bertucci • Vincent Bezuidenhout • Michele Borzoni • Francki Burger • Francesca Cao • Andrew Carlson • Samantha Contis • Pradeep Dalal • Paola Davila • Suruchi Dumpawar • Rian Dundon • Max Dworkin • Tracy Dyan Edser • Marten Elder • Lisa Elmaleh • Samuel Falls • Miguel Fernandez • Ayala Gazit • David Gilbert • Adela Goldbard • Kate Greene • Aldo Guerra • Fermín Guzmán Martínez • Andrew Hardman • Lizzie Leigh Horan • Simangele Kalisa • Alfredo Karam • Matthew Kime • Katie Kingma • Ray Klimek • Gabriela León • Joshua Lutz • Julie Mack • Colin Montgomery • Nandini Muthiah • Elisabeth Oppenheimer • Juan Orrantia • Monique Pelser • Jiang Pengyi • Sasha Phyars-Burgess • Ariane Questiaux • Ernesto Ramirez • Nicole Ranucci • Rahul Sujatha Ravindran • Thabiso Michael Sekgala • Elizabeth Stamplis • Will Steacy • Elaine Stocki • Kate Stone • Motohiro Takeda • Cory Treadway • Devon Ward • Robert Watermeyer • Grant Willing • Huang Xiaoliang • Suyeon Yun

www.tierneyfellowship.org

AI WEIWEI: INTERLACING

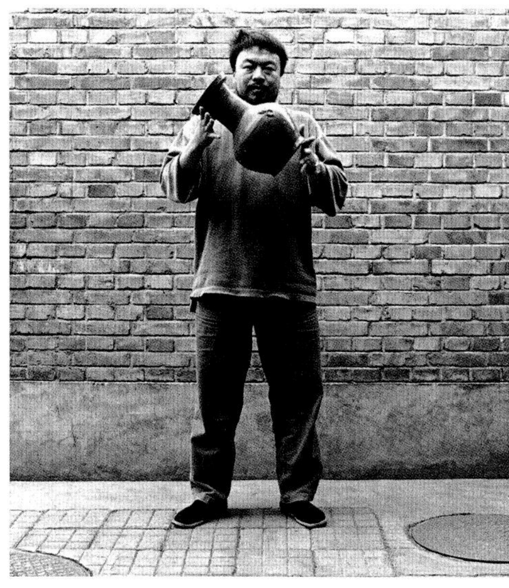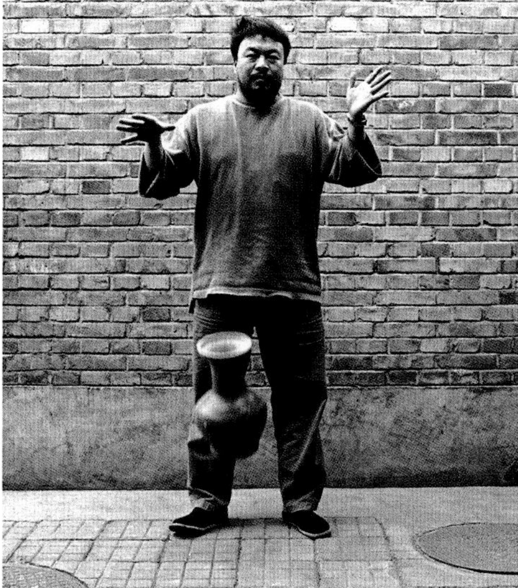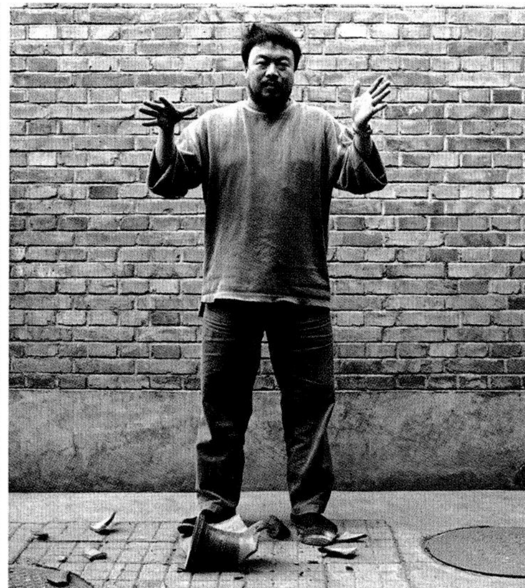

The insistent question "Where is Ai Weiwei?" was ubiquitous during the Chinese artist's recent disappearance and detention. Yet behind this question, urgent as it was, hovered another query: *Who* exactly is Ai Weiwei, the artist that the Chinese government considers so dangerous? Ai's rise in the art world during the past few years has been meteoric, yet he has remained strangely elusive, not least because of the breadth and hyperactive pace of his work—as an artist, architect, designer, blogger, activist, and iconic media figure.

In its recent show, Fotomuseum Winterthur focused on yet another facet of this artist's work: photography. Conceived in close collaboration with Ai, the exhibition had to be installed in his absence, but the disappeared artist, visible in many photographs, haunted the show like a spectral presence. The exhibition made it clear that photography is not just another aspect of Ai's sprawling œuvre; rather, it is a thread that seems to tie it all together, intersecting as it does with all his work's many areas. Consequently, the show and the exhaustive accompanying catalog (published by Steidl) allow the viewer a comprehensive overview of Ai's artistic and activist practices, as well as of his personal life.

Ai was born in 1954, the son of poet Ai Qing, who was at the time banished to the remotest northeast China by Mao Zedong for "revisionist thought." The young artist studied at Beijing Film Academy, and then in 1983 moved to New York, where he briefly studied with painter Sean Scully at Parsons. After dropping out of school, Ai spent time in the East Village "aimlessly hanging around with friends," as he says. Most importantly, he discovered the work of Marcel Duchamp. "After Duchamp, I realized that being an artist is more about a lifestyle and attitude than producing some product. A way of looking at things," he later declared. Ai produced

his own readymades and, most importantly, took more than ten thousand black-and-white photographs, which he developed only upon his return to Beijing in 1993. They show a group of Chinese expatriate artists, hanging out on the fringes of the East Village art scene, living the bohemian myth. Another series of images focuses on the poet and occasional photographer Allen Ginsberg, whose images of his Beat friends seems to be echoed formally in Ai's New York photographs: composed with casual precision, printed with black frames or as film strips, and with handwritten captions at the bottom.

Time and again throughout his work, Ai has photographed himself, consistently relating this self-documentation back to his persona. But in the late 1980s and early '90s Ai's focus began to shift from his personal environment to public spaces. He documented the Tompkins Square Park riots of 1988 and incidents of police brutality on New York streets. The city is shown as a battleground of opposing forces—government versus inhabitants—that have a claim on its territory. Ai would later return to this topic in his documentation of the rapidly changing urban landscape in China. In his later New York photographs, the act of taking pictures becomes political in itself, since recording riots and violence is a partisan act. As is evident in the exhibition, the power of this act would later be increased by the digital media, which would allow Ai not just to take pictures, but also to disseminate them freely on the Internet, thus actualizing their potential effect.

THIS PAGE: *Dropping a Han Dynasty Urn*, 1995; OPPOSITE, TOP: *Anton Wei, Lorimer Avenue Apartment, Brooklyn*, 1983. From the series *New York Photographs*, 1983–93; BOTTOM: *June 1994.*

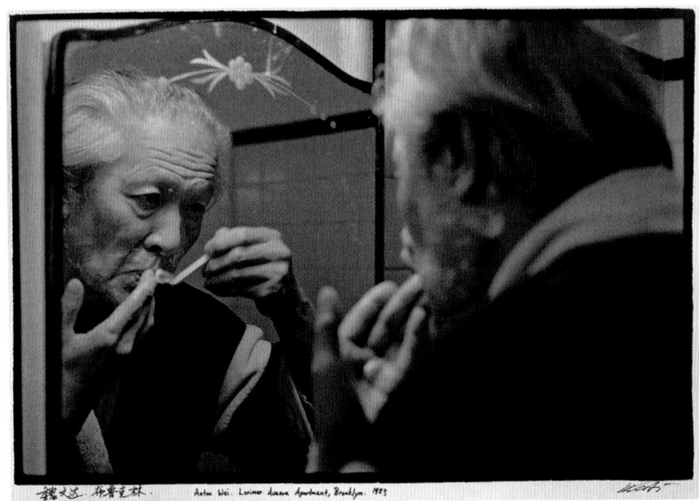

After his return to Beijing, Ai extended his practice into architecture, eventually collaborating with Swiss architects Herzog and de Meuron in the design of the Beijing National Stadium (known as the "Bird's Nest"), built for the 2008 Olympics. Until around 2005, Ai's involvement in photography remained conceptually concise and project-oriented, in sharp contrast to the voluminous output of his New York years. A large-format 1995 triptych shows him iconoclastically dropping a Han dynasty urn. An equally aggressive stance is projected by his 1995–2010 series *Study in Perspective*, which shows his extended left arm, with the middle finger upright, in front of landmarks all over the world. The ambiguous gesture measures his distance, his relative position vis-à-vis these symbols of power, and at the same time literally "gives them the finger." As his contribution to the 2007 Documenta, Ai famously flew 1,001 Chinese people from all walks of life to Kassel as a living installation; they are portrayed in the series *Fairytale Portraits* (2007).

Ai's involvement in architecture triggered a renewed involvement in photography, this time in a documentary mode. He photographed the construction of the "Bird's Nest" and the simultaneous building of the new Beijing airport in painstaking detail. The resulting series makes it obvious that the artist's interest in architecture lies more in the process rather than in the final result. Another work, *Provisional Landscapes* (2002–8), consisting of hundreds of photographs, provides a critical perspective on urban development in contemporary China. The photographs show sites where traditional buildings and neighborhoods were torn to down to make room for large-scale construction projects. In photographs like these, one realizes perhaps why Ai is considered dangerous by the Chinese government. Rather than celebrating economic growth, the photographs question the frantic pace at which China is currently growing.

In 2005 Ai acquired a digital camera and began blogging, at first on the Chinese platform Sina; then, after that immensely popular blog was shut down by the government, he switched to Twitter, which he accessed via a proxy server. Ai used the Internet to publish a vast stream of images and comments on current affairs, his art projects, and his personal life. His activism became increasingly provocative—he published, for example, the names of children who died in improperly built schools during the earthquake in Sichuan province in 2008. Ai exhaustively and non-hierarchically documented his own life as well as his artistic and activist practice on his blog, effectively fusing them—an enactment of his Duchamp-inspired notion that art is first and foremost a way of living. ◐

—Martin Jaeggi

Ai Weiwei: Interlacing *was presented at the Fotomuseum Winterthur, May 28–August 21, 2011; it will be on view at the Jeu de Paume, Paris, February 21–April 29, 2012.*

Martin Jaeggi is an independent critic and curator in Zurich.

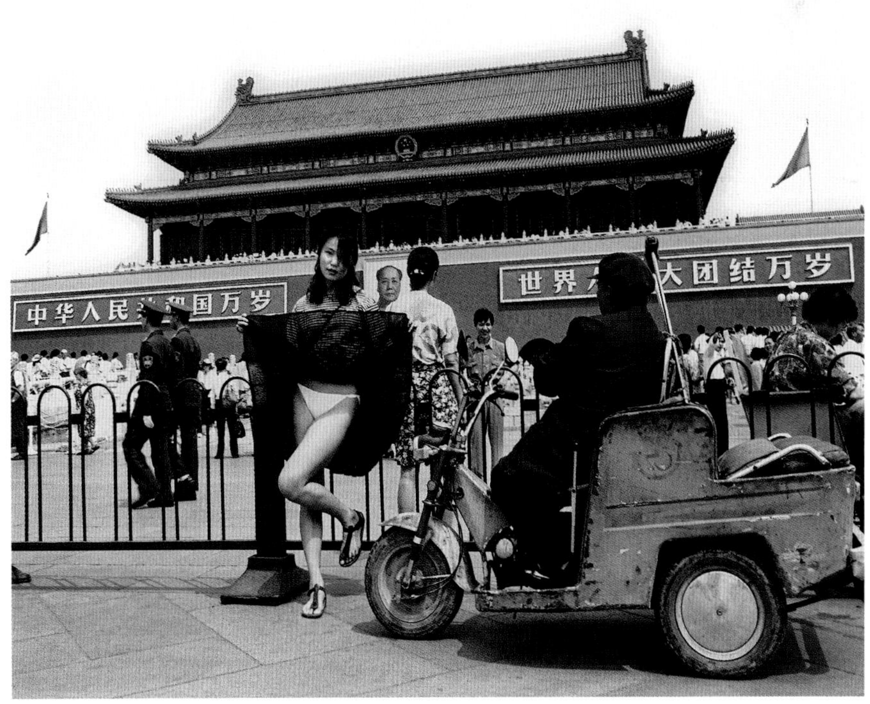

WANG QINGSONG: WHEN WORLDS COLLIDE

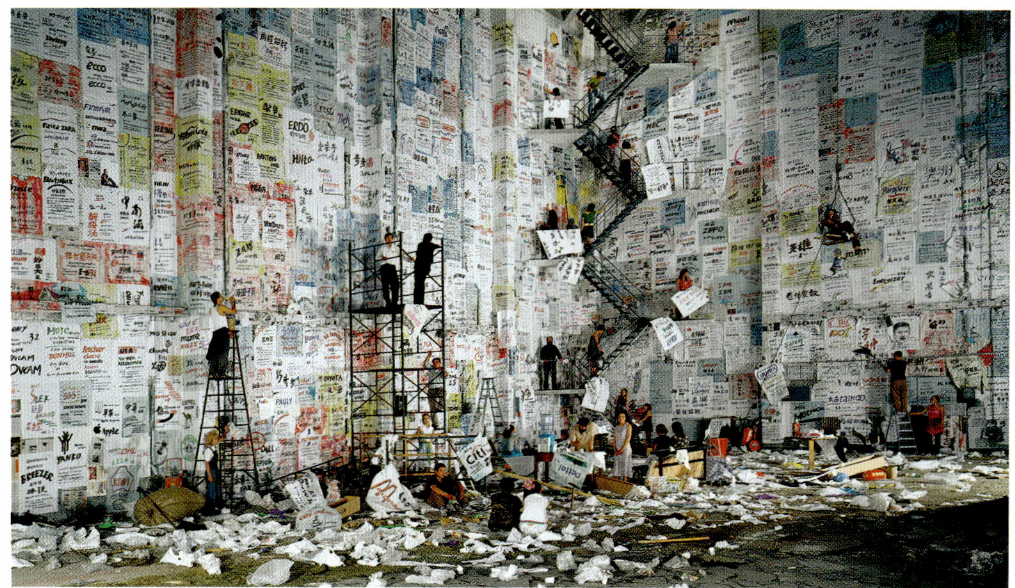

"I find no change in the destinies of intellectuals in China."

He targets recent history with humor and sorrow. In *Competition* (2004), he stands with a megaphone before a huge wall of mock advertisements, a takeoff on walls of competing Red Guard faction posters during the Cultural Revolution. In *Sentry Post* (2002), migrant workers, many of them wounded, are barred from city residence by barbed wire as Wang prepares to hurl a Molotov cocktail into their midst.

These photographs are large-scale, wickedly sardonic, over-the-top, impressive, and highly theatrical. Recently, Wang has been making equally biting short videos. His 2008 work *123456 Chops* is a grim, sped-up account of a man relentlessly chopping up a goat carcass until all that remains are bloody particles. Wang's intent was to condemn the wholesale acceptance of violence in popular entertainment, followed by desensitization. It is hard to watch.

When Communism falls, or even wavers, artists seize the luxuries of criticism—thinly veiled by parody and pastiche—and rebellious subject matter. Meanwhile, capitalism and its discontents rush in. In Eastern Europe and Russia, after the Wall fell in 1989, and in China after Deng Xiaoping's economic reforms of the early 1990s, visual arts cudgeled previous regimes and flaunted nudity. Artists also appropriated Western art even more eagerly than Western postmodernists did, evidently believing that once-prohibited art must be admirable and important. After a while, unease with the West and precipitous movement toward it set in; then the invasion of commercialism was widely attacked.

Wang Qingsong is a prominent figure in one chapter of this story, a position recognized by the International Center of Photography with a recent show curated by Christopher Phillips. Beginning in the late 1990s, Wang's photographs revised the venerable Chinese tradition of copying famous works: he reconfigured them as blasts at the contemporary worship of material goods and loss of age-old values. Once, he posed as a many-armed Buddha on a Coca-Cola pedestal with his hands grasping a cell phone, a CD, American cigarettes, and Chinese and American currency; even the holy figure who said material desires brought suffering has become prey to them. Wang's signature work, *Night Revels of Lao Li* (2000), riffs on a tenth-century painting of a court official who, unable to effect imperial reforms, withdrew to a life of debauchery, upon which the emperor sent an artist to spy on him. In Wang's update, he plays the spy, and Li Xianting (a noted critic who lost his job as editor of a top art magazine for championing experimental art) plays the court official. "After so many years of Chinese history," Wang says,

The sales of Wang's work finance his projects. The size—the ICP show wasn't quite spacious enough to do him justice—and ambition of his photographs mirror his nation while skewering its ills. They depend on the inexpensive labor and materials that have made China the supply house to the West, and on the accelerating global art market to fund the work. Art that bites may find that social and political forces bite back: Wang says: "I'm helpless in that I can't really stop the trend for embracing consumerism. It's a global trend. . . . Many kids in China already think Coca-Cola is a Chinese brand." His project to photograph re-created battle scenes from Western art ran afoul when a Chinese newspaper reported that he was producing pornography, because the "dead" in his works were naked. Wang's negatives were confiscated and never returned.

And then there's Ai Weiwei. . . . Ⓐ

—Vicki Goldberg

Wang Qingsong: When Worlds Collide *was presented at the International Center of Photography, New York, January 21–May 8, 2011.*

Vicki Goldberg's most recent book, *The White House: The President's House in Photographs and History,* just released from Bulfinch, follows the house, its occupants, and its visitors, from the 1840s to 2010.

Wang Qingsong, *Competition,* **2004.**
©/courtesy Wang Qingsong

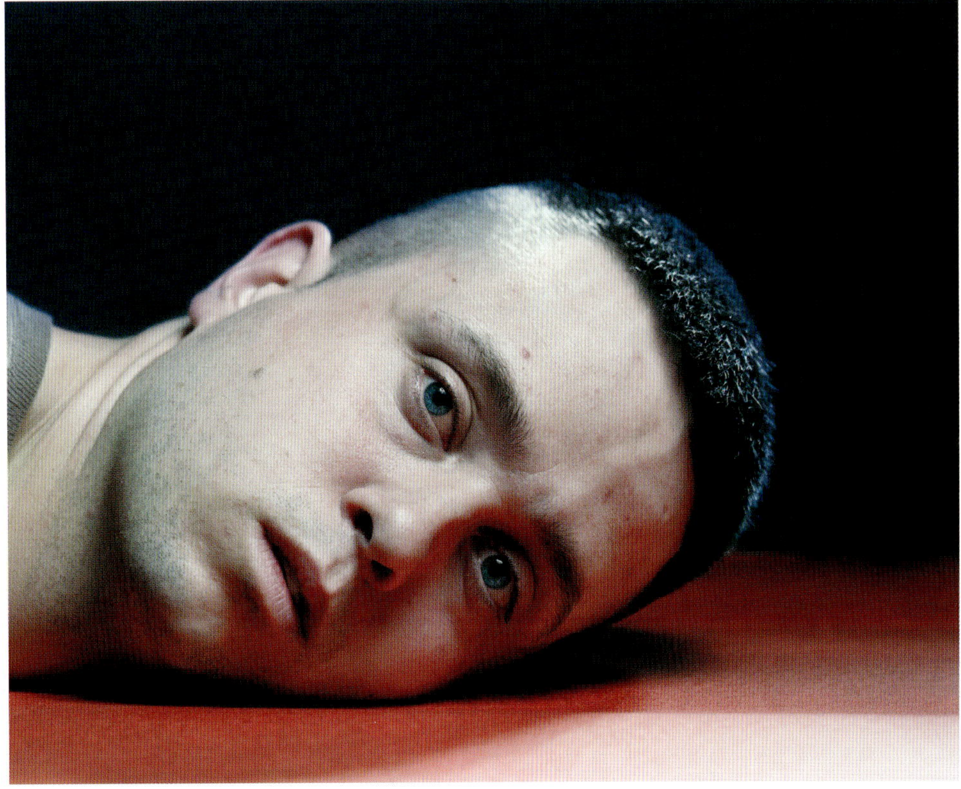

Soldier: Bruno—355 Days in Iraq

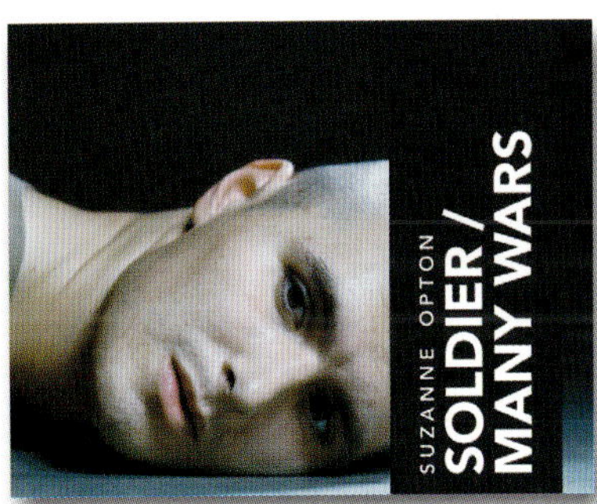

Suzanne Opton
Soldier/Many Wars

Essays by Phillip Prodger
and Ann Jones

9.5 x 12 inches
39 four-color plates
104 pages, hardcover

ISBN 978-0-9833942-0-4

$60 USD

AVAILABLE THROUGH D.A.P.

In the two series collected in the volume, *Soldier/Many Wars,* photographer Suzanne Opton photographs American Soldiers close up, laying their heads before the camera, and American veterans who are draped. The subjects of the *Soldier* series are all young, active-duty soldiers from the Iraq and Afghanistan wars. Reviewing them for *The New Yorker,* photography critic Vince Aletti wrote: "The posture is vulnerable and startling intimate, as if these young men and women were facing someone in bed or on a stretcher… Opton catches soldiers both on guard and off, looking out and inward simultaneously, and we can only imagine what they're thinking, what they've done, and what they dread." The project received extensive press coverage and even sparked a heated debate about America's image of the military. The *Many Wars* series presents portraits of veterans from American wars over the past 70 years, most of whom are in treatment for combat trauma. Through interviews by the photographer, we learn how war has affected their lives. Both bodies of work were selected by Martin Paar for the Brighton Photo Biennial in 2010.

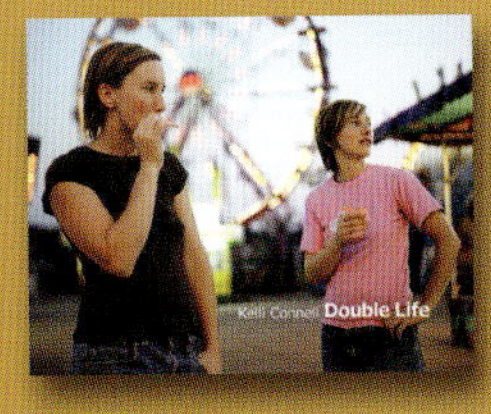 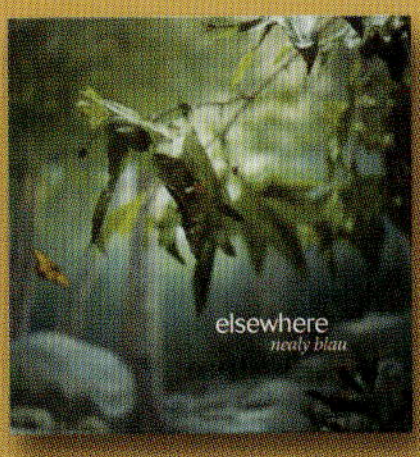 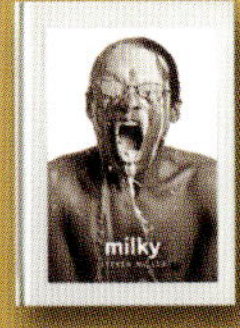 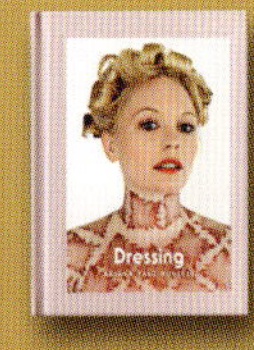 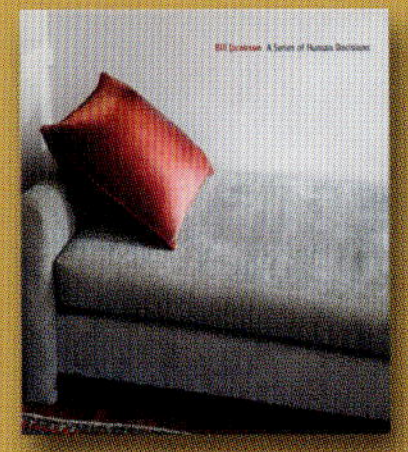 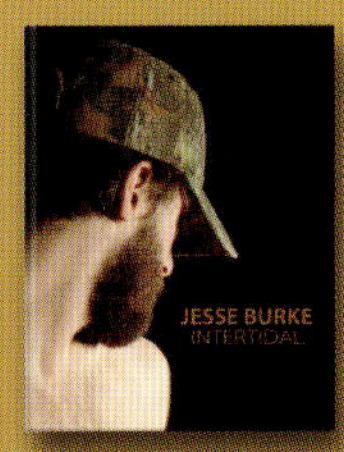 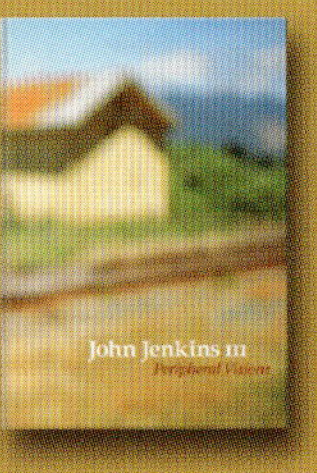 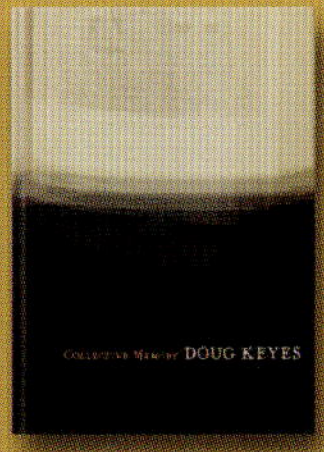

Special **Collector's Edition Prints** for each book are available consisting of a signed, limited edition print with a signed book.

THE WORKER-PHOTOGRAPHY MOVEMENT

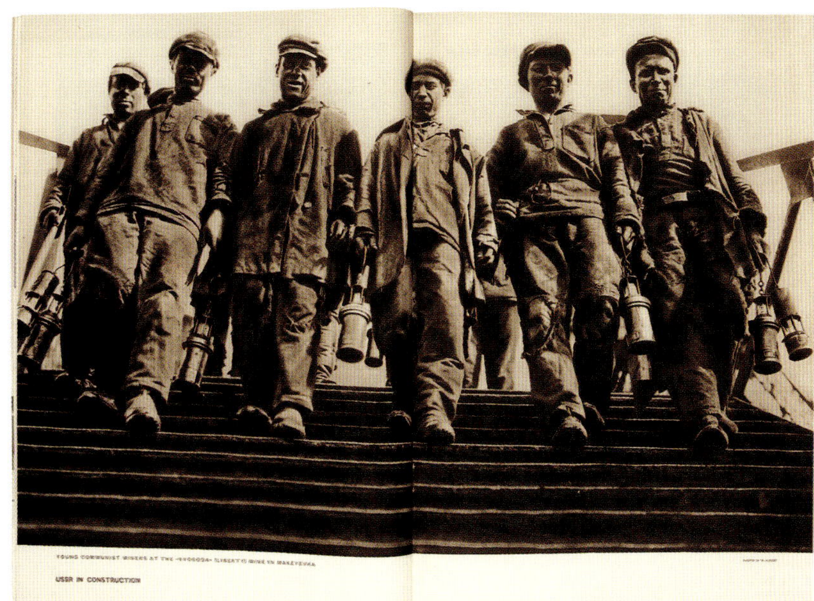

Slightly eclipsing a strong installment (despite severe budget cuts) of the annual PhotoEspaña festival, was an exhibition at the Museo Nacional Centro de Arte Reina Sofía in Madrid focusing on workers' photography during the years between the World Wars. *A Hard, Merciless Light, The Worker-Photography Movement, 1926–1939*, curated by Jorge Ribalta, was a tour de force and extraordinarily timely, considering Europe's precarious economic state.

This exhibition, featuring more than one thousand objects—magazines, photographs, films, posters, and more—contextualized various strands of photography made by workers, from the American Photo League and Farm Security Administration to images produced during the Weimar Republic in Germany and the early Stalinist years of the Soviet Union, along with lesser-known worker-related photographic movements across Europe.

The photographers of the German magazine *Arbeiter-Illustrierte Zeitung* (*AIZ*) and its Soviet cognate, the Russian Association of Proletarian Photo Reporters (ROPF), called for entries from workers, in addition to those from professional photographers and illustrators. The use of "amateur" worker photographers was key in the effort to depict working conditions from the standpoint of actual laborers. In his catalog essay, Ribalta describes how many of the photographers featured in the show—such as Eugen Hellig, John Heartfield, and Willi Münzenberg (of *AIZ*), and Maks Alpert and Arkady Shaikhet (of the ROPF)—sought to move photography away from "pure visual effect" toward its use "as a weapon for the socialist transformation of reality."

In 1931 *AIZ* published a monumental project, "24 Hours in the Life of a Moscow Worker Family"—the Filippovs—featuring

work by Alpert, Shaikhet, and Semen Tules. "24 Hours" was an in-depth description of the conditions faced by the proletariat. The piece combined an almost anthropological approach, depicting a setting (the Donskaya 59 district of Moscow tenements), imagery from factory life, workers' recreation, as well as the family's living conditions at home. This vibrant montage was typical of the era and greatly influenced by Aleksander Rodchenko's 1933 magazine project *USSR under Construction*. The Soviet Filippovs inspired a parallel project by Erich Rinka on "the German Filippovs." The ideological differences behind two are notable: the Soviet work emphasizes a hopeful future for the proletariat under the Soviet Socialist system, while the Weimar-era German version stresses the misery of workers under capitalism. *A Hard Light* thus draws out the political uses of similar photographic productions by situating works within their respective economic and social contexts.

In Western Europe, as in the United States, however, professional photographers dominated. Images produced by lesser-known artists such as Kata Kálmán and Kata Sugár (both Hungarian), and Irena Bluhová (Czech), describe the poverty of workers and displaced persons in the wake of World War I and the onset of the Depression. Unlike most of the photographers working in Germany and the USSR, who tended to adopt a more contextual approach, these photographers produced mostly portraits, opting to show the individual faces of workers in the 1920s and '30s. Their focus on discrete persons was clearer in the more capitalist West than in the East, where class-oriented politics dominated approaches to worker photography. With the rise of Nazism in Germany, *AIZ* was forced to disband in 1936; many of its photographers fled to Paris or the United States. In the Soviet Union, Stalin's purges effectively shut down the ROPF.

Images from the Popular Front days of 1930s France and the era of the Spanish Civil War also stand out in this exhibition. The influential French magazine *Regards* positioned these social movements in relation to the French Revolution, drawing comparisons through the use of montage or overt symbolism between demonstrations of hundreds of thousands of people and

THIS PAGE: From the Soviet magazine *USSR under Construction*, no. 3, 1931; photograph by Max Alpert, Young miners in the Svoboda mine of Makeyevka. OPPOSITE, TOP RIGHT: Front cover of the German magazine *Arbeiter-Illustrierte Zeitung aller Länder*, no. 17, 1931; photograph by Tina Modotti. BOTTOM LEFT: Lothar Reubelt, *Delivery of Food to the Ones in Need*, Steyr, Austria, 1932.

USSR under Construction: Museo Nacional Centro de Arte Reina Sofía (Library and Documentation Center); *AIZ*: Museum of Fine Arts, Houston; Ruebelt: IMAGNO/Collection of Christian Brandstätter, Vienna

the storming of the Bastille in 1789. (The issue from July 14, 1935, for example, superimposed figures in costumes from the French Revolution onto crowds demonstrating for the Popular Front.) Highly celebrated photographers, including Robert Capa and David "Chim" Seymour, were also active in Paris in the mid-1930s and documented strikes and workers in mass demonstrations.

The use of photography as propaganda and documentary evidence during the Spanish Civil War is frequently associated with the work of Capa, Gerda Taro, and Henri Cartier-Bresson; the images of the conflict by German photojournalist Walter Reuter are less known. The reconstruction of a 1937 show, *Exposición de las juventudes* (Youth exhibition), gathered Reuter's images of Madrileños awaiting air raids, huddled in shelters and bombed-out buildings, as well as various soldiers. Poster makers from both right and left appropriated images by Reuter (sometimes the same images) in their campaigns to win support or defame their opponents. John Heartfield's poster imagery of the miseries of the Spanish Civil War and appeals against Franco and his supporters, Hitler and Mussolini, were also well illustrated in *A Hard Light*.

There was a poignancy in the fact that this exhibition happened in the area of the actual battlegrounds of the Spanish Civil War—but more immediately, the Reina Sofía show took place just a few hundred meters from Puerta del Sol, where the greatest demonstrations in Spain's post-Franco history transpired last summer: up to a hundred thousand people, known as *los indignados* (the indignant ones), peacefully protested for social change and against high youth unemployment and the destruction of the social safety net under the force of International Monetary Fund-mandated reforms. Similar protests were carried out throughout Spain. The images of the demonstrations flooding

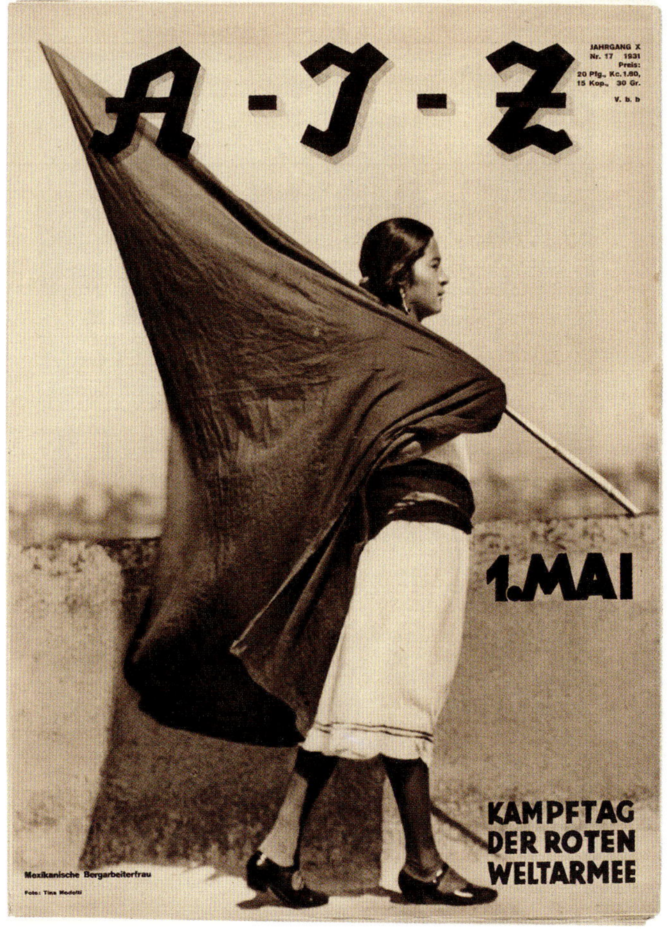

the media were mirrored and even anticipated by the workers' photography on display at the Reina Sofía. Still, the peaceful demonstrations are a mark of how far democracy has become embedded in Spanish society. To be sure, 2011 is not 1936, but the absence of violence in the face of massive unemployment is a sign that the democratic political process has taken hold.

The exhibition's title is from a phrase by Edwin Hoernle, a contributor to *AIZ*'s cousin, *Der Arbeiter-Fotograf*. It was necessary, said Hoernle, to "proclaim proletarian reality in all its disgusting ugliness, with its indictment of society and its demand for revenge . . . we must present things in a hard, merciless light." The Spanish light may be just as hard today, but times have changed. ◐

—Bill Kouwenhoven

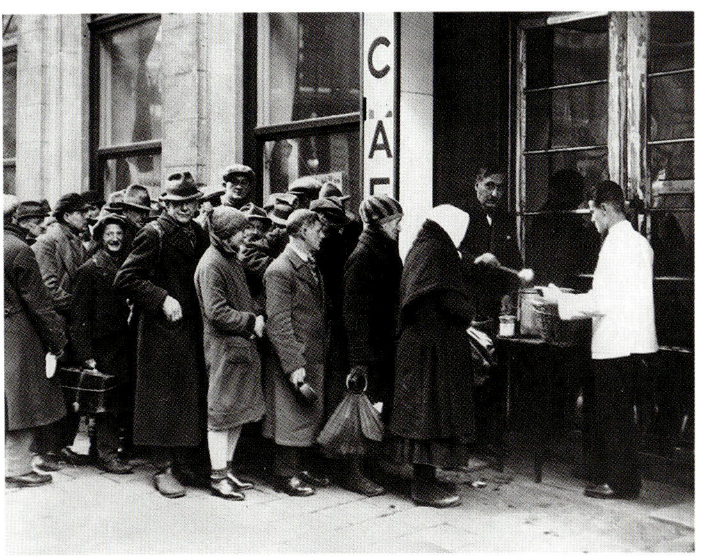

A Hard, Merciless Light: The Worker-Photography Movement, 1926–1939 *was presented at the Museo Nacional Centro de Arte Reina Sofía, Madrid, April 4– August 22, 2011.*

Bill Kouwenhoven is the international editor of London-based *Hotshoe Magazine* and author of *Nuevas Historias: A New View of Spanish Photography and Video Art* (Hatje Cantz, 2006).

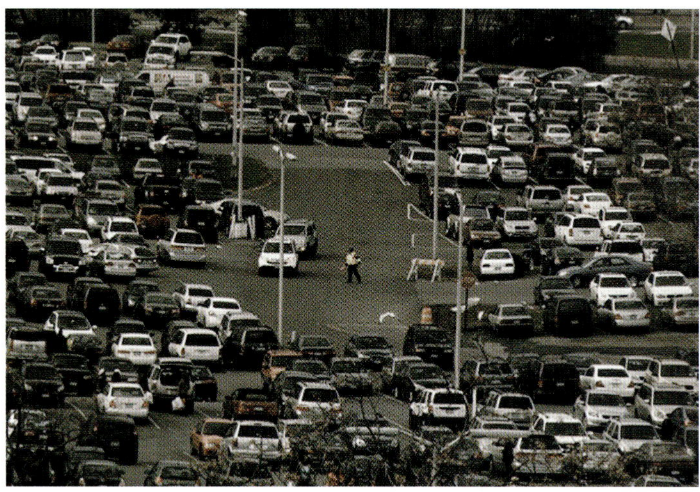

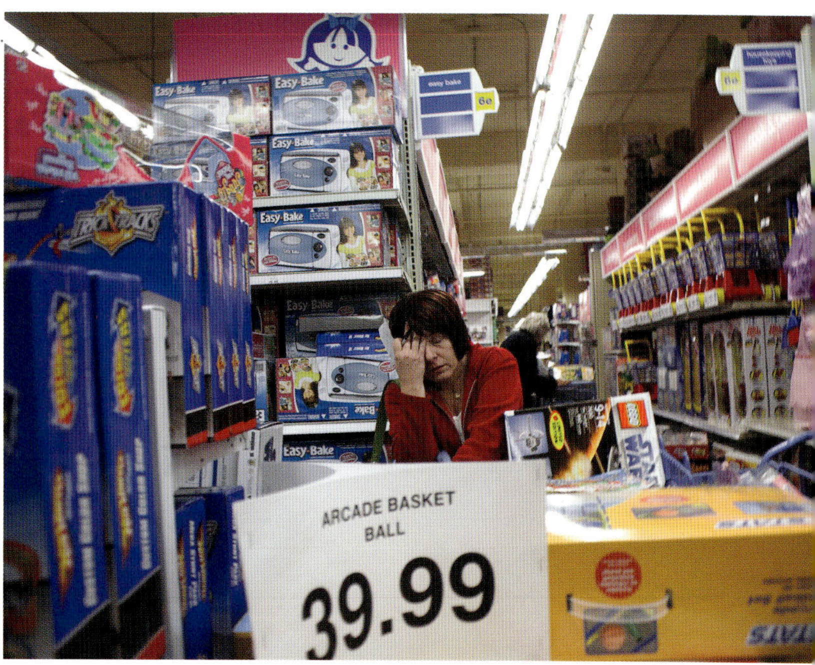

PICTURE BLACK FRIDAY

A PROJECT BY JOHN SAPONARA

Every year, Black Friday rings in the yearly holiday shopping season in the United States, with hundreds of thousands of people getting up before sunrise to line up for deals; as soon as the stores unlock their doors, they are besieged by customers. On Black Friday 2008, security-guard Jdimytai Damour was trampled to death by the crowd of shoppers as he tried to hold back crazed bargain-seekers at a Walmart in Long Island. The media coverage of the event was mostly over by the end of that Thanksgiving weekend.

   The photojournalism project *Picture Black Friday*, launched in 2009, is an open call for photographers throughout the United States to go out and produce images that document the day—however they see it, on their own terms, wherever they are. The artists approach the event from any angle, returning sometimes with single images, sometimes with a mini-photo-project. Together the photographs provide an investigation and analysis of the combination of forces—an unstable economy, financial desperation, excitement, fear, need, greed, and a distinctly American cultural tradition—that culminate the morning after Thanksgiving. Ⓐ

—J.S.

All photographs made for the project *Picture Black Friday*, 2009 and 2010. THIS PAGE, CLOCKWISE FROM TOP LEFT: Tracy Brown, Cross County parking lot, Westchester, New York; Caitie McCabe, Toys "R" Us, Yonkers, New York; Shawn Rocco, 5 A.M., Best Buy at Renaissance Center, Durham, North Carolina; Alexandra Lethbridge, Macy's, New York City; OPPOSITE, CLOCKWISE FROM TOP LEFT: Sandy Carson, Austin, Texas; Ruben Natal-San Miguel, 125th Street, New York City; Matt Furman, 4 A.M., Best Buy, Altoona, Pennsylvania; Dan Koeck, Discount store, Fargo, North Dakota; Jeffrey Kane, 10:30 P.M., Thursday, Target, Hooper Avenue, Toms River, New Jersey; Michael D. Wilson, Bloomingdale, Illinois.

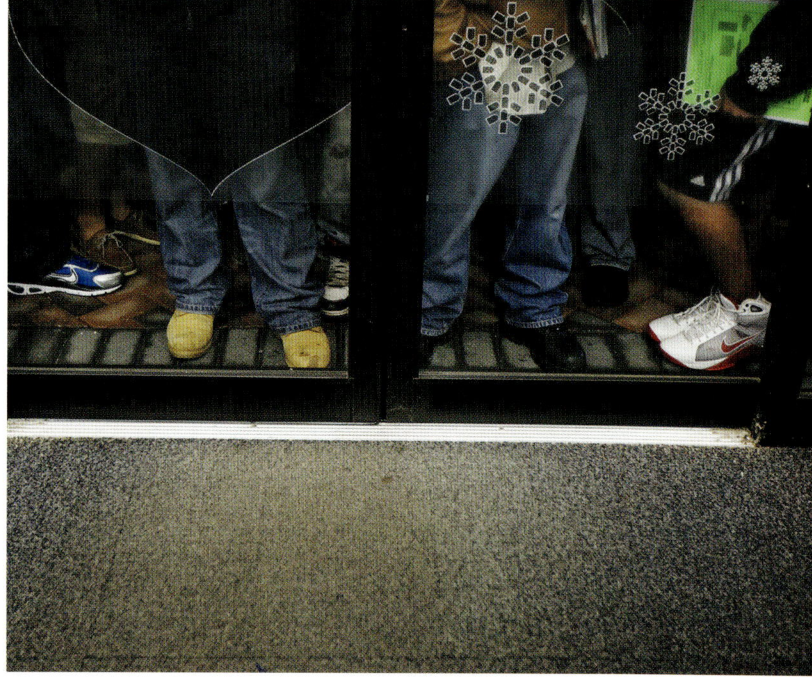

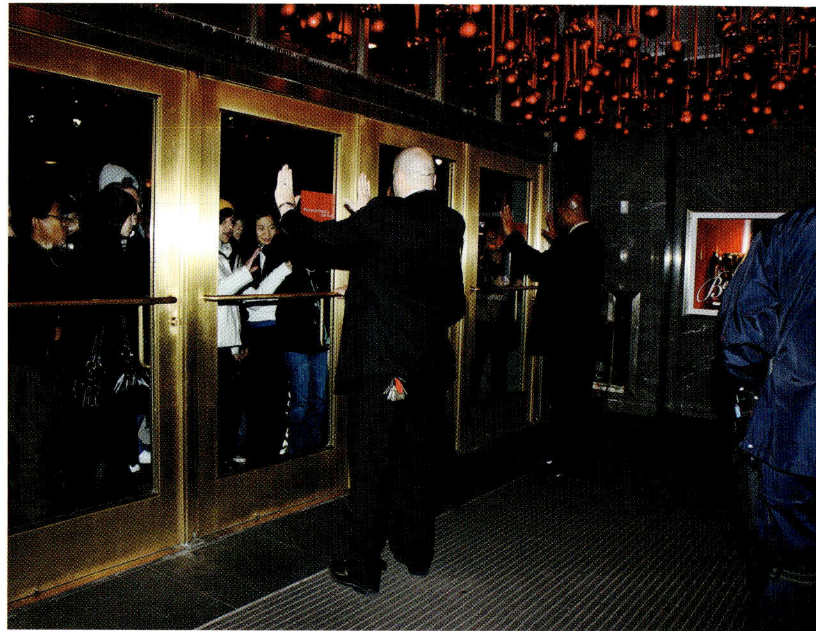

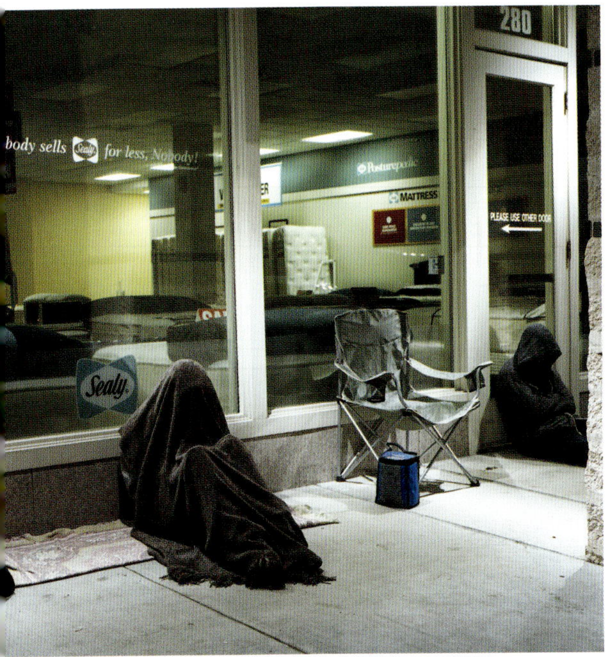
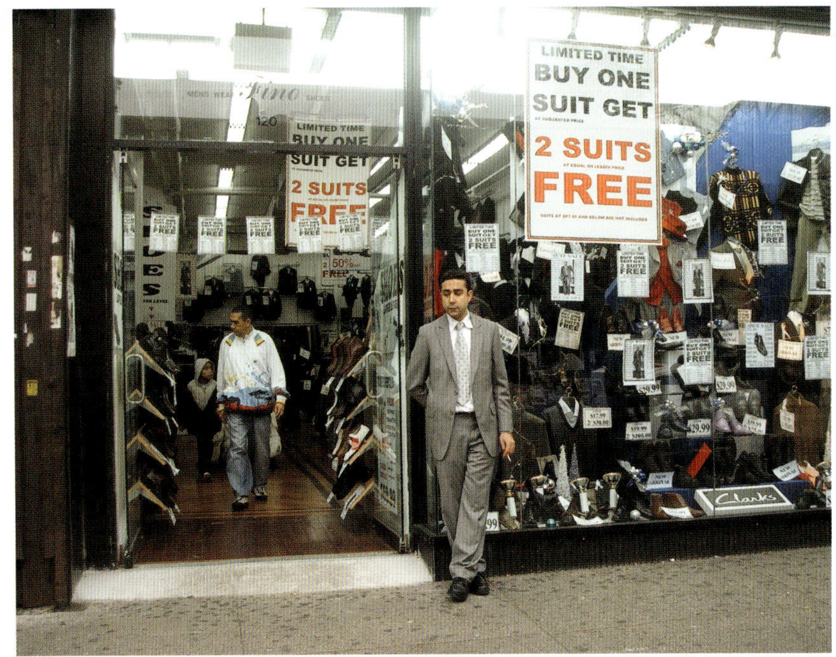

LIMITED TIME
BUY ONE
SUIT GET
2 SUITS
FREE
Clarks

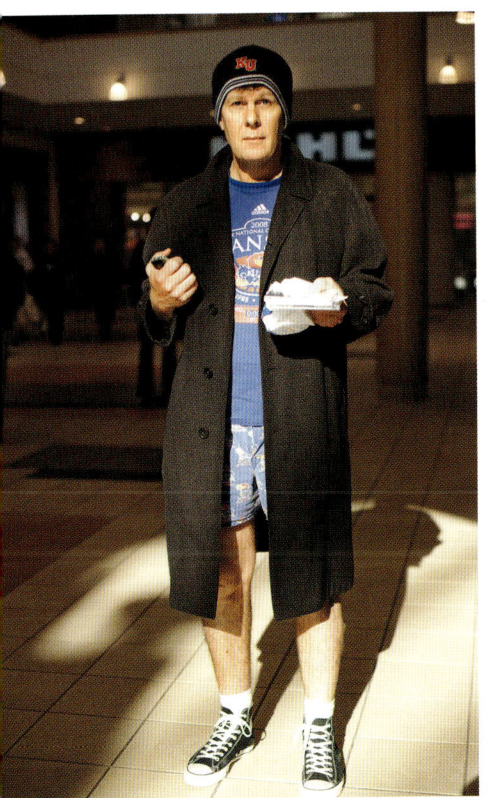
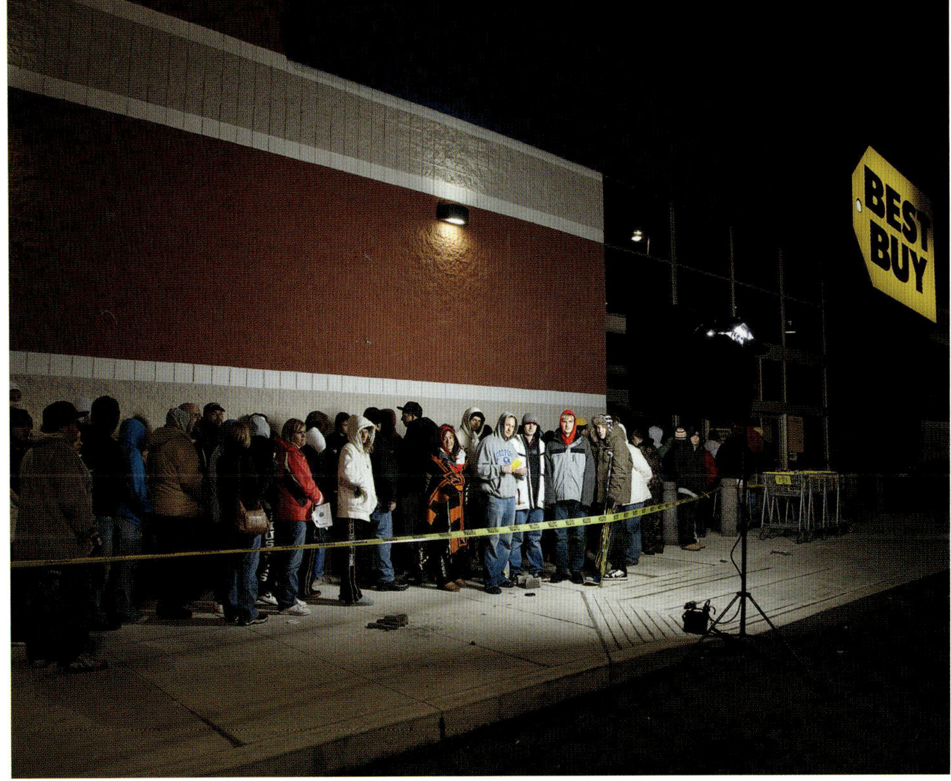

BEST
BUY

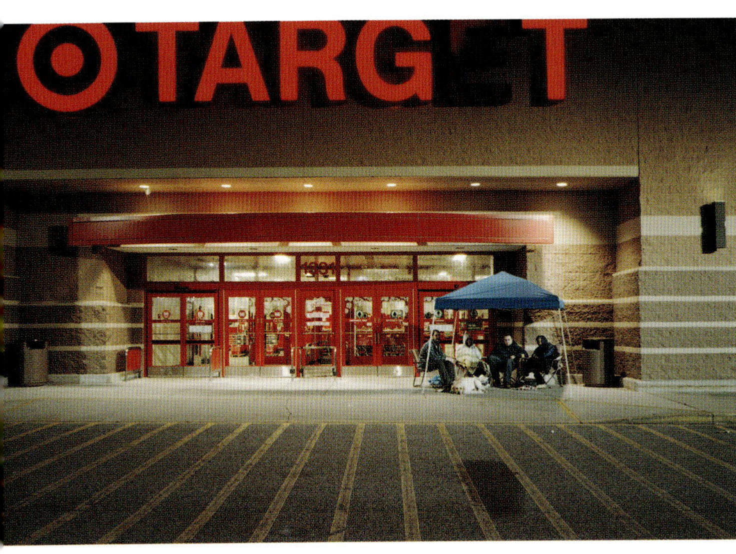

TARGET

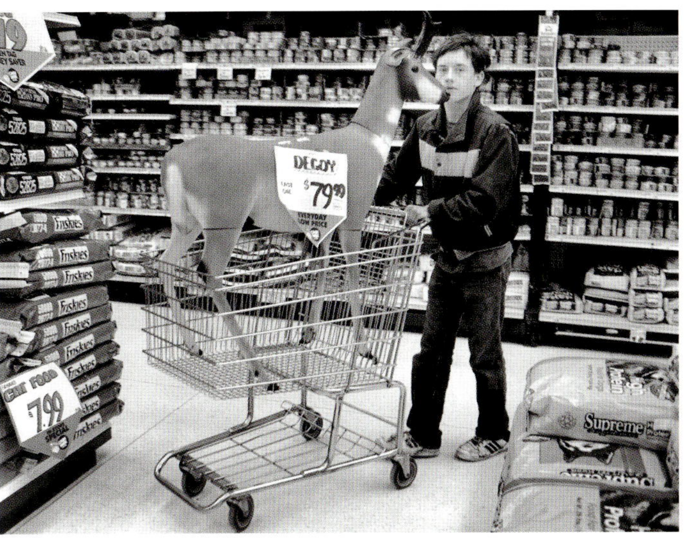

DECOY
$79.99
$7.99
Friskies
Supreme

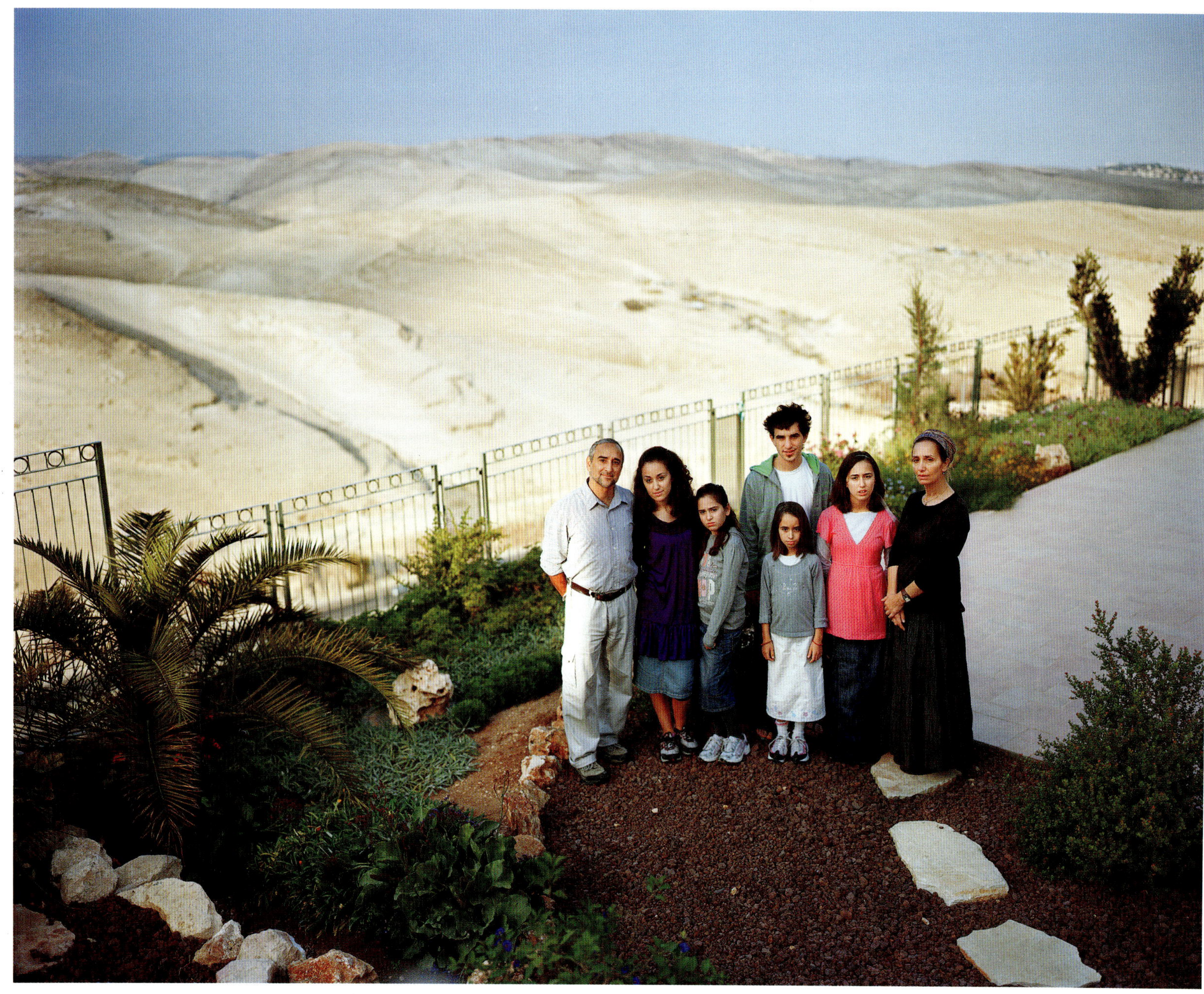

SETTLERS

PHOTOGRAPHS AND NOTES BY NICK WAPLINGTON

These images are from a work in progress titled *Settlers*, which I began in 2008. By "settlers," I refer to Israeli Jewish immigrants currently living in the area they call "Judea and Samaria," but which is more commonly referred to as the West Bank. This is the area of the former state of Palestine that was controlled by Jordan from 1948 until 1967, when it was annexed by Israel.

As this annexation has not been sanctioned by the United Nations, any Israeli building in this area is deemed to be in violation of international law and is seen as an act of aggression by the four million Palestinians who continue to call the area their home.

The settlers, however, consider Judea and Samaria to be part of the biblical land of Israel, which they believe was given to them by God four thousand years ago. Furthermore, they firmly maintain that that the lands that were captured by Israel in the 1967 Six-Day War are rightfully theirs to settle. Their building projects continue.

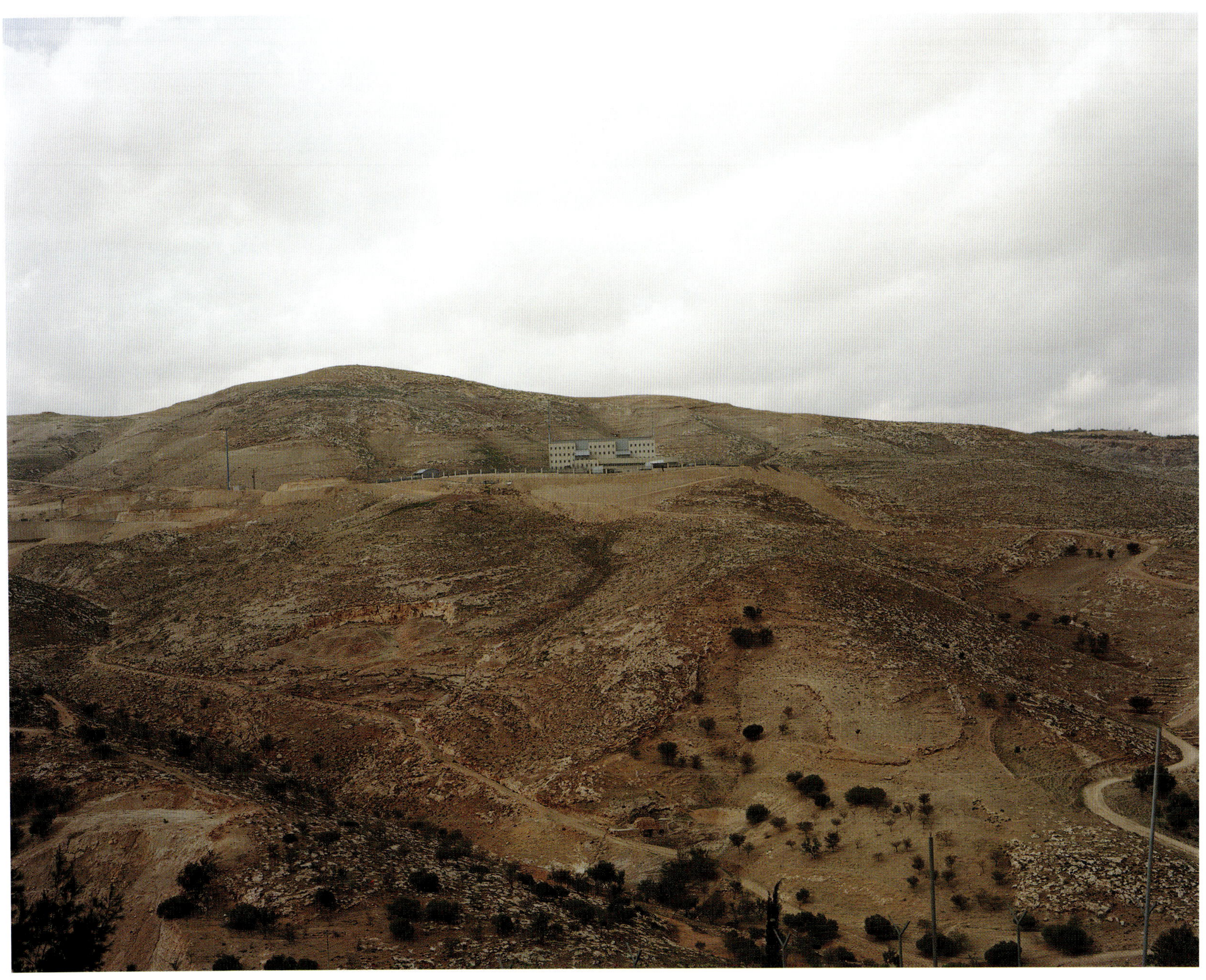

All photographs 2008–11.

OPPOSITE: This family portrait was made in the high desert city of Ma'ale Adumim, a large settlement built on the edge of the Judean Desert, close to Jerusalem on Highway 1, the major freeway that transverses the center of Israel from Tel Aviv to the West Bank and the Dead Sea.

The city sits atop the highest hill between Jerusalem to the east and the Jordan valley to the west. (*Ma'ale adumim* means "red hill" in Hebrew.) Planning of the city was started soon after the capture of the West Bank from the Jordanians in 1967. Construction began in 1975 with only a few hundred basic housing units. Now, with more than thirty thousand inhabitants, shopping malls, schools, and even an art museum, Ma'ale Adumim is considered a city by the Israeli government.

The settlement's inhabitants are both secular and religious, and consist of people from across the Jewish diaspora who made *aliyah* (emigrated to Israel), as well as Israeli-born residents. The family in this photograph is originally from Australia.

THIS PAGE: This is the headquarters of the Israeli police force for Judea and Samaria. Situated on a hill between East Jerusalem and Ma'ale Adumim, the building officially opened in 2008 and is staffed by officers previously stationed in Jerusalem. It is the first building in a proposed new development block currently known only as "E1." If completed, E1 will include 3,700 new housing units, plus social amenities such as schools and welfare services, and will link Jerusalem and Ma'ale Adumim.

The Palestinians say this plan is part of a larger goal to encircle East Jerusalem completely, thus confining Palestinian urban planning to an ever-smaller area, while cutting the eastern part of the city off from Palestinian villages in the West Bank. The Israelis contend that the development of E1 will thwart the contiguity of Palestinian construction, development that will hamper Jerusalem and isolate Ma'ale Adumim. They are eager to build up the area as quickly as possible.

Many families who move from Israel "proper" to the West Bank see themselves as the "new pioneers": modern-day counterparts of the original Zionists who arrived from Europe in the early twentieth century. Their stated goal is to settle all the biblical lands of Israel.

Like many settlers, this family lives in a development that is built on the probable site of a town that existed in ancient Israel, in this case Teqoa. This modern community is located in the Gush Etzion district, close to Jerusalem. It came into being in 1975, and now has four distinct neighborhoods covering a few miles stretching from the vicinity of Bethlehem in the west down into the Judean Desert in the east. The last of these, called Teqoa D, has a New Age feel, with teepees and organic farming, and is inhabited by a number of young people with dual U.S. and Israeli citizenship.

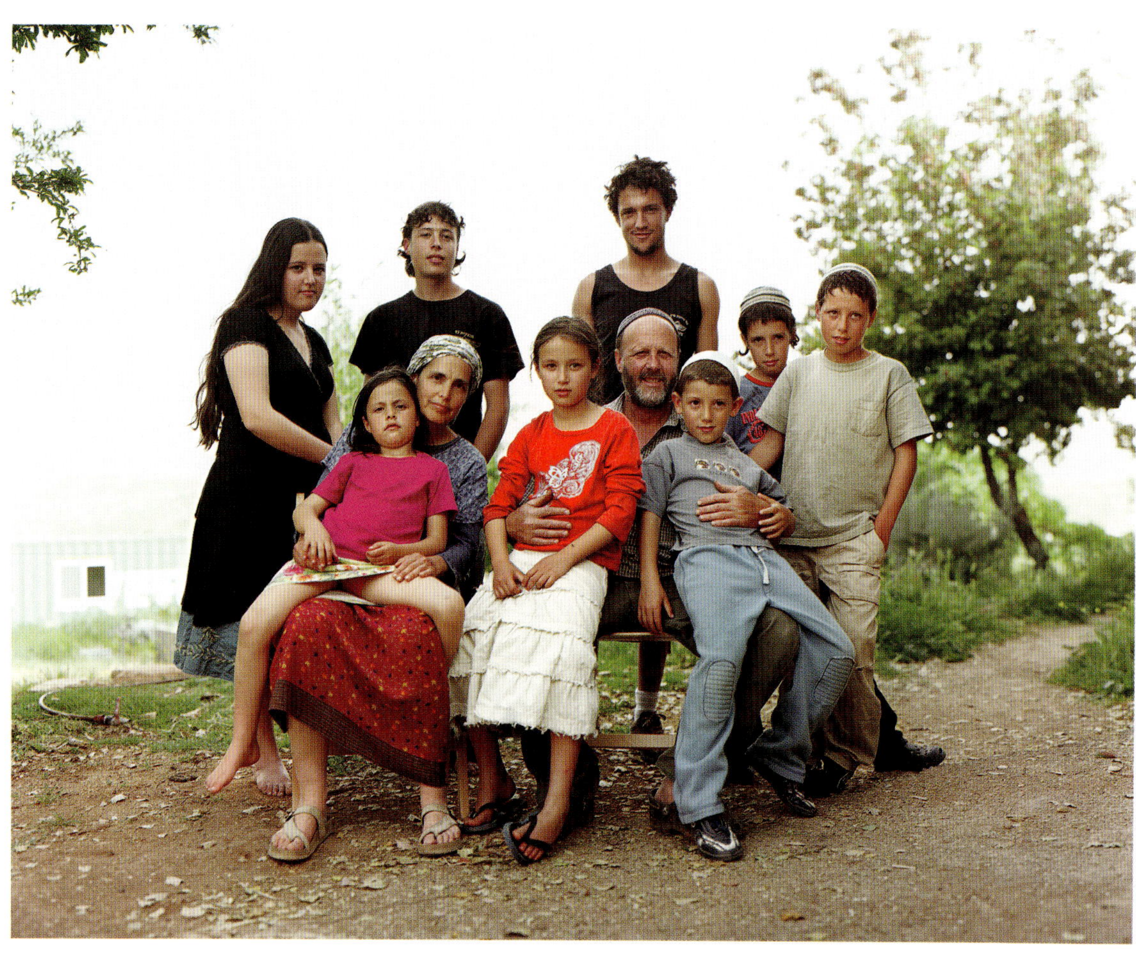

Some settlements give rise to more contention than others, but few are more disputed than Psagot. Built on Tawil Hill in the 1980s, the settlement holds a high vantage point for monitoring movements in the nearby Palestinian city of Ramallah. It also prevents the urban sprawl of Ramallah from moving to the east—in fact, Arab construction in the area is forbidden by the Israeli government.

The proximity of Psagot and Ramallah is disconcerting; settler houses literally face Arab houses here, and it is possible to walk down the hill shown in this image and look into the windows of Palestinian houses below. Despite this nearness, the communities do not mingle, and Psagot residents generally keep themselves apart from their Palestinian neighbors.

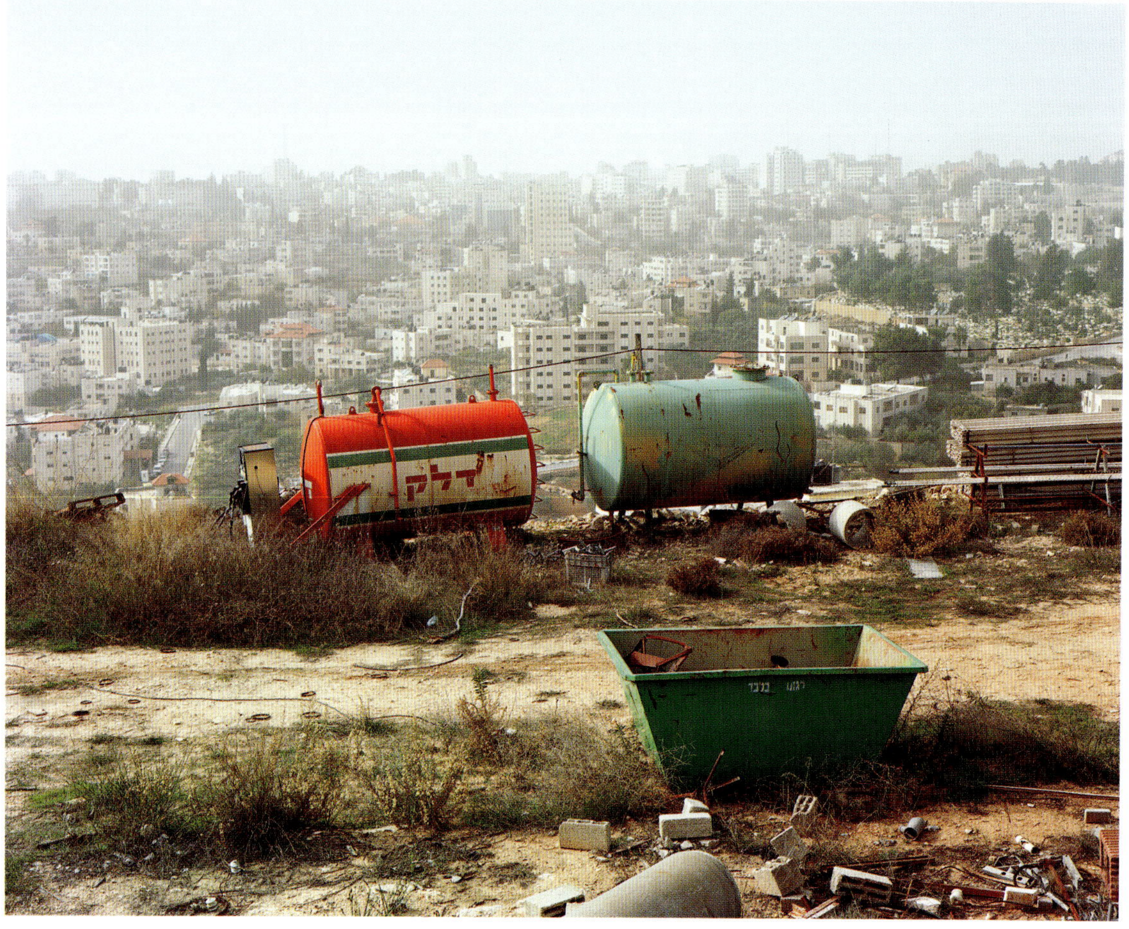

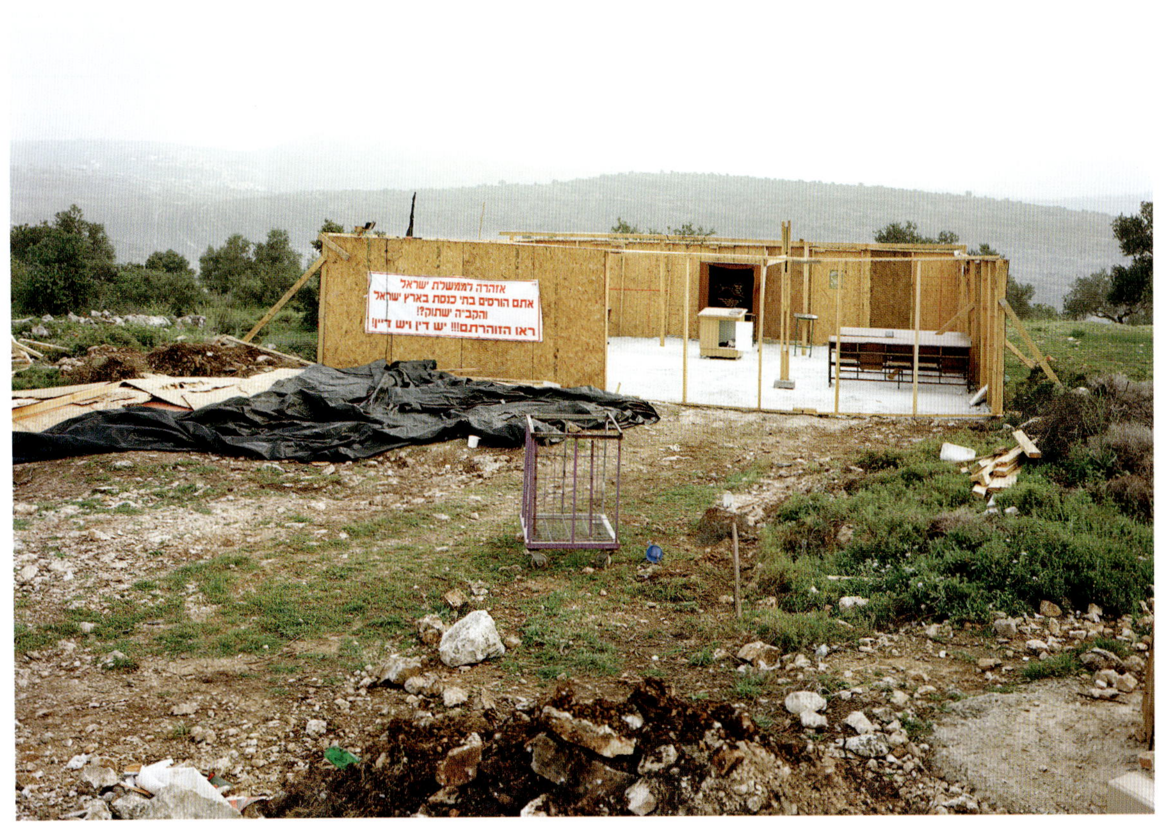

This wooden structure is a synagogue built by the inhabitants of Nahliel. A tiny religious community in central West Bank, Nahliel is located at the heart of the Ramallah governorate: Bir Zeit is to the east and Beitillu to the west. The defining structure of Nahliel is the large gate across the main road at the valley's head; this gate controls access to the Ramallah road and is closed to Palestinians.

When the Israeli government announced a building freeze in 2009, the inhabitants of Nahliel decided to build their temple on Palestinian land, just outside the gate. This led to a number of standoffs between the settlers and the Israeli security forces over the next few months; the army would destroy the synagogue, and the inhabitants of Nahliel would rebuild it. It is worth noting that such battles go on daily in the West Bank between the Israeli security forces and the settlers without any participation or interference from the Palestinians.

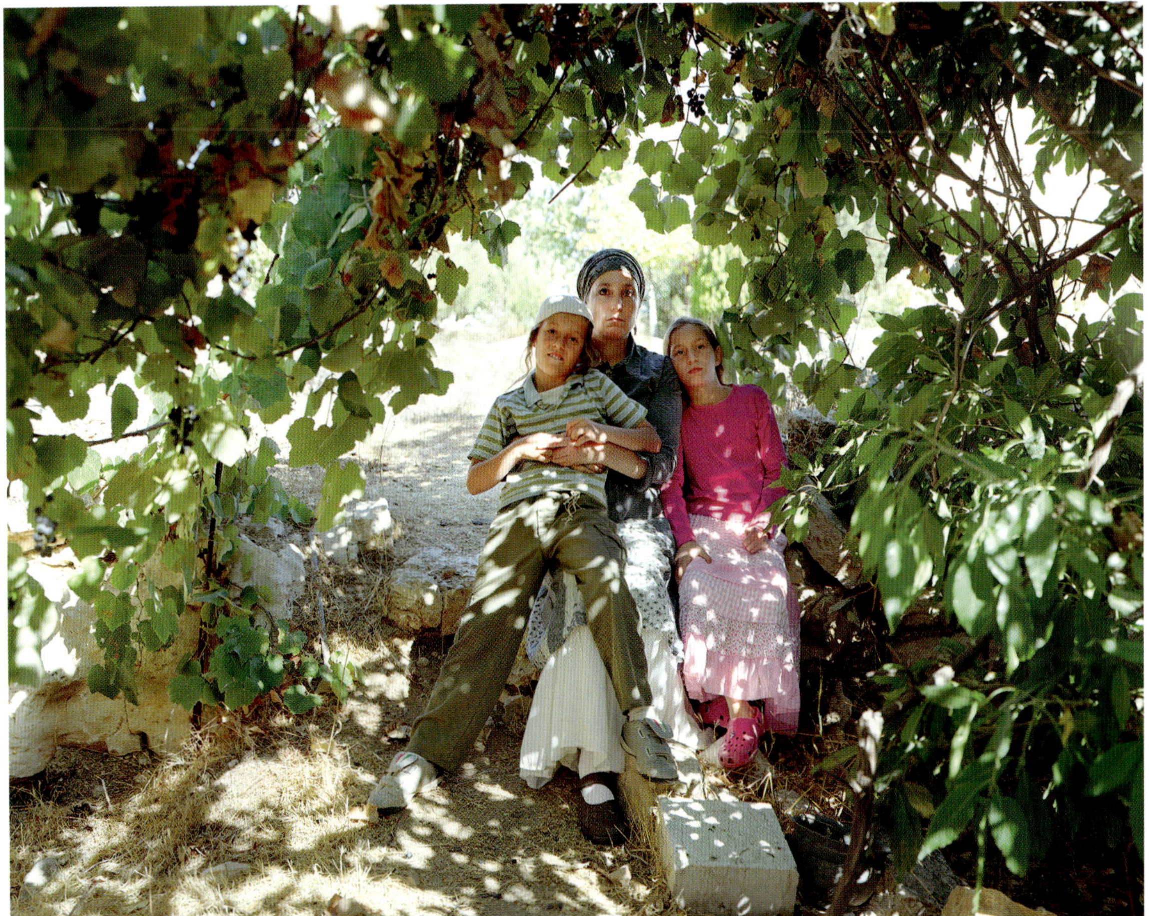

This woman is the widow of a settler who was murdered several years ago. She and her two children live in the settlement of Bat Ayin in Gush Etzion. Bat Ayin is a mainly Breslov religious community (a branch of Hassidim) of around a thousand people; they practice organic farming and holistic medicine, and they ride horses; the community also houses a yeshiva. Unusually, Bat Ayin has no perimeter fence. Despite its peaceful principles, Bat Ayin has also been home to a number of settlers convicted of terrorist offenses.

The killing of this woman's husband, however, was unprovoked: he was praying at a spring (*mikvah*) that is visible from his hillside house when he was killed by two Palestinian men from the nearby village of Khirbet Safa. His widow continues to live in the house she shared with her husband.

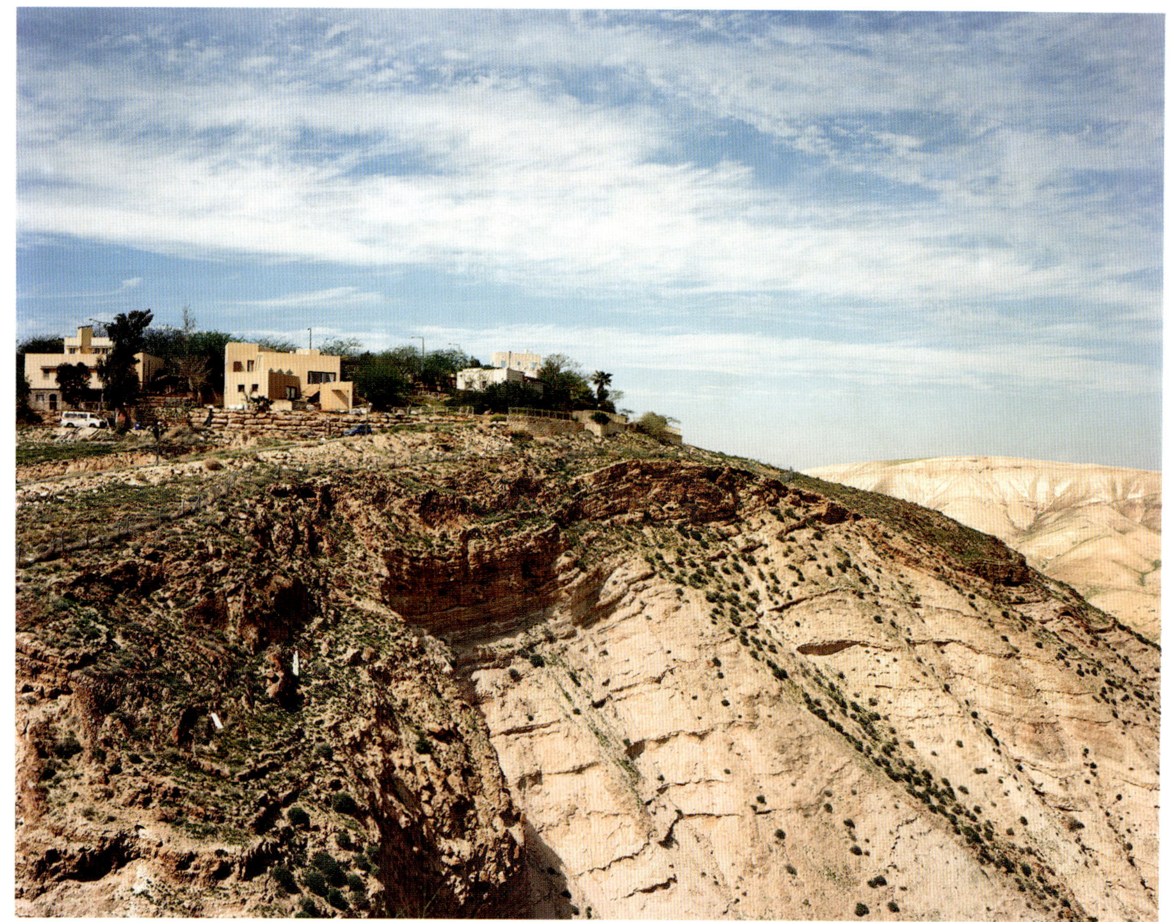

The village of Alon (top) is on top of an escarpment located approximately halfway between the Dead Sea and Jerusalem. It is far enough into the Jordan Valley never to get cold but close enough to the city to commute in fifteen minutes. The settlement is heavily guarded; an appointment is required to enter. Inside, it is an open and friendly place with a strictly observed population ratio of 50 percent religious families to 50 percent secular. The family photographed here is originally from the United States, the father from Boston and mother from Los Angeles. On the wall is a picture of the American jazz musician and civil-rights activist Nina Simone.

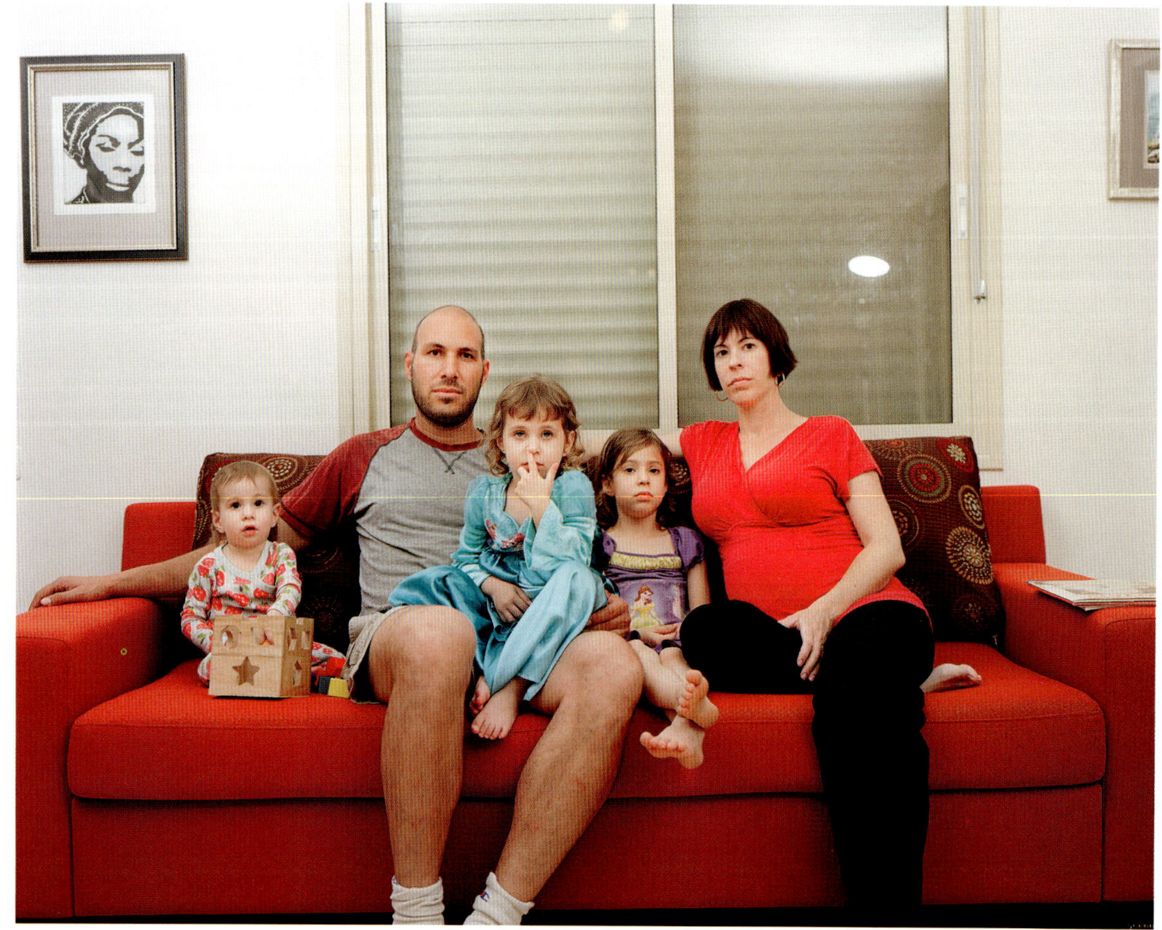

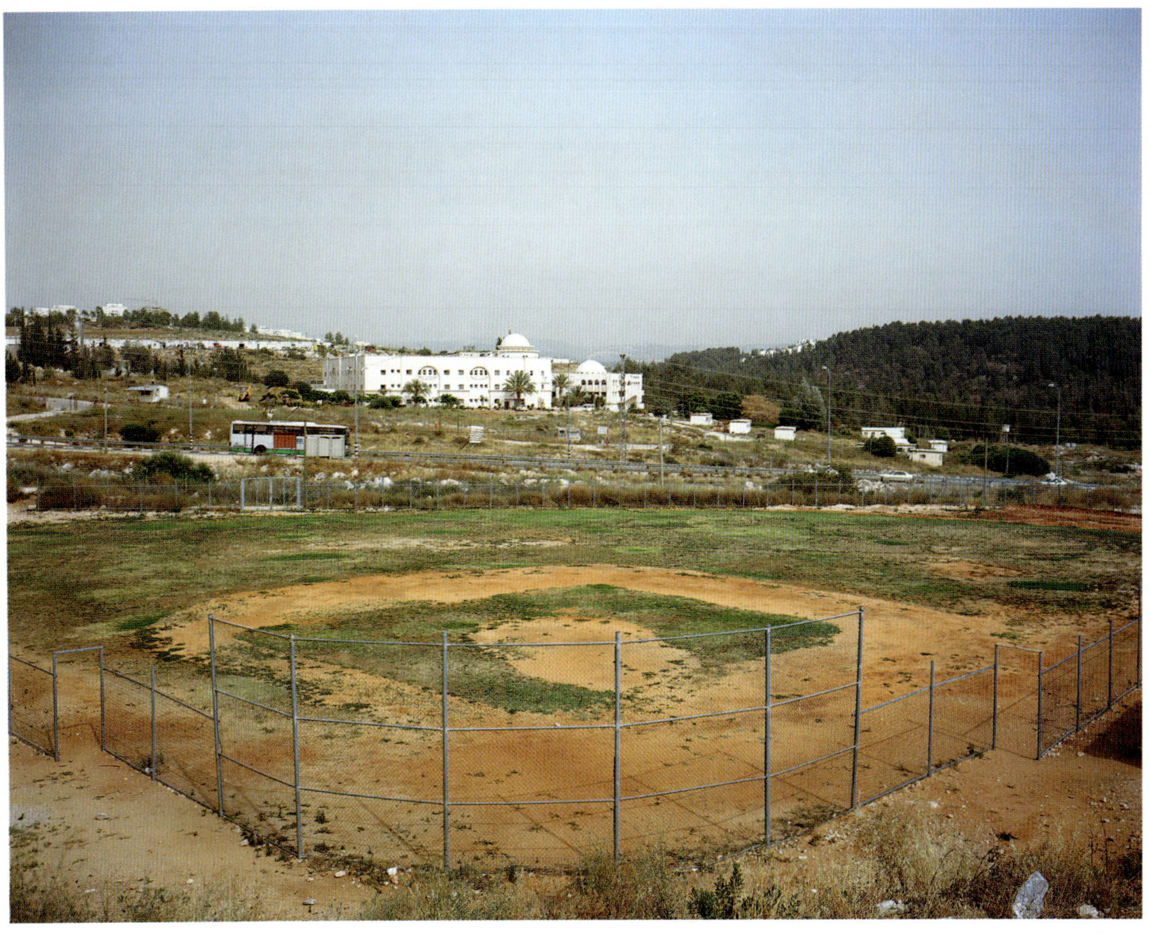

With its baseball diamonds and basketball courts in full swing on Friday mornings, Hashmonaim (top) is one of the most American of the Anglophone settlements in the West Bank. Situated within commuting distance of Tel Aviv, this village has been affectionately dubbed "Little Florida" by some of the people in the area. Founded in 1983 near the new city of Modi'in Illit, Hashmonaim stands only a couple of hundred yards inside the green line that separates the West Bank from Israel. It is one of a string of settlements built along the former border with Jordan just inside the ceasefire line, thus occupying this eye line of the hills looking down on the coastal plane of Israel.

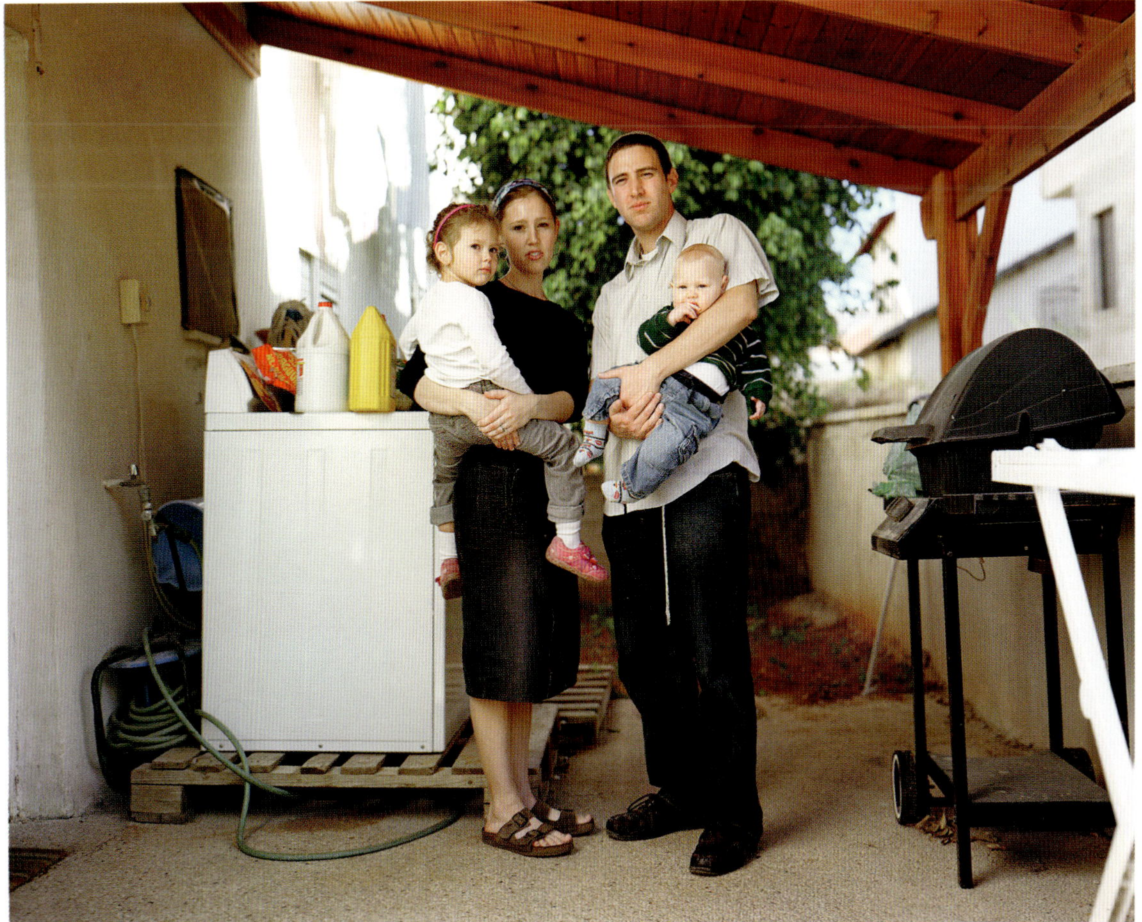

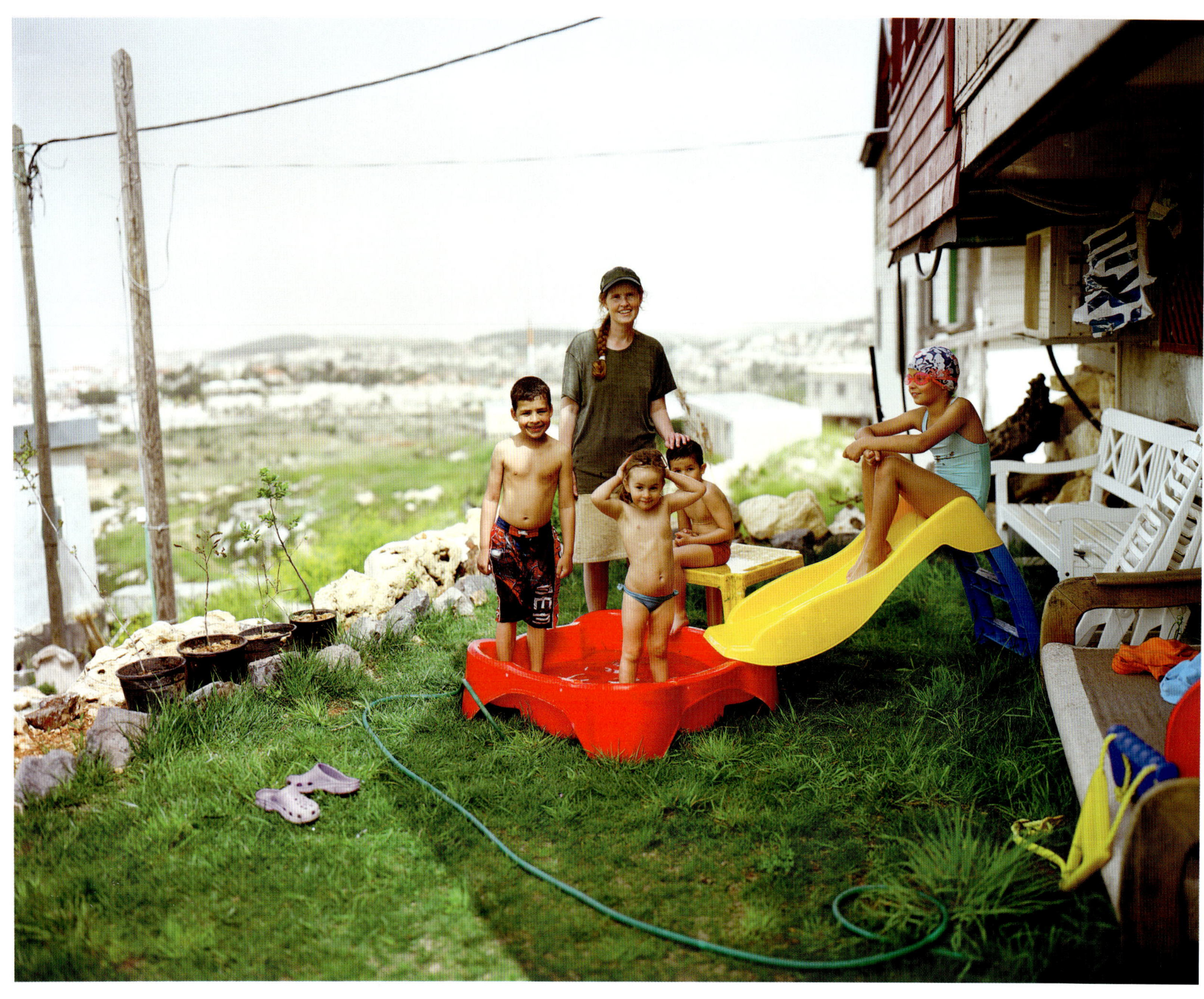

This is the outpost of Givat Hahish. The woman pictured is a Norwegian convert to Judaism. There are a number of converts living in the West Bank, many of them former Christians who came to study the bible and converted. This family lives next door to another family of converts from Boulder, Colorado. The nearby community of Alon Shevut has many hundreds of Peruvian converts who emigrated to Israel en masse in the 1990s with their German pastor, who also converted.

It is often easier for people from other countries to convert, move to Israel, and be given tax breaks and building rights in the West Bank than it is for Arab locals whose families have lived on the land for centuries to get access to housing or building permits.

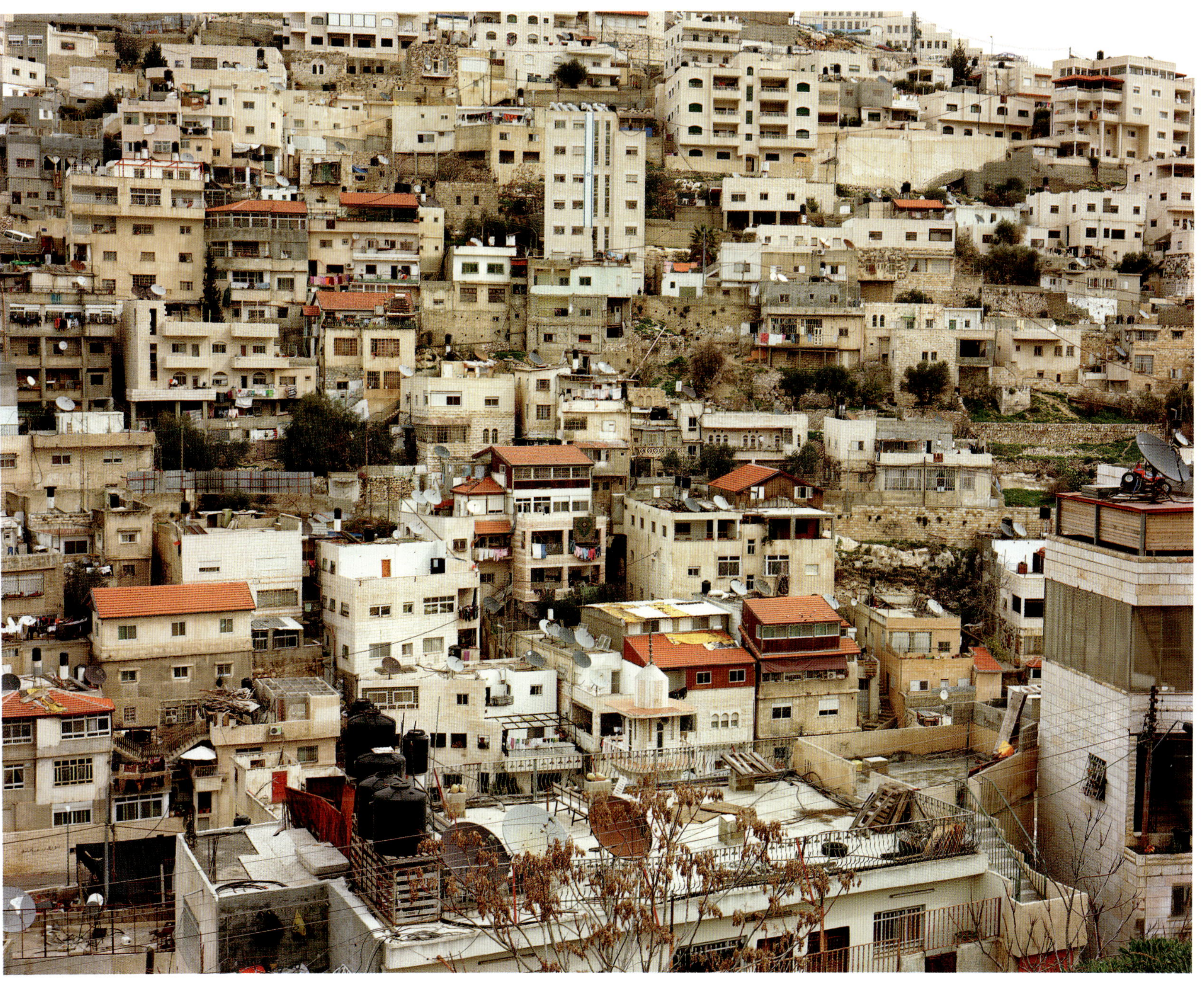

The building with the Israeli flag draped down it (at the center top of the frame) is Beit Yonatan. It is located in Silwan, a predominantly Palestinian area of East Jerusalem directly south of the Old City. In recent years Jewish settlers have established a number of footholds in Silwan, and Beit Yonatan is one of the most notorious. Built illegally and subject to a demolition order from the Israeli government, the building continues to house six settler families, who are protected by Israeli soldiers and police.

Beit Yonatan has become a symbol for a wider battle for control of Silwan, where Palestinian houses are slated for demolition to make way for the new City of David shopping mall and park. Shoring up Israeli claims on this territory is an ongoing archaeological dig for the remains of the original City of David. After twenty years, the dig has yet to find any conclusive proof of the city's location on this spot, but it has literally undermined a number of Palestinian homes that stand above the tunnels.

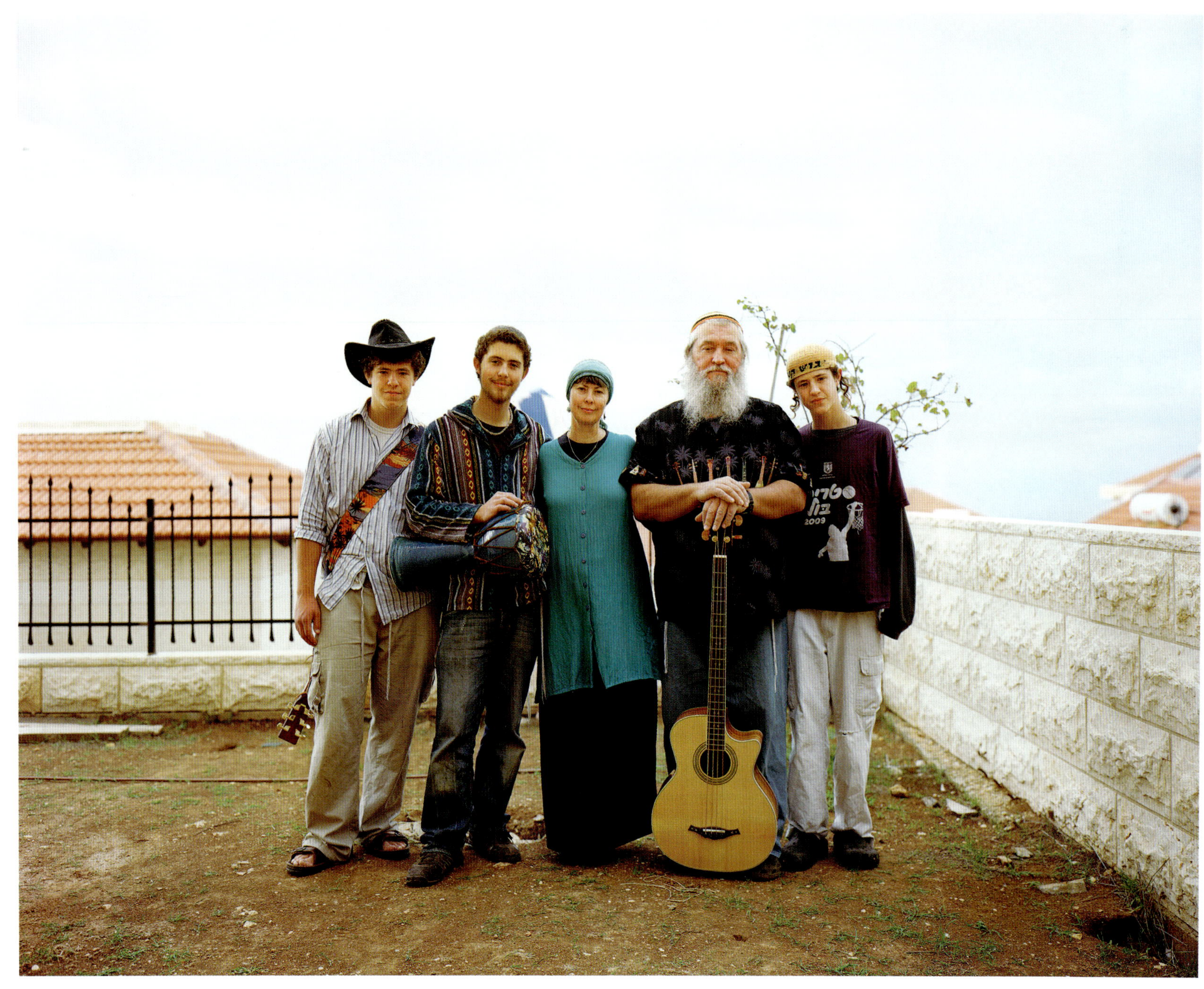

This family is made up of new immigrants to Israel from Baltimore, where the father served with the U.S. Navy. Upon his retirement, he moved the family to the Anglophone settlement of Neve Daniel in the West Bank and took up music. Neve Daniel proudly hosts the highest-situated synagogue in Israel, a pizza/sushi takeout restaurant, and good transportation to both Jerusalem and Hebron.

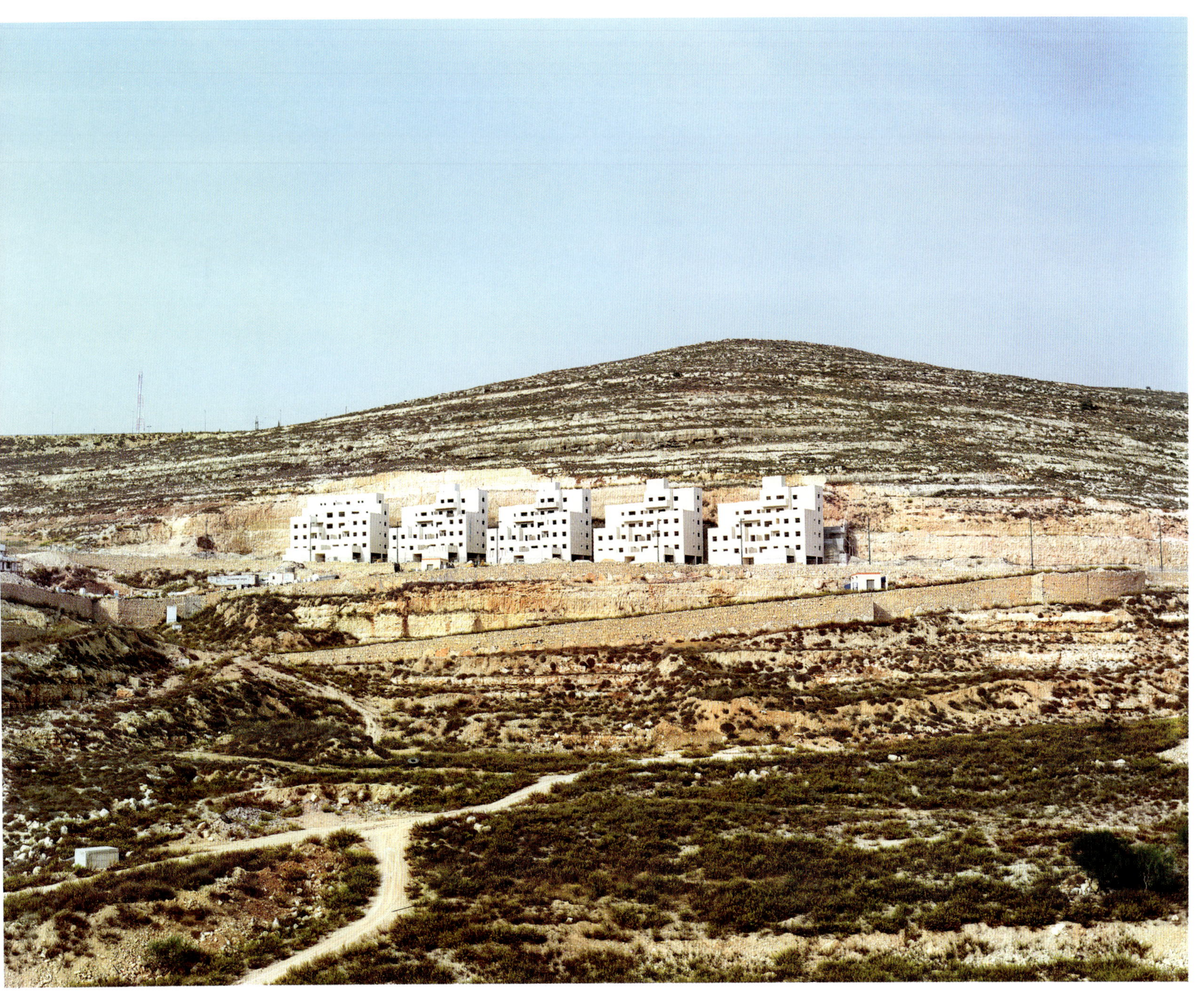

These new buildings form part of the "under-construction" settlement of Agan Ha'Ayalot, built along the corridor of Highway 443 that connects Jerusalem to Tel Aviv by cutting through the territories. Falling under the jurisdiction of nearby Giv'at Ze'ev, this purpose-built settlement will house members of the Haredi (ultra-Orthodox) community. As the number of Haredi within the total population of Israel has grown in recent years, so has their determination to stand apart from the rest of Israeli society. New towns such as Agan Ha'ayalot will permit them to carry on their separate existence. Many in Israel oppose the Haredi's exemption from military service, the social welfare that allows them to study the Torah full-time, and more recently their segregation of Orthodox schools along Ashkenazi and Sephardic lines, whereby children of the two branches of Judaism are not allowed to mix.

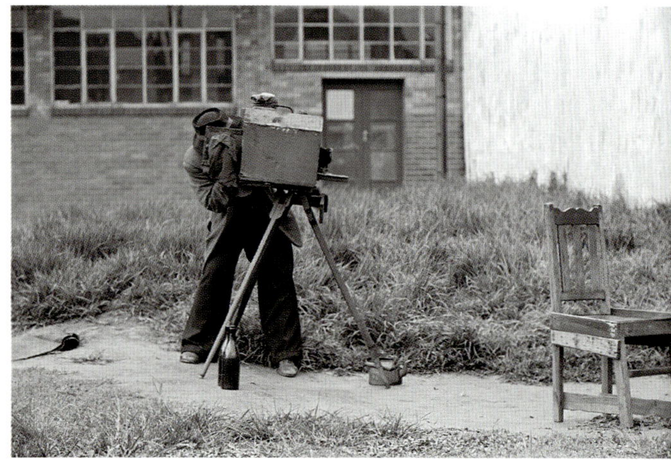

ABOUT THOSE PHOTOGRAPHS . . .
TJ AND *DOUBLE NEGATIVE*

**Bronwyn Law-Viljoen interviews
David Goldblatt and Ivan Vladislavić**

Photographer David Goldblatt and writer Ivan Vladislavić recently published a remarkable collaborative project, TJ/Double Negative *(Umuzi, 2010), a volume of photographs and a novel, packaged handsomely together in a paper slipcase. The two books share a preoccupation with the South African city of Johannesburg, where both artists live and work. For* TJ, *Goldblatt selected images from a vast body of work on the city going back to the late 1940s. In* Double Negative *Vladislavić tells the story of the young photographer Neville Lister, whose encounter in the city with the elder master Saul Auerbach has a profound influence on his life. The pair of volumes received the 2011 Kraszna-Krausz Award for best photography book.*

Bronwyn Law-Viljoen met with Goldblatt and Vladislavić to discuss their unusual collaboration, their thoughts on photography and literature, and the relationship between fiction and history.

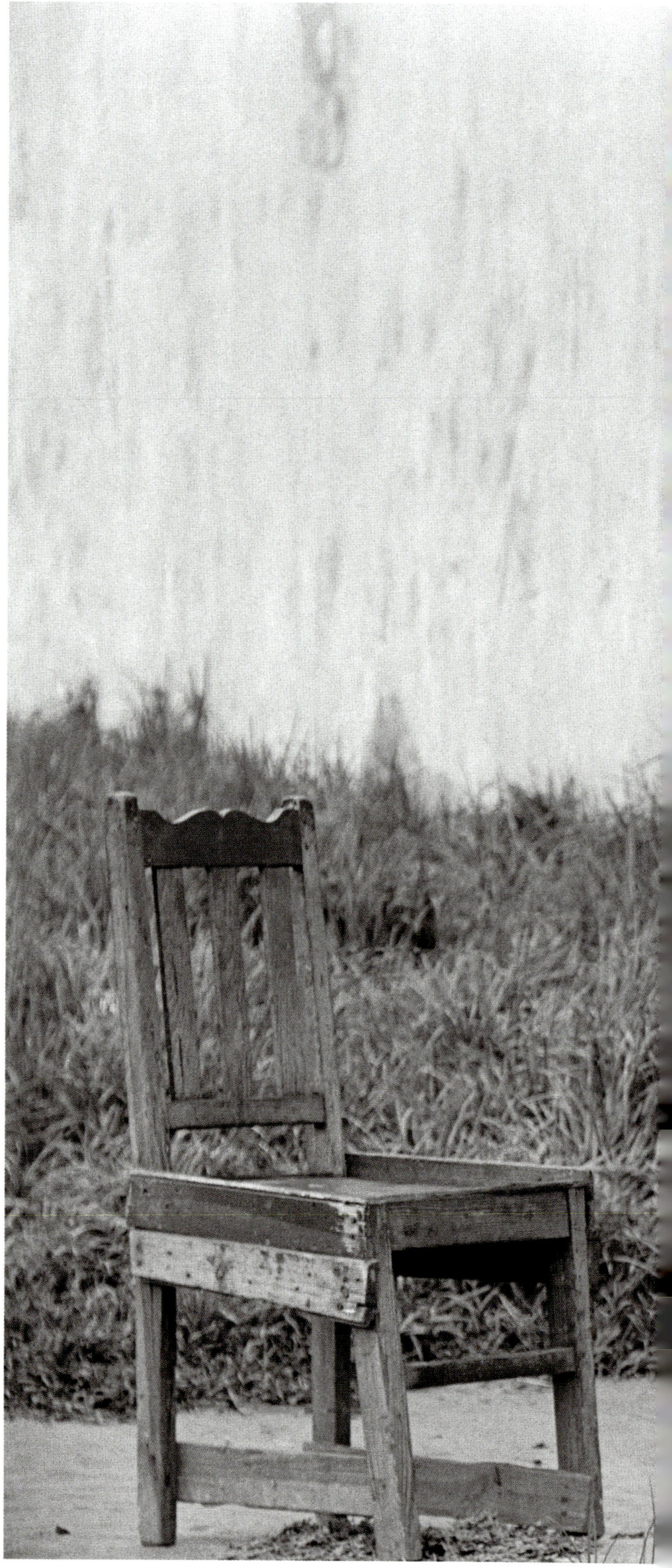

BRONWYN LAW-VILJOEN: I began preparing for this interview by thinking of some of the great literary/photographic pairings of the past. Walker Evans and James Agee's *Let Us Now Praise Famous Men* is of course the starting point for many discussions about the relationship of photography and text. But there are others: the novelist John Banville smuggled some of Josef Sudek's photographs out of Czechoslovakia and then wrote a history of Prague using Sudek's pictures. Richard Powers's 2008 novel *Three Farmers on Their Way to a Dance* is directly based on a photograph of three young men by August Sander. And the novels of W. G. Sebald have spawned an entire academic industry devoted to understanding the writer's enigmatic use of

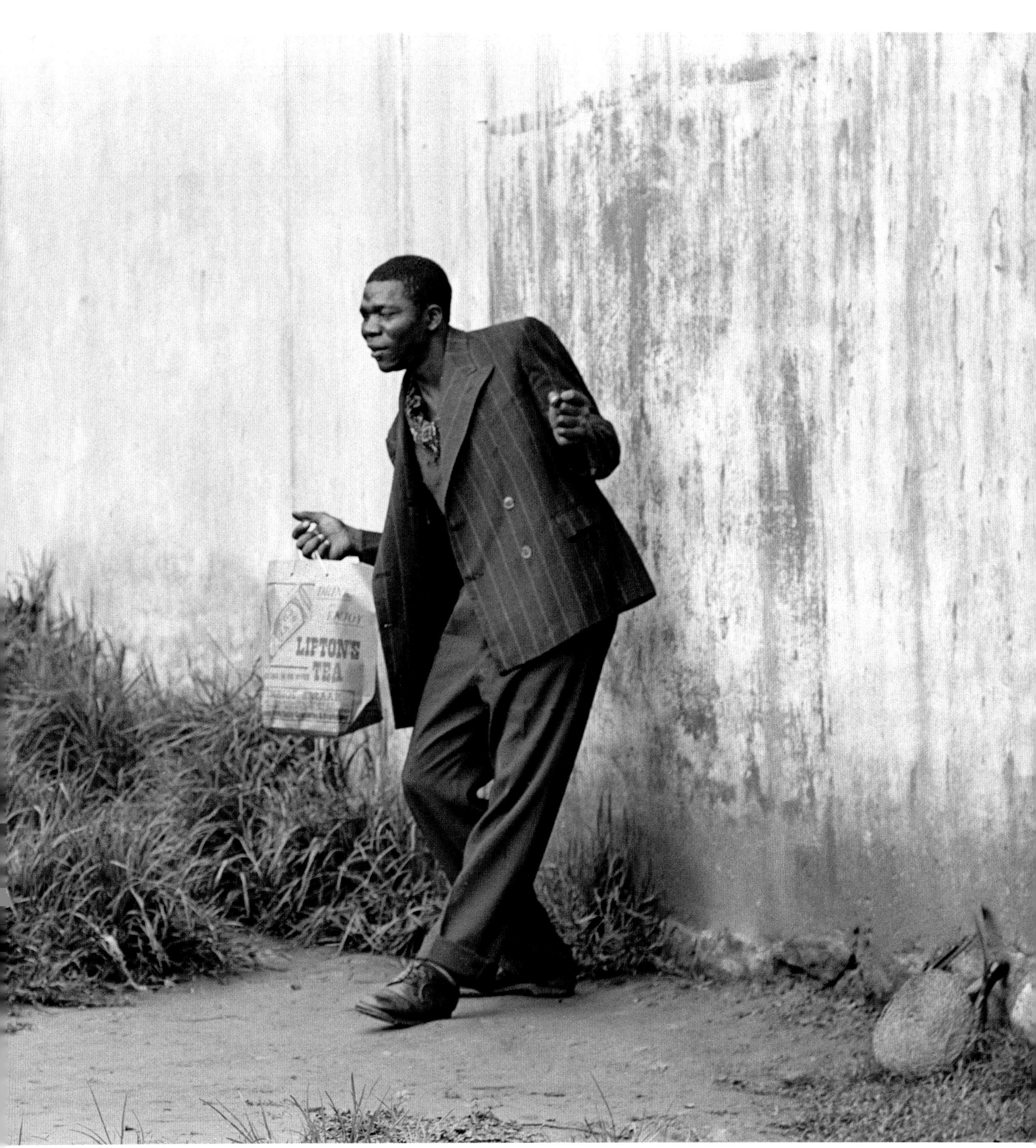

LIPTON'S TEA
ENJOY

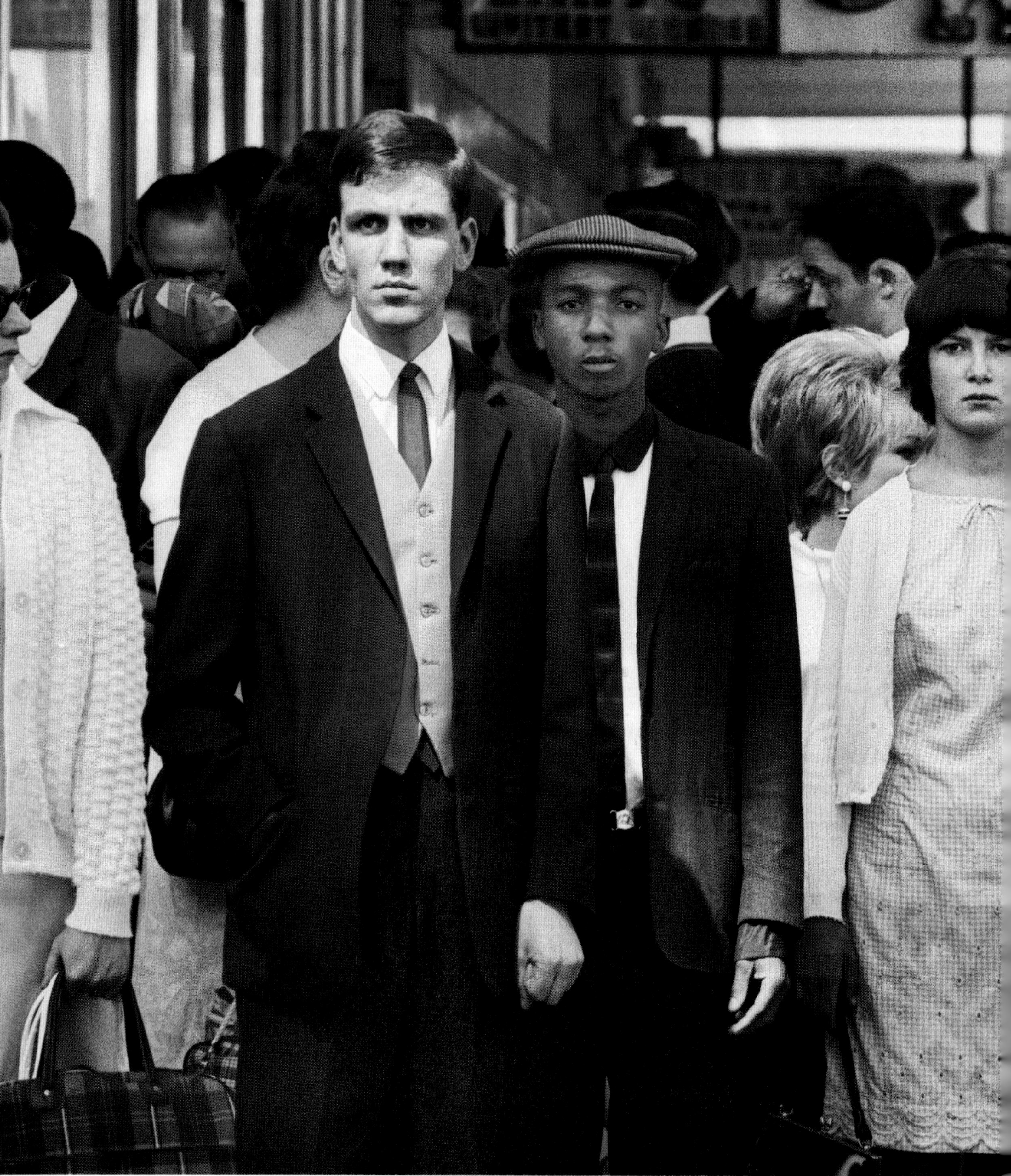

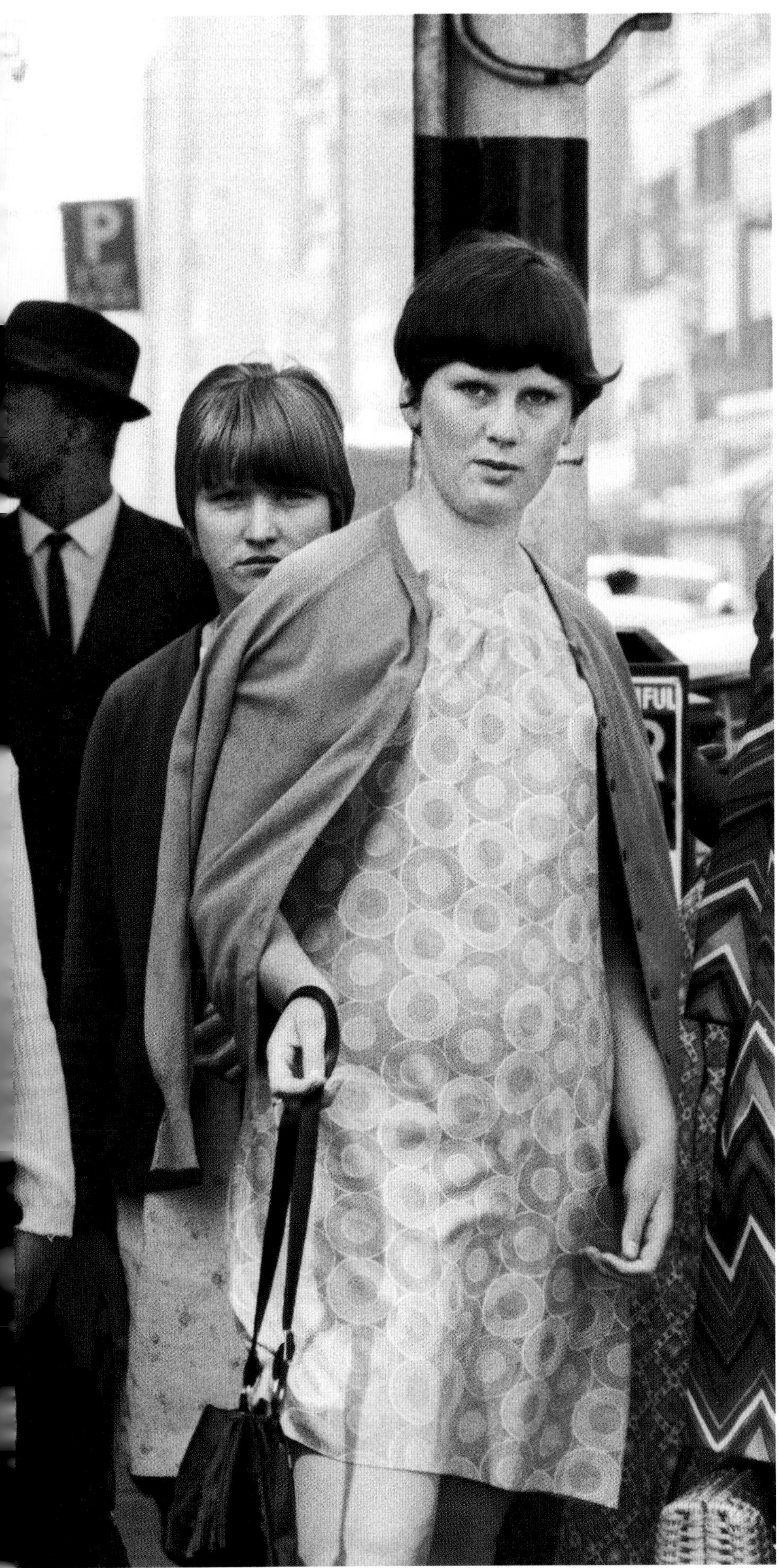

photographs. Did you have any precedents in mind when you began this project?

IVAN VLADISLAVIĆ: I didn't have any specific precedents in mind, although Sebald really interests me. His use of photographs is completely his own—I am intrigued by the relationship between the text and the photographs: they almost cancel each other out in some places, rather than working together.

Still, I didn't have a particular model in mind. I didn't want to be held too tightly either to a journalistic practice or to some critical commentary on the photographs. So my approach from the beginning was to have the photographs in the corner of my eye and to pursue my own literary process as much as possible.

DAVID GOLDBLATT: Neither did I. In fact, to be honest, after our initial discussions, Ivan and I had hardly any conversations other than mutual support. When finally he gave me a preliminary script I was taken aback—it was completely different from anything I had expected. I worked with Nadine Gordimer on the books *On the Mines* [1973] and *Lifetimes: Under Apartheid* [1986]. With those projects, it was quite different: we collaborated closely on the whole thing.

IV: I had been given an early selection of the photographs that were to go into the book to use as "reference material," but in the end, quite a different selection made it through. It may well be that some of the images that shaped my text unconsciously in crucial ways are not in the *TJ* selection at all.

BLV: How was the project conceived? Did it begin with the photographs or with an idea for a novel about a photographer? Or with an idea for a book on Johannesburg?

DG: Ivan and I, over a period of some years, have shared a certain delight in our rather twisted views of things in the world, and of Johannesburg in particular. I invited Ivan to come out with me while I was working. Out of that came a clearer determination to collaborate in some way. I imagined that he would contribute some kind of literary essay to the project. I had in fact spoken to other people about contributing to a book like this. But Ivan expressed the desire to be the sole writer and to write specifically for this work—

PAGES 34 and 35: Portrait photographer and client, Braamfontein, 1955; LEFT: On Eloff Street, 1967.

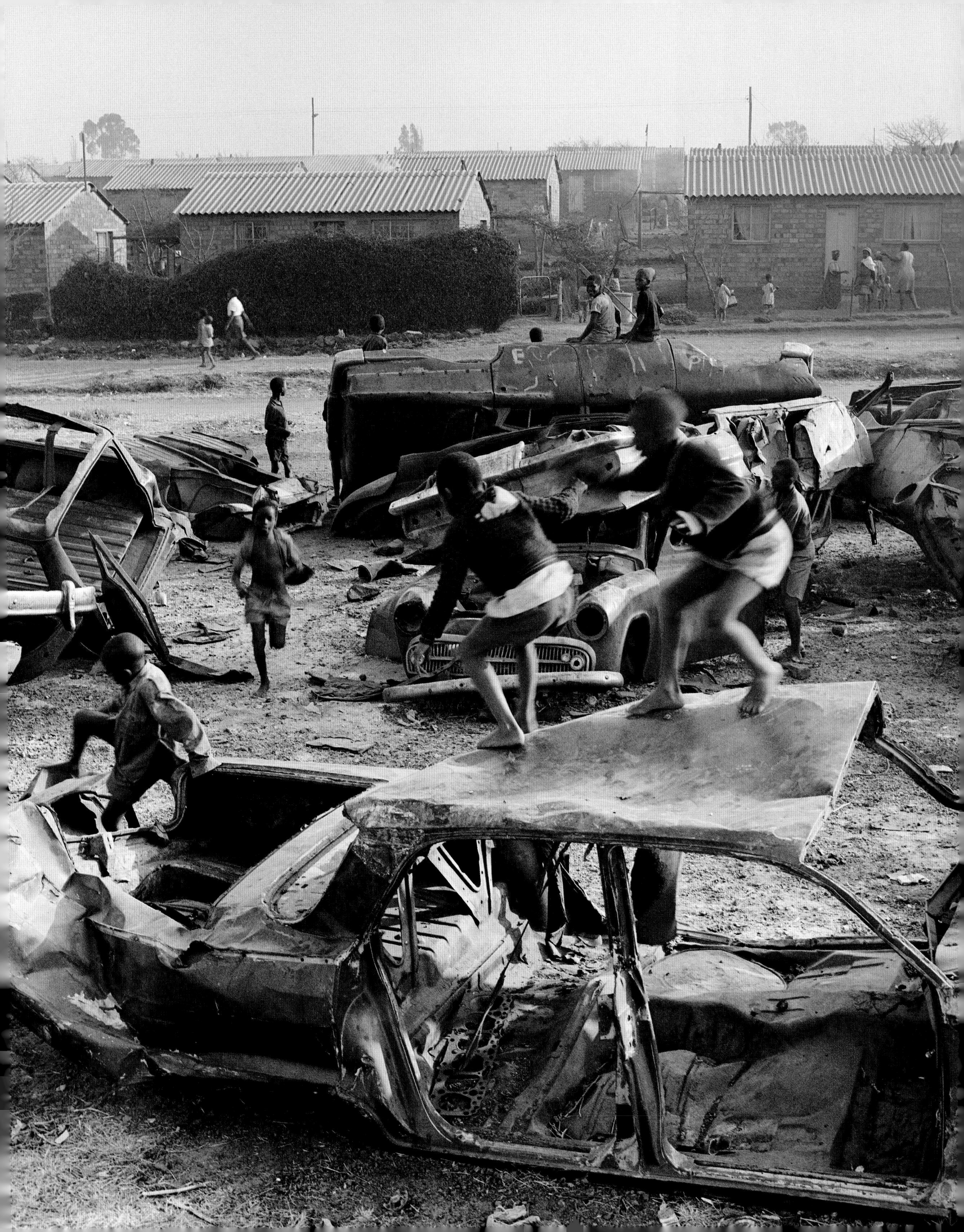

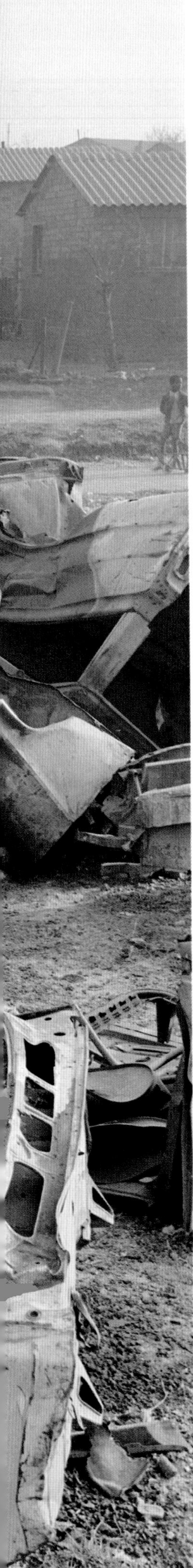

in other words, not to contribute a kind of minor-key part, but to write a major work. At that point, the collaboration assumed a different, much more definite character.

IV: Before starting *Double Negative*, I had worked alongside visual artists and with photographers—including, notably, Joachim Schönfeldt, who asked me to write a text in response to some "illustrations" he had made; the book that eventually grew out of that was my novel *The Exploded View* [2004]. And in fact some of the work from my *Portrait with Keys* appeared in David's catalog *51 Years* [2001]. So that primed me for this project.

With *Double Negative*, I was at a point in my writing trajectory where I didn't want to do any more documentary or nonfiction pieces about Johannesburg. I wanted to write a novel. Of course, it was immensely appealing to collaborate with David, but the only way I could find of going forward was to say to David that I wanted to write a fiction work. And, to his credit, he didn't bat an eyelid.

BLV: Ivan, it seems to me that of the two "tasks" in the project, yours was the more difficult, since David's photographs of Johannesburg were, for the most part, already in the world. Were you daunted by the thought of having to work around the images, or against them?

IV: It was daunting at the start. It would have been easier to write a short story or an essay. Having said I'd write something more ambitious, the thought that I would now have to generate an *entire novel* while David waited, drumming his fingers, was daunting. I know that these things cannot be rushed and so it was not a case of saying I would have a draft ready in three months. David's attitude was always that I should take as much time as I needed. In the end the whole process, from concept to publication, took about five years.

The other daunting thing was writing alongside such a tremendously powerful body of work. It would have been quite easy to get absorbed by it—not in a positive way. I had to try to write something that would have its own power and weight, that would hold together and have its own integrity, and not be just providing some kind of feeble commentary to the photographs.

I also had something else to push against: while my novel was to be set in Johannesburg, I didn't want it to be *about* the city in the same way as my last few books. That became a point of resistance for me.

BLV: While Ivan was working all this out, David, were you making photographs that were specifically for this project?

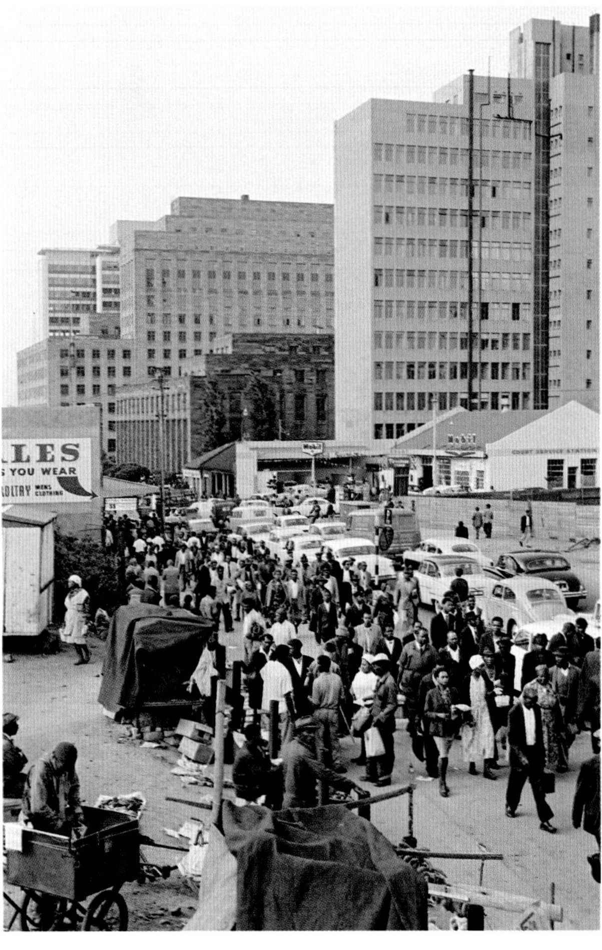

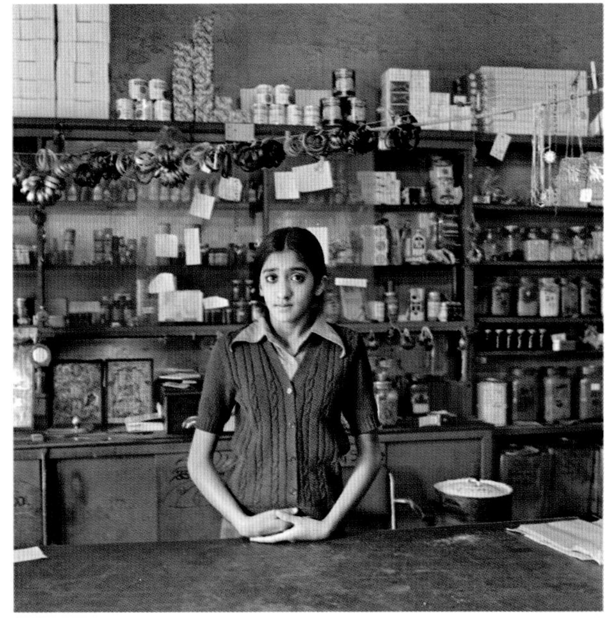

LEFT: Playground, Chiawelo, September 1972; ABOVE: Evening exodus from the city. Blacks stream to Westgate Station for trains to Soweto; whites in their cars head for the northern suburbs, 1964; BELOW: Yaksha Modi, daughter of Chagan Modi, in her father's shop before its destruction under the Group Areas Act, 17th Street, Fietas, 1976.

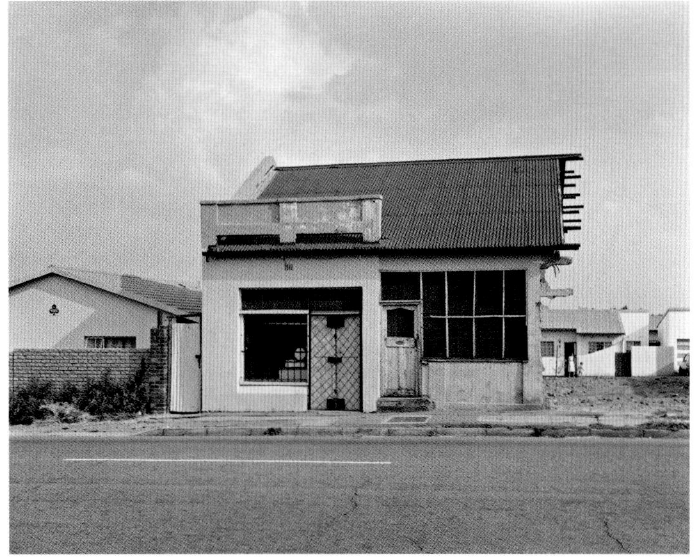

DG: Well, the realization that we were now going to look at Johannesburg made me aware that I needed to consider what I had done in relation to what is happening now, and react or respond to that—and that was for me a major step. Because what was happening in the city, and to some extent in the country, was very worrying, and that made me look more closely at things to see if I could find a way in, photographically.

BLV: David, can you talk about your view of history and how it is reflected in this project, in your own "making" of history in the book?

DG: When I started looking back at my work I realized that it was an enormous mass of *stuff*. By no stretch of the imagination could it be called a picture of Johannesburg. Apart from two magazine assignments, I have never set out in any way to "represent" the city. That made putting this book together both more difficult and easier. Easier in that I didn't claim to represent Johannesburg and therefore I was free to put the material together in any way, but more difficult in that, once I started putting it all together, it became obvious that I had no clear sense of the city. Having said that, I am very aware of history, and that became much more sharply defined to me when I started to put this together.

BLV: Ivan, can you talk a little about the notions of history that you are invoking in the novel?

IV: One of the things that inspired my novel was a conversation I had with Jonathan Hyslop, the social historian. We had been to see the twentieth-anniversary staging of the play *Sophiatown* at the Market Theatre [in Johannesburg], and we got talking about having been at the first opening of the play in 1986 and then at the rerun in 2006. It was around the time when I was starting to think about what David and I were going to do. Watching the play again, twenty

years later, more than a decade into democracy, I was struck by how much its meaning had changed because the context of its reception was so different. Out of that grew the idea of having cross-sections through time in the novel—presenting three distinct periods that would allow me to explore how things shift and change over time. I had this three-part structure before I knew it would be the story of the relationship between two photographers.

BLV: The image that opens *TJ* is of a portrait photographer. To what extent was this project an "analysis" of photography itself? It seems to me that the book is partly about the recording process that photography is, that one of the layers of the book is a conversation about the act, the work of taking a photograph.

IV: Again, this focus was part of my resistance—my saying let me *not* write another novel about Johannesburg, let me rather deal with how we see Johannesburg and the world at large. In doing this, I could draw on the stylistic shift in David's work over time— all the pictures are taken in Johannesburg, but what intrigues me is how his focus and way of taking photographs have changed.

DG: I have long since put aside questions about the legitimacy of taking photographs and the nature of taking photographs. I just take photographs. That's been my position all along. Perhaps at some point in selecting photographs for this book I had moments of doubt about going from the rather straight-up photographs to the rather oddball pictures that I did in my car mirror, but I thought: It doesn't really matter to me; these pictures are another aspect of this world that I inhabit.

I photograph what is interesting to me. There's very little self-consciousness in my work in that sense. I do what I think is appropriate to the thing I am interested in.

IV: Taking a photograph used to be a very deliberate, slow act. But that has changed—now it's often incidental, something people do while they are doing something else. I am interested in that as an analogy for shifts in how we experience things—how we write about things, for instance. I've tried to refract this idea through the book, by using different modes of writing to suggest different ways of seeing.

BLV: David, how do you respond to the rather ambivalent representation of the photographers in the novel? The photographer Saul Auerbach is held up, at least by some of the characters in the novel, as the artist par excellence, but Neville treats him with a mixture of admiration and circumspection. Through Neville we are witness to one of the ways Auerbach makes photographs. Neville admires the simultaneous randomness and purposefulness of the making of two photographs in Bez Valley. [*Bezuidenhout Valley is a suburb of Johannesburg. To make these photographs, Auerbach* *climbs a hill with Neville and a British journalist, from where they have a good view of the valley. They each pick a house and then they drive to those houses to photograph whoever lives there.]* Does this in any way reflect your own way of making images?

DG: I think Ivan has both a critical view and a strongly empathetic view of the character. He uses Auerbach as a vehicle for questions about photography, about the city, about attitudes, not the least of which is the question of randomness. I found the Bez Valley incident very interesting because it touches on aspects of me, or someone like me. Auerbach is a believable character in the story and Ivan has accurately discerned the process by which a guy like this works.

The question of randomness is interesting, because I *do* employ it. My photography might be very deliberate, but I enjoy the randomness. It is, for me, always associated with a very definite commitment to whatever comes out of that randomness. Recently I decided to look at the intersections of latitude and longitude in South Africa and to go to every one of them and make a photograph, until I found that it was actually very boring—because sometimes there was fuck-all there! And that made me realize that although I am committed to randomness I am absolutely not a conceptualist. I can't just hook myself to a concept and follow it through. I need something outside of my own "inside" that engages me, provokes me, makes me want to photograph.

IV: It intrigues me that a photograph, one instant out of an infinite number of possibilities, becomes such an enduring, constantly referenced thing, and comes to stand for so much.

I'm concerned with the random in my own writing process. It's an extraordinary idea—it's not so much the question of randomness in itself, as David says, but what you do with the material once your choices are made.

I often have the sense when I'm writing that every paragraph could be different, that every word could be changed. (This is what comes from having worked as an editor.)

BLV: Can we talk about fiction? What seems to happen in this project—partly because the novel and the book of photographs lie side by side—is that photography is read in the light of, or even as fiction, and the novel is read in relation to the usual "burden of truth" that has always been the province of photography. David, are you able to look back at your work over so many years, and see

not *fiction* so much but a way of working that is not dissimilar from the way in which the novel writer constructs "truth" or "history"? I suppose what I am suggesting is that this project takes the photographs out of one realm into another. In a sense they become "literary"—creative in the way that the novel is creative.

DG: *Creative* is a word that I distrust in relation to this. They are certainly literary in the sense that I see photographs as paragraphs of writing. They need to be as carefully considered, word for word, constructed, and then finally put together as a good piece of writing. To me they are very closely associated.

IV: I think there is a kind of magnetism between the novel and the photographs. If you've bought them in this package, you can't read the novel without certain descriptions in it triggering memories of the photographs that you've seen. This was precisely the fascination of writing *Double Negative*: to create that uncomfortable fit. The relationship between the two works also interests me because I think that a lot of contemporary writing is in this gray area between fiction and nonfiction. In fact, I don't know how else you write fiction except by referencing things you have seen, read, heard, dreamed, imagined. What this project hopefully does is make the connection to the field of references more obvious, more conscious. Writers always work on the edge of things they want to ignore, that they don't want to acknowledge, that they want to forget. One could say that the act of forgetting is central to the making of fiction. So writing consciously alongside a very powerful, recognizable body of work makes clear what writers are doing all the time.

DG: There is no question in my mind that literature—sometimes a piece of nonfiction, perhaps a sentence that I've read somewhere, perhaps a whole book—continuously rubs off on the way I am working and what I am seeing. Which does not mean that every

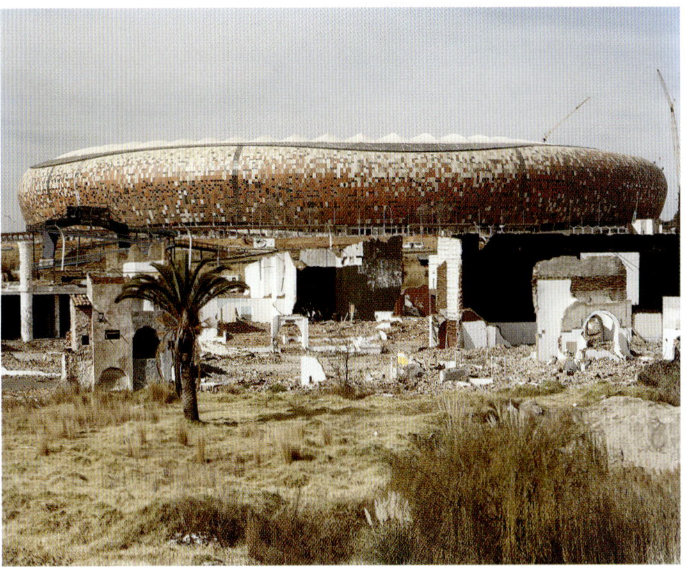

OPPOSITE: Hassimia Sahib's butcher's shop, truncated but still in business after the neighbor's half of the building was destroyed under the Group Areas Act, March 8, 1986; RIGHT: Near Soweto: Soccer City Stadium and the ruins of Shareworld. The stadium, built for the 2010 World Cup, cost 3.3 billion rand to complete (a budget overrun of 800 million rand). Shareworld, intended as a theme park catering to the people of Soweto, was built and went bankrupt in the late 1980s, June 6, 2009.

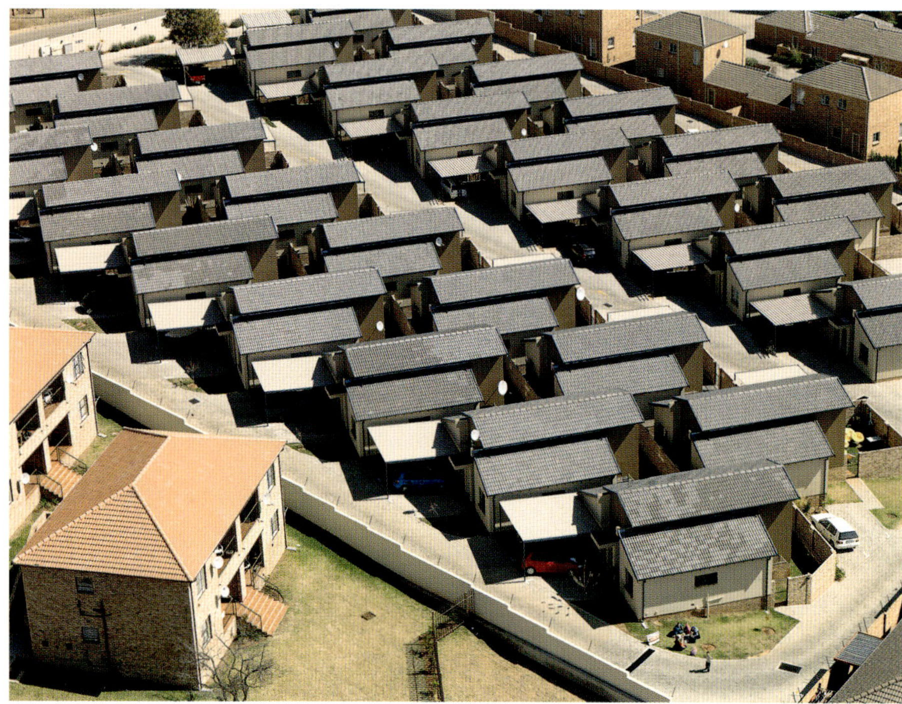

time I pick up the camera I am thinking of Dostoevsky. It's just a feeling, a way of being, almost. There are several writers in South Africa who have been particularly relevant for me in that sense—along with Ivan, there's Gordimer, Herman Charles Bosman, Barney Simon, early Athol Fugard—all these people, in one way or another, have given me that feeling of these two things rubbing up against each other. Every time I go to a photograph I did of a little fruit shop somewhere in Lorentzville I am very conscious of Vladislavić. Not that I expect to find any description of that shop in his work, but I know, without thinking about it, that if he and I had been at that street corner at that particular moment we would have bounced off each other.

BLV: There's an inflection in the way you take photographs that draws on a literary strand. That photograph of the portrait photographer at the start of *TJ* is a case in point—it is a very "literary" photograph. Of course it tells a historical story about black portrait photographers, but when we see the same image again, this time as a diptych, later in the book, it has become a novelistic device.

IV: Many of the photographs offer a narrative, as still and frontal as some of them are. The one on the cover of David's book is a perfect example: it tells a story. Then again you could also read the caption as a short story—even without the photograph.

BLV: David, in your photographs, people seem to construct themselves before the camera. Ivan, in the novel, you too suggest that this is possible and have characters "remake" themselves during the course of the story.

IV: One of the exciting things about South Africa is that it is a society in which we've had to reinvent ourselves. It is not a static, solidified society. Though of course it's not just South Africa. It's the contemporary world in which so many people have the need to reinvent themselves. Even if they don't always have the means at their fingertips. ◐

ABOVE: In Johannesburg's northwest, cluster-housing "estates" have sprouted in poorly planned profusion. Here, behind the invariably electrified perimeter walls, middle-class blacks and whites live in previously unthinkable proximity, and even neighborliness, August 15, 2009; RIGHT: Refugees from Zimbabwe sheltering in the Central Methodist Church on Pritchard Street, Johannesburg, March 22, 2009.

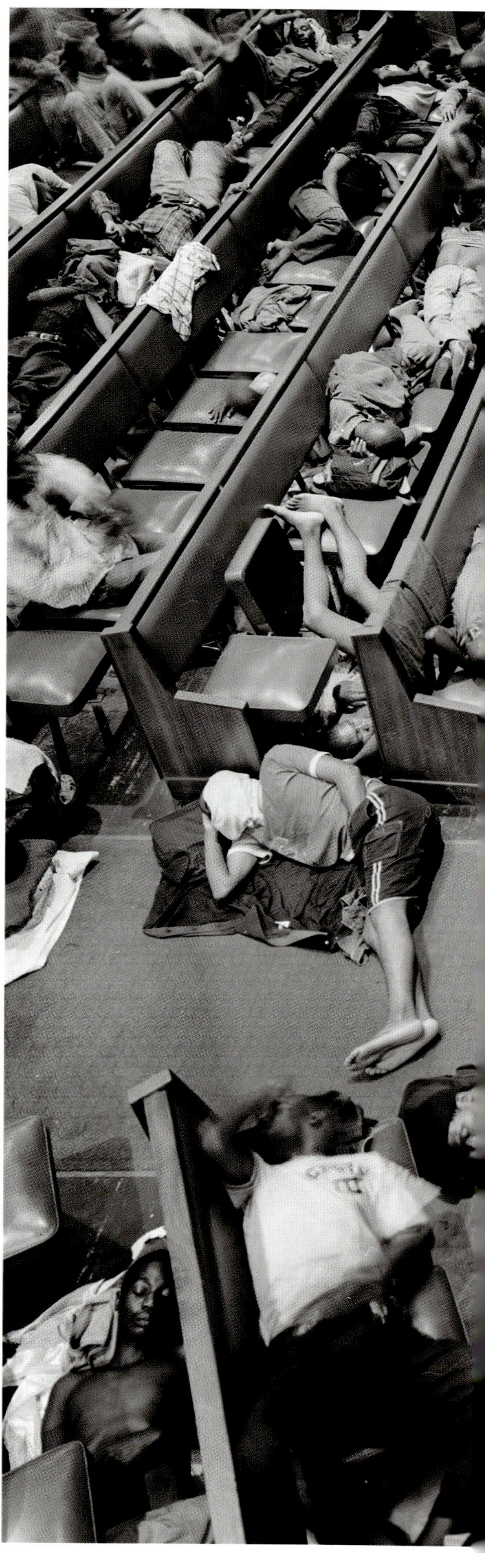

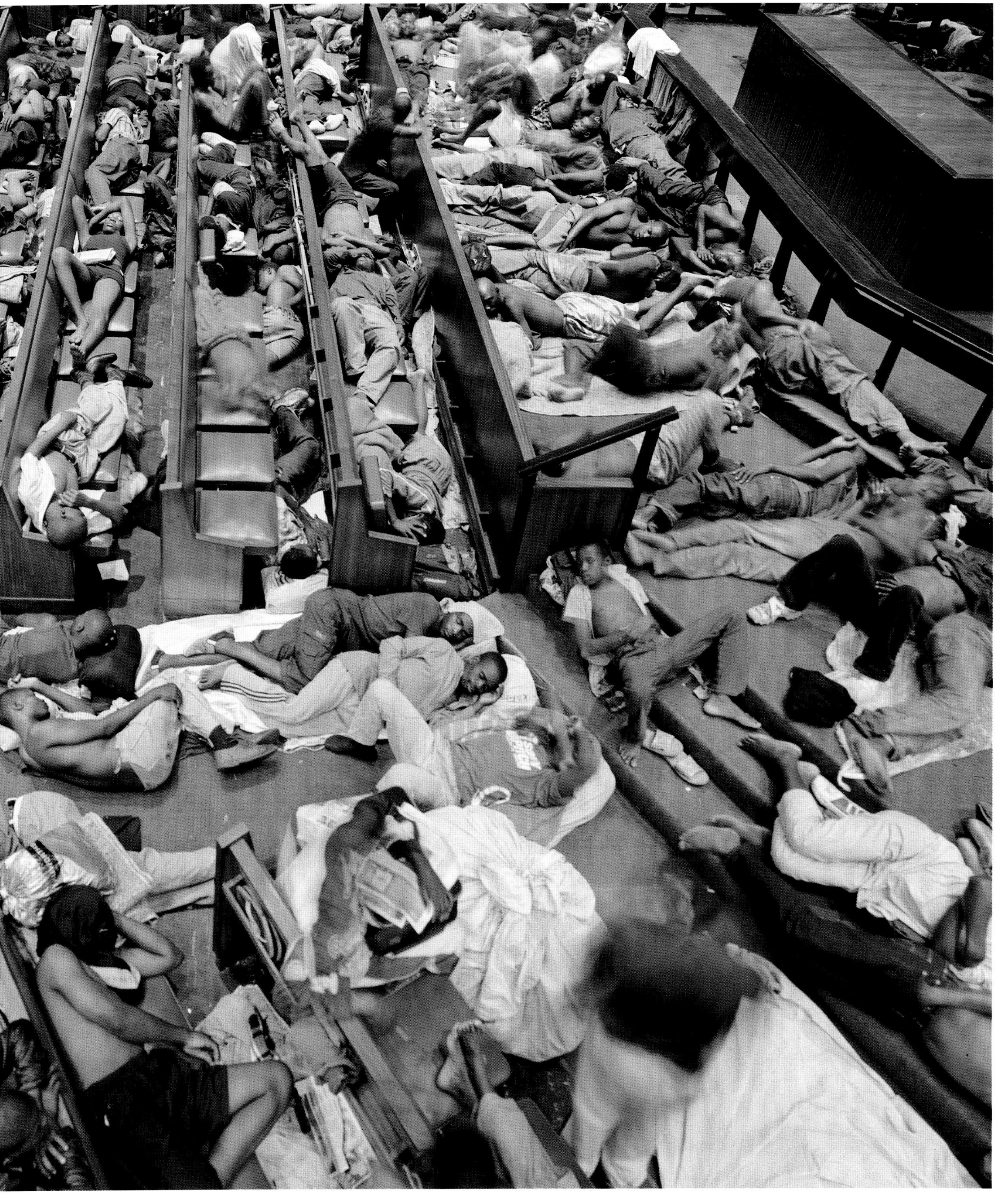

FORM AND PRESSURE

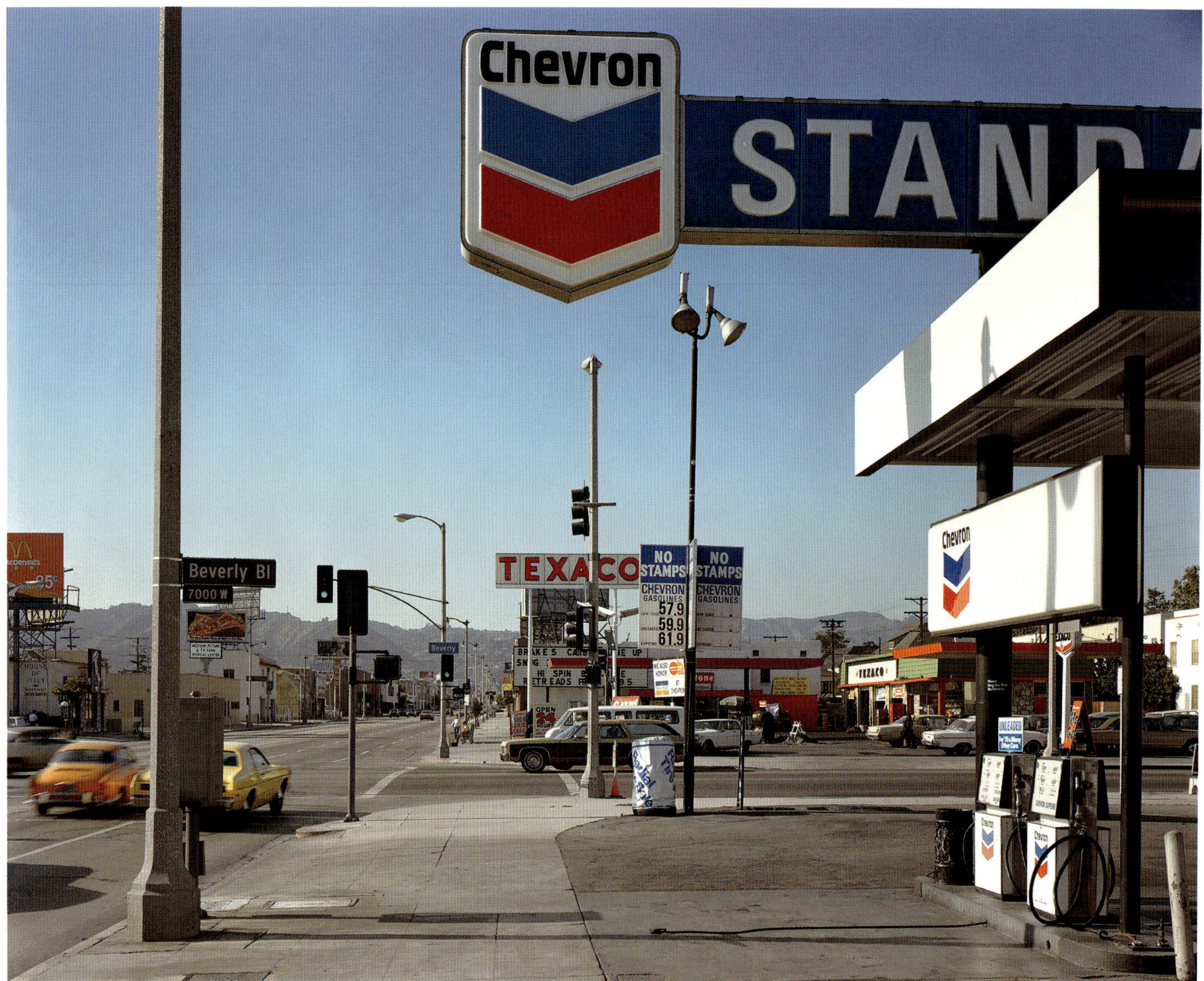

BY STEPHEN SHORE

I made this photograph at the intersection of Beverly Boulevard and La Brea Avenue in Los Angeles on July 21, 1975. I was at the start of a commission from the great architect Robert Venturi, to explore the contemporary American landscape. I was drawn to this scene because it seemed to be such a quintessential Los Angeles experience: the gas stations, the jumble, the signage, the space. I was also, for my own personal reasons, exploring visual structure. For the previous two years, since I had been using a large-format camera, questions would arise, seemingly on their own. They were questions about how the world I wanted to photograph could translate into an image. They were, essentially, questions about structure.

For about a year, my work had been moving toward greater structural complexity. Look at the picture opposite, made in 1974, a year before the Los Angeles image. Both of these pictures happen to be based on one-point perspective with the vanishing point in the center of the image. The Los Angeles photograph is much denser; there is more information to organize. I was also interested in how the frame of the picture forms a line that all the visual elements of the picture relate to. It is the image's proscenium, as it were. I recognized that when three-dimensional space is collapsed into a flat picture, objects in the foreground are now seen, on the surface of the photograph, in a new and

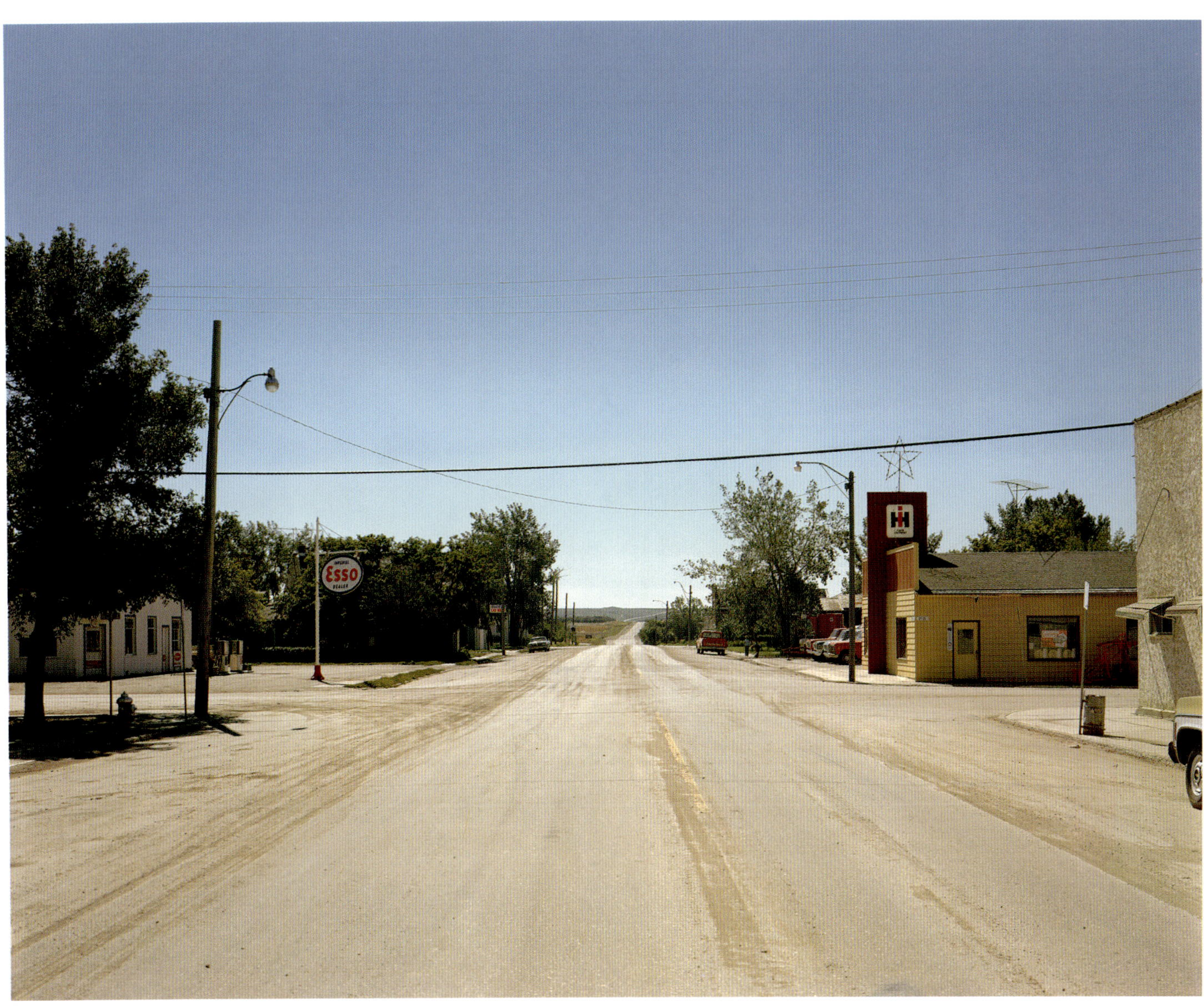

precise relationship to the objects in the background. Look, for example, at the relationship between the "Standard" sign and the light pole underneath it in the Los Angeles photograph. I was interested in seeing how many of these visual interstices I could juggle on a single image.

When I took the Beverly and La Brea picture, I saw it as a culmination of this process of juggling ever-increasing visual complexity. At the same time, I recognized that I was *imposing* an order on the scene in front of me. Photographers have to impose order, bring structure to what they photograph. It is inevitable. A photograph without structure is like a sentence without grammar—it is incomprehensible, even inconceivable. This order is the product of a series of decisions: where to position the camera, where to place the frame, and when to release the shutter. These decisions simultaneously define the content and determine the structure.

I use the term *structure* rather than *composition* because *composition* refers to a synthetic process, such as painting. A painter starts with a blank canvas. Every mark he or she makes

OPPOSITE: Stephen Shore, Beverly Boulevard and La Brea Avenue, Los Angeles, California, June 21, 1975; ABOVE: Stephen Shore, Proton Avenue, Gull Lake, Saskatchewan, 1974.

Both photographs courtesy the artist and 303 Gallery, New York

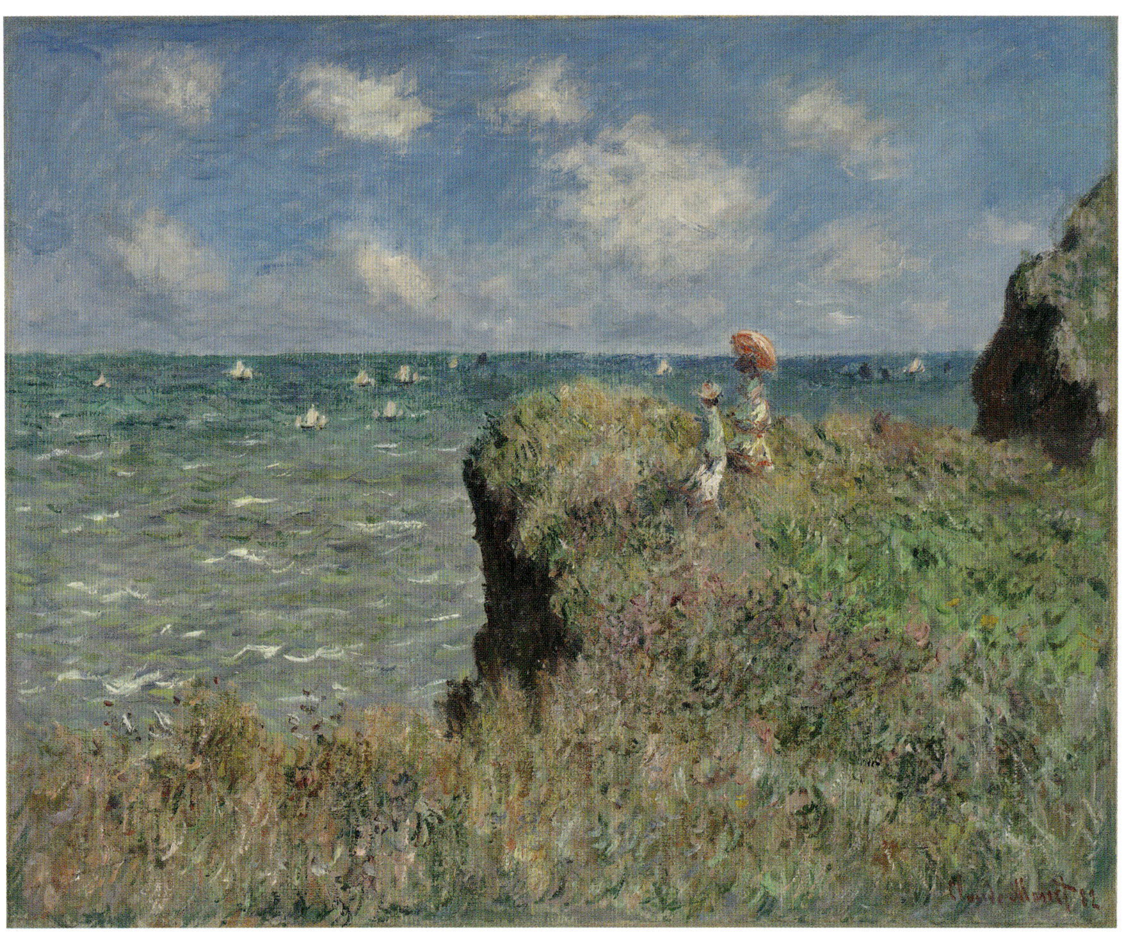

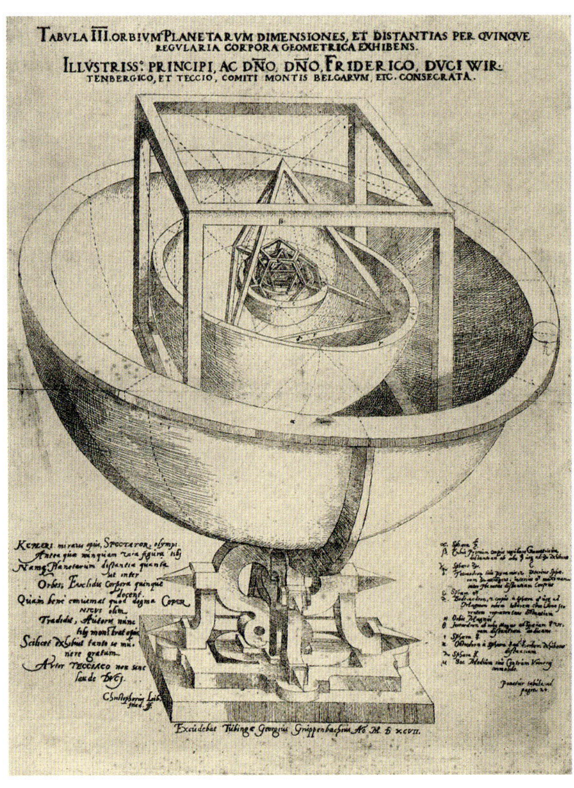

adds complexity. A photographer, on the other hand, starts with the whole world. Every decision he or she makes brings order. *Composition* comes from a Latin root, *componere*, "to put together." (*Synthesis* comes from a Greek root, *syntithenai*, which also means "to put together.") A photographer doesn't "put together" an image; a photographer selects.

Think about the relationship of the world to the observer in an analytic interaction—for example, an astronomer trying to grasp planetary motion. In 1595 Johannes Kepler, at the time a follower of Copernicus, had an epiphany about the organization of the heliocentric universe: that each planet follows a circular orbit— the circle being a perfect form—and each orbit is described by a Platonic solid, one nesting inside the other. This complex idea was rendered in the illustration at left, published in Kepler's 1596 *Mysterium Cosmographicum*.

LEFT: Illustration from Johannes Kepler's *Mysterium Cosmographicum*, published by Georg Grüppenbach in 1596; ABOVE: Claude Monet, *Cliff Walk at Pourville*, 1882; OPPOSITE: Paul Signac, *The Road in Gennevilliers*, 1883.

Kepler: New York Public Library/Photo Researchers, Inc; Monet: Mr. and Mrs. Lewis Larned Coburn Memorial Collection, 1933.433, The Art Institute of Chicago; Signac: Musée d'Orsay, Paris, France/Réunion des Musées Nationaux/ Art Resource, New York

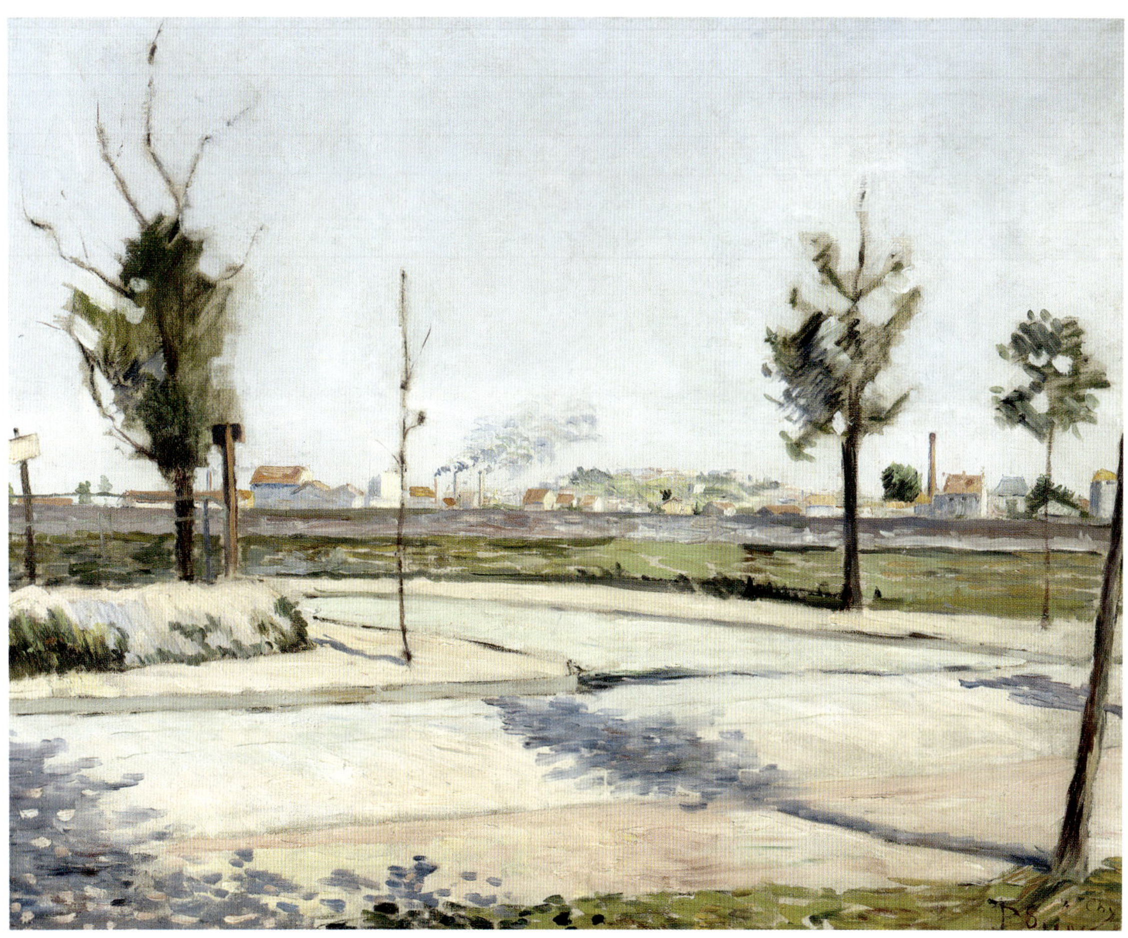

By 1605 Kepler, having worked with the Danish astronomer Tycho Brahe, and having had access to Brahe's more exact calculations of planetary motion, realized that the orbits could not possibly be circular, but had to be elliptical. Reality did not fit into Kepler's previous, idealized preconceptions. So he discarded his circular model and replaced it with an *elliptical* one. Structure brings order to our perceptions. It can clarify them but also impose our preconceptions on them. There are times when our preconceptions butt heads with reality.

Some artists have attempted to find a mode of expression that is less mediated by the visual conventions of their predecessors. This goal is a horizon that keeps receding. For example, the Impressionists broke from the historical, classical, or religious content of academic painting and found a technique that acknowledged the application of paint on the canvas. In doing so they developed their own language with their own conventions.

These two paintings were made in the early 1880s by Claude Monet (opposite, top) and Paul Signac (this page). The Signac is of almost nothing: an empty lot, a factory in the distance, scraggly trees. It is at once random and balanced. It seems photographic in the way the tree on the right is cut off by the frame

and in the way that tree's shadow is treated with the same attention as any object in the picture. But what is most impressive is that it looks like real life. It is not trying to be beautiful. It apparently has not been filtered by a refined sensibility. Even as the Impressionists broke with the visual conventions of the academic painting of their day, so Signac in this one picture transcends the conventions that even the radical Impressionists imposed.

In *Hamlet*, Shakespeare has the young prince give an acting lesson to the group of players he has brought to Elsinore. Hamlet tells them:

Suit the action to the word, and the word to the action; with this special observance, that you o'erstep not the modesty of nature; for anything so overdone is from the purpose of playing, whose end, both at the first and now, was and is, to hold, as 'twere, the mirror up to nature; to show virtue her own feature, scorn her own image, and the very age and body of the time his form and pressure.

At first Hamlet defines the relationship of form and content (or "action" and "word"). Form—structure—is not an aesthetic nicety

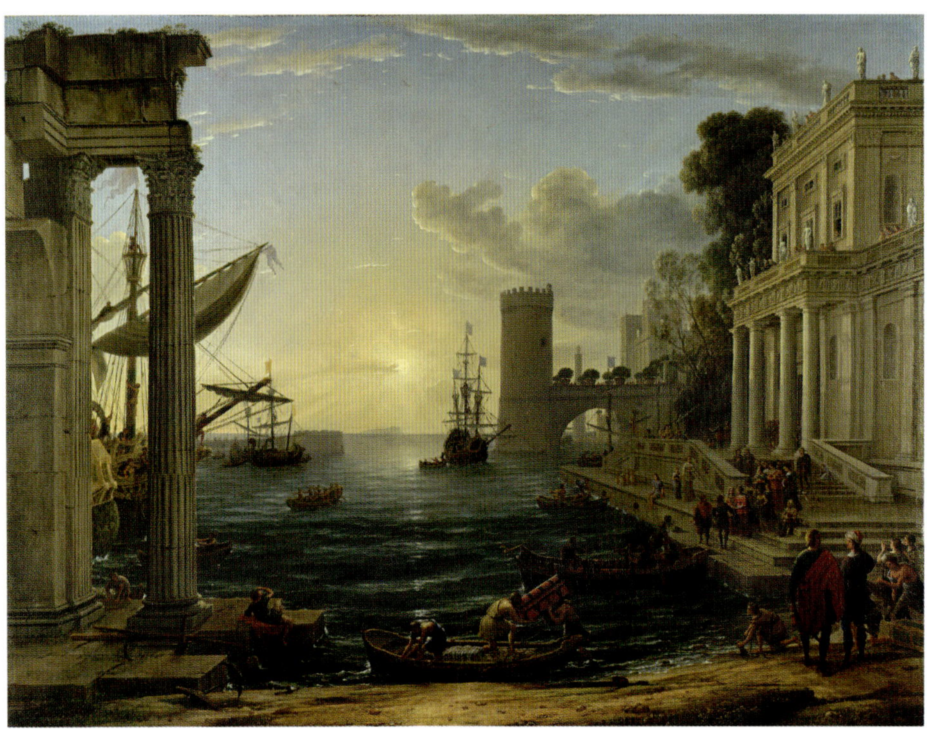

applied to content. It is not art sauce poured on top of content. It's an expression of understanding. But, Hamlet reminds us, "o'erstep not the modesty of nature." This is a plea for the structure not to call attention to itself, but to be *seen through*, to be transparent. He then goes on to suggest the scope of the content. Now, theater and literature and film may be better at exploring "virtue" and "scorn" than photography, but then there is this final line: "[To show] the very age and body of the time his form and pressure." This is within the realm of photography. A photograph can aspire to this.

When I was making the photograph at Beverly and La Brea, as I was figuring out where precisely to position my camera to make sense of all of the visual relationships I was trying to coordinate, I realized that while I was grappling with the visual facts in front of me, I was imposing a truly classical pictorial organization upon them. It brought to my mind the landscapes of Claude Lorrain (whose life overlapped Kepler's), which often have one-point perspective and include vertical objects near the sides to give tension to the edges and activate the illusion of space.

This troubled me. I was imposing a seventeenth-century solution to a twentieth-century problem. It was an elegant formal solution, but it didn't express the form and pressure of this age. Like Kepler realizing that his assumptions did not account for the facts, or like Signac recognizing the visual conventions of his day, I was aware that I was imposing an organization that came from me and from what I had learned; it was not really an outgrowth of the scene in front of me. With this in mind, the next day I went back to the same intersection and made the photograph on the facing page.

As I approached the intersection for a second time, I asked myself if I could organize the information I wanted to include *without* relying on an overriding structural principle, as I'd done the day before. Could I structure the picture in a way that communicated my experience of standing there, taking in the scene in front of me? Sometimes I have the sense that form contains an almost philosophical communication—that as form becomes more invisible, transparent, it begins to express an artist's understanding of the structure of experience.

One of the most eloquent descriptions of the deep interaction between form and content was written in the fourteenth century by the Persian poet Mahmud Shabistari:

The speck of dust that sparkles in a beam of light is nothing by itself, but by external cause obtains existence and apparent form: but as without the dust no form appears, so without the form neither does the dust exist.

Like a speck of dust in a beam of light: you cannot see the dust without the light, nor can you see the light without the dust; you can't see content without form, nor can you see form without content. ◐

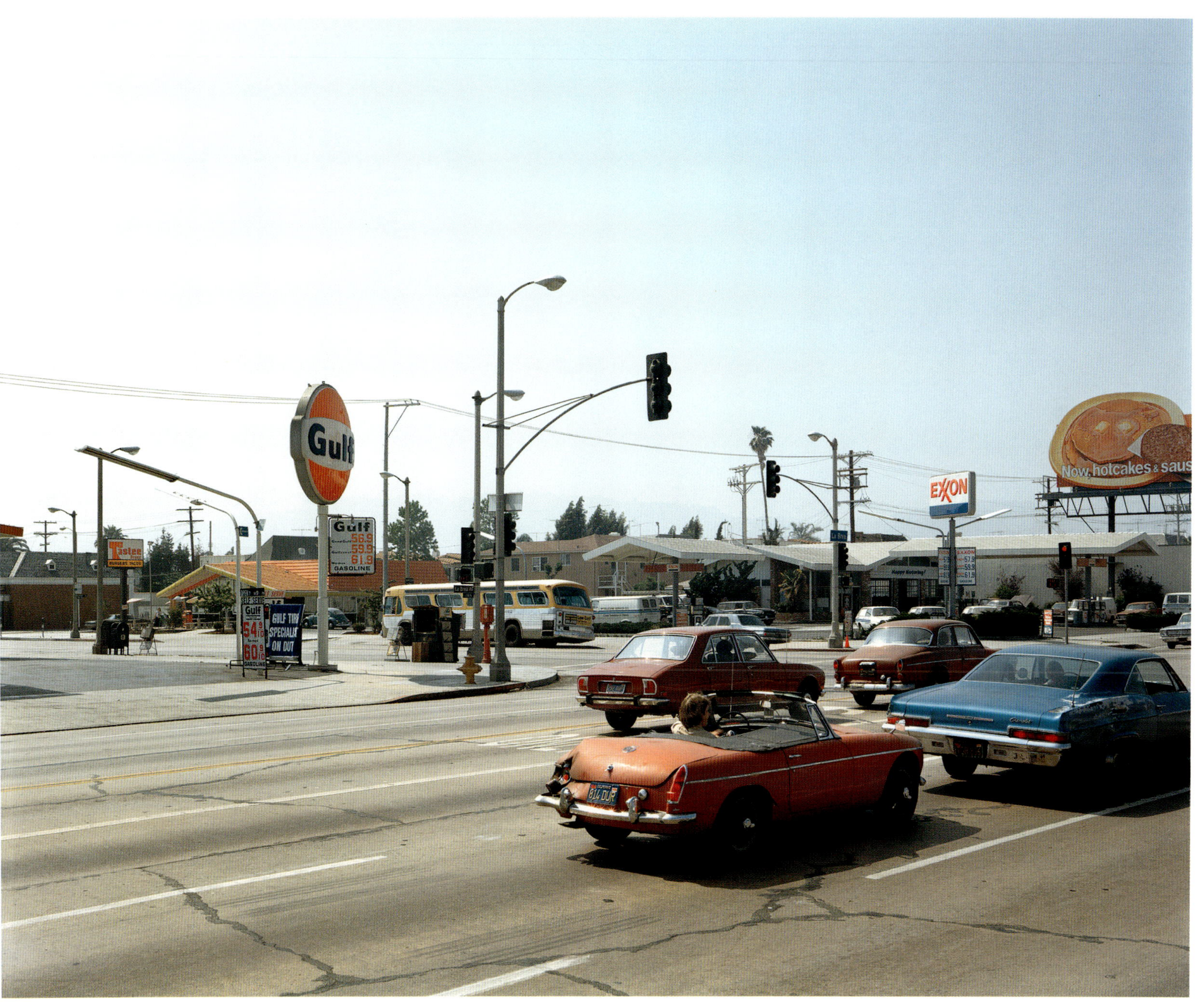

OPPOSITE: Claude Lorrain, *Seaport with the Embarkation of the Queen of Sheba*, 1648;
THIS PAGE: Stephen Shore, Beverly Boulevard and La Brea Avenue, Los Angeles, California, June 22, 1975.

Lorrain: © National Gallery, London/Art Resource; Shore: courtesy the artist and 303 Gallery, New York

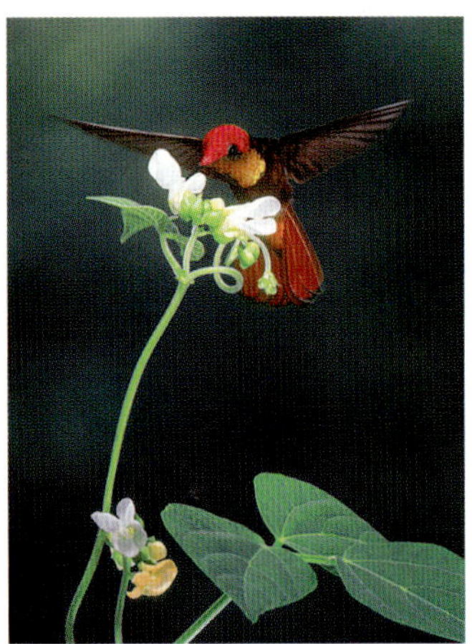

THE LIVES OF THE SAINTS

CHARLES BOWDEN

Hummingbirds appear before dawn, a whirring and darting at the feeders. Black silhouettes maneuver in the faint gray. The great blue heron alights on the power pole, the sun slips over the mountain. Delphiniums begin to glow with faint lavender and intense blues. The zinnias come on cheap and crass.

I am just up the river, fifty miles from the killing ground of Ciudad Juárez.

The dead follow me. I sit at a table and put secret graveyards on a map, one I cannot publish because such an act would lead to the murder of my sources.

I listen to the birds, the dead slowly drown out the songs.

I hear stories.

Everything seems normal here with miles of pecan groves lining the river under a blue sky.

But I hear stories.

I read old things with fresh eyes. "People travel to wonder at the height of the mountains, at the huge waves of the seas, at the long course of the rivers, at the vast compass of the ocean, at the circular motion of the stars," says St. Augustine, "and yet they pass by themselves without wondering."

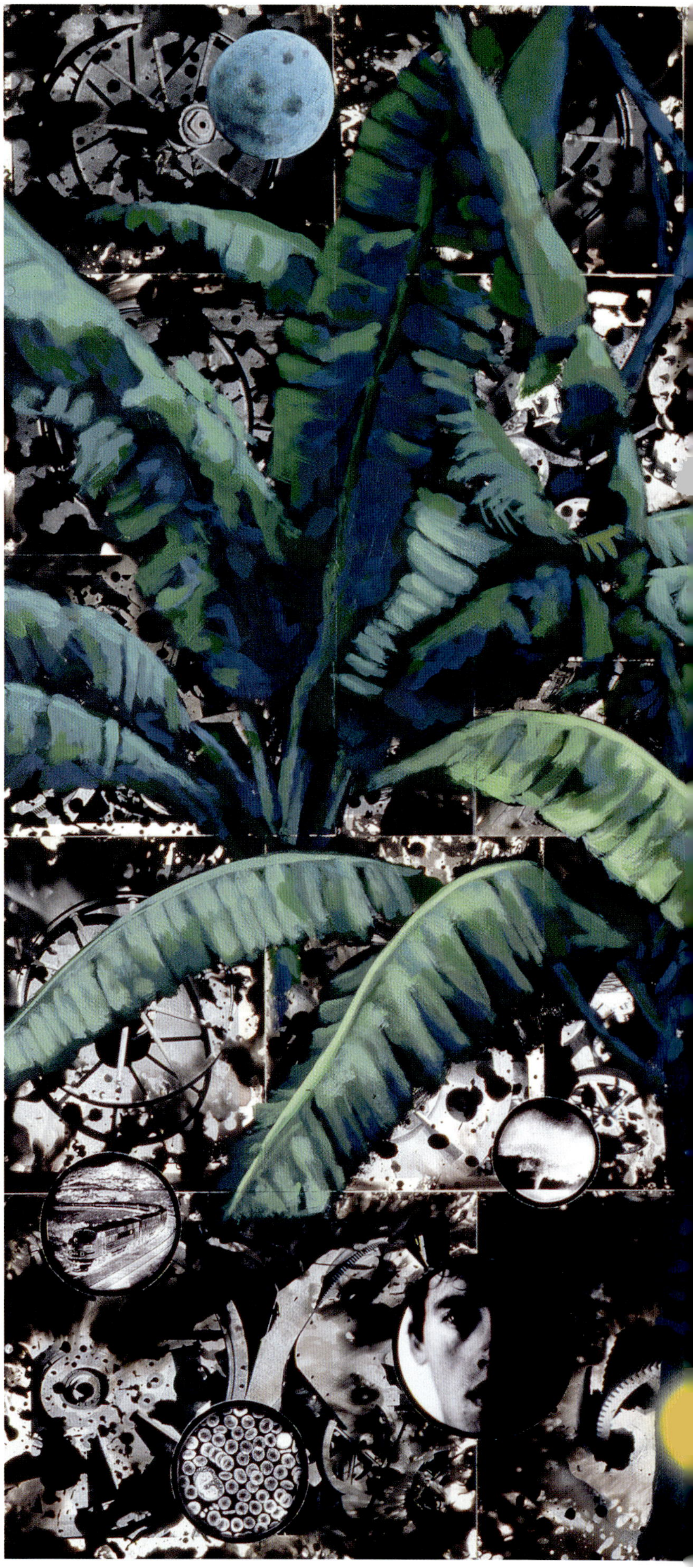

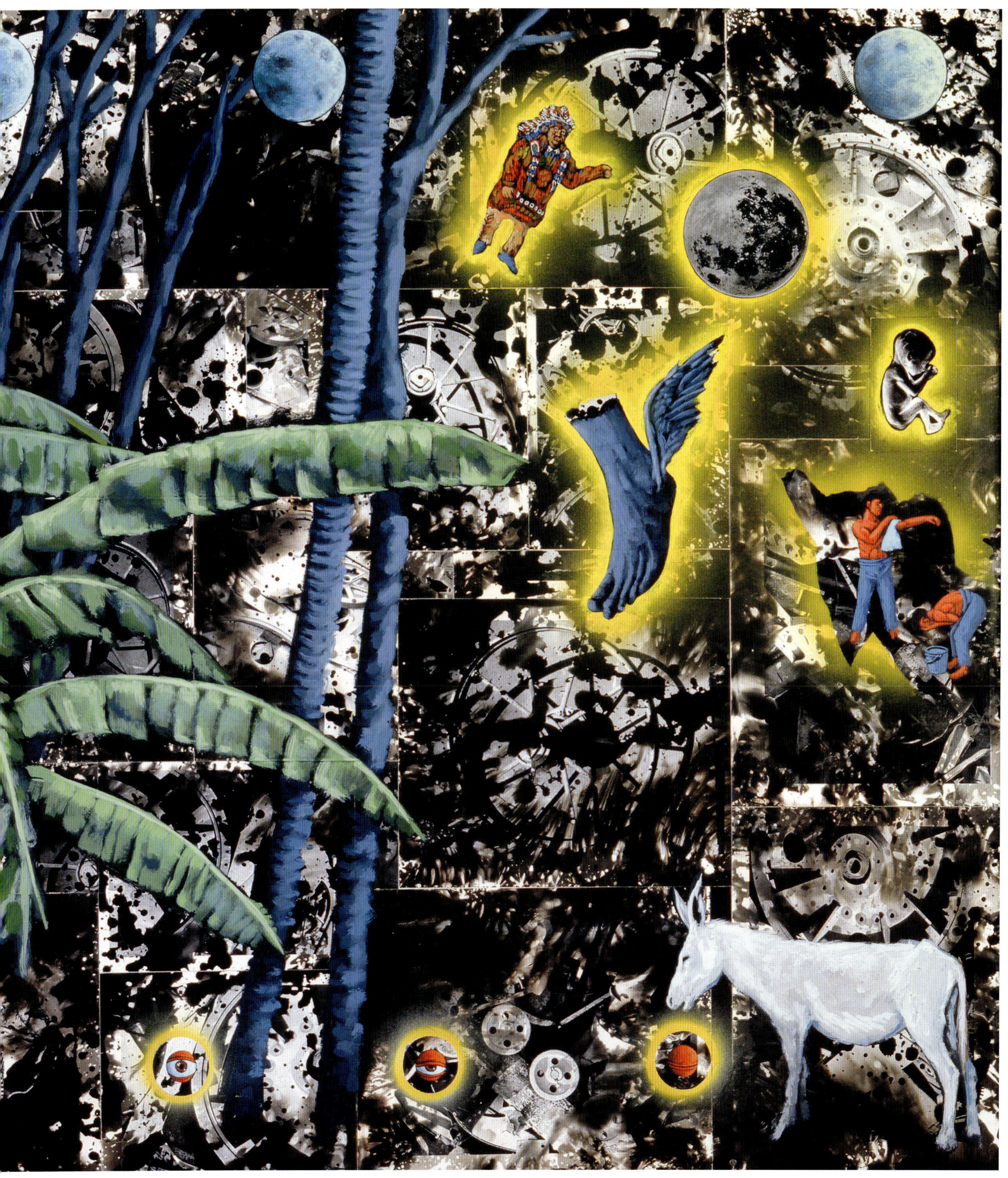

The hummingbirds near Patagonia, Arizona, sip almost two gallons at the feeder, then, vanish at dusk. I have come here to erase Juárez from my mind.

I have failed.

The moon rises late in the night hunting through a veil of clouds. Music joins the purl of water wandering the creek and around eight P.M. four men in hoods line up eighteen people in a drug clinic in Ciudad Juárez and kill them. The authorities describe the scene as a river of blood coating the hallway. A chained dog was killed also. Visitors report there is a smell of death in the air.

To the east of me, a rancher is slaughtered.

To the west of me, a border-patrol agent is slaughtered.

And pretty much to the south of me, a seventeen-year-old Mexican guy is slaughtered on the line—the agents say he was throwing rocks.

I listen to songs of New Orleans and plan my exit to the bayous and the brown, sullen waters of the big river. I want to stop hearing the stories, I want to forget, or at the very least, I want to cease to learn.

The river and delta are drugs I need.

Upstream in Arkansas, I am talking to a man painting a wall in an elementary school on the delta. The June air burns. He went up to Detroit in the '80s, after Nam, after his wars on native ground for civil rights, went up and got into the crack trade and after a while his organization was doing $50 million a year. He wants to write this down, get the killing in Nam down too.

I ask him if he is clean.

He says: "I won't lie to you, no sir, I am not clean."

I ask him what he is using.

He says: "Everything."

I know the feeling. That is why I am on the delta, that is why Juárez seems to keep me on a leash. That is why I keep wanting to hit someone. That is why I just want some peace.

The man keeps painting the wall in the school.

Everything.

But just before dawn as I watch a mouse wander the patio, I realize there is really no way to leave. What I seek is where I am and where I will arrive after all the miles of highway.

One of the hummingbirds at the feeder, a blazing species called *Rufous*, migrates twelve thousand miles each year, and yet every place it alights finds what it just left behind—insects and nectar to devour. The bird lives in motion to stay where it begins and ends.

The waters of the sea evaporate and wander back to the headwaters as clouds and then the rain falls and the journey down the river renews.

In an hour, the gray light will seep into the sky and a roar will come as they return to the feeders.

Maybe I will wander past myself, full of wonder.

There is the matter of food and drink, also.

There has been a delay because a man sits in front of me and he says that people are sometimes hard to kill.

I feel the door closing behind me and I know it will not be easy to get out of this room.

Once, he explains, he took a contract to murder a very tall and fat man. So when that man entered the room, he hit him in the back of the head with a hammer.

But the man did not go down. He simply turned and said: "Is that any way to greet someone?"

It took a lot of blows to kill him.

The other day I cut catfish filets, very thin, in the style of southern Louisiana. I washed them in a bath of egg and buttermilk, then dredged them through cornmeal and seasoning.

Another day I rolled out noodles, cut an inch wide with ragged edges. The sauce is made from crushed red pepper, oil, uncured bacon, garlic, tomatoes, cream, pecorino cheese shredded fine.

The need rises. I slice fresh *ciabatta*, douse with good olive oil, cover with diced tomatoes, anchovies, garlic, sea salt, and basil. An explosion on the tongue, I uncork the bottle and watch the moss draping down from the trees by the swamp slowly sway.

Such things are not details if you go down by the river.

You must learn to say yes before you can endure the people who say no.

The other day a man told me my problem was simple: I had never been tortured.

When I started out, I planned to farm and eventually die surrounded by fine fields and fat cattle. The raw smell of red clover in the meadow has been the fragrance I wished to wash over my life.

In the third or fourth century A.D. an old man dies in North Africa and leaves this epitaph: "Here lies Dion, a pious man; he lived eighty years and planted four thousand trees."

I wanted to be like that man. He almost certainly planted olive trees, a featured crop of the region. The early fathers of the African church had abundant light for their lamps and could write the mysteries of the faith all night long to the envy of their Italian colleagues.

But there was a change in the air at the same moment when Dion left his summary of his life. St. Jerome, looking out at a small child, sketched this view of that world: "In such a world

PAGE 50, TOP LEFT: Luis Mazariegos, *Ruby Topaz (Chrysolampis mosquitus)*; PAGES 50–51: David Wojnarowicz, *Where I'll Go After I'm Gone*, 1988–89; OPPOSITE: David Wojnarowicz, *Fever*, 1988–89.

Mazariegos: © Luis Mazariegos; Wojnarowicz: courtesy the Estate of David Wojnarowicz and P.P.O.W. Gallery, New York

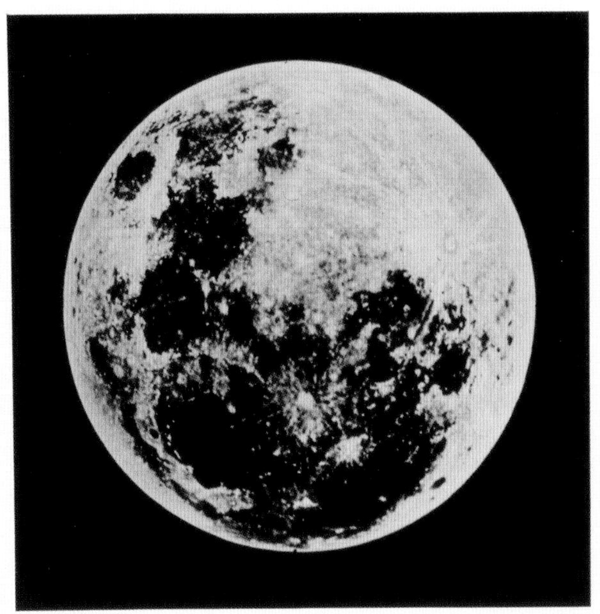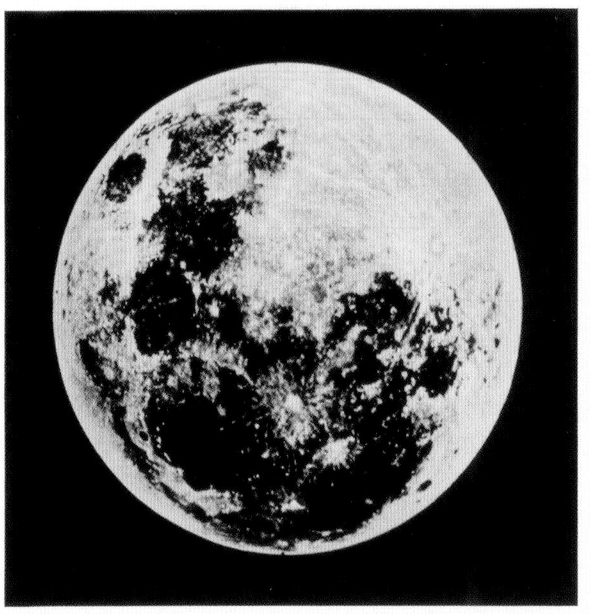

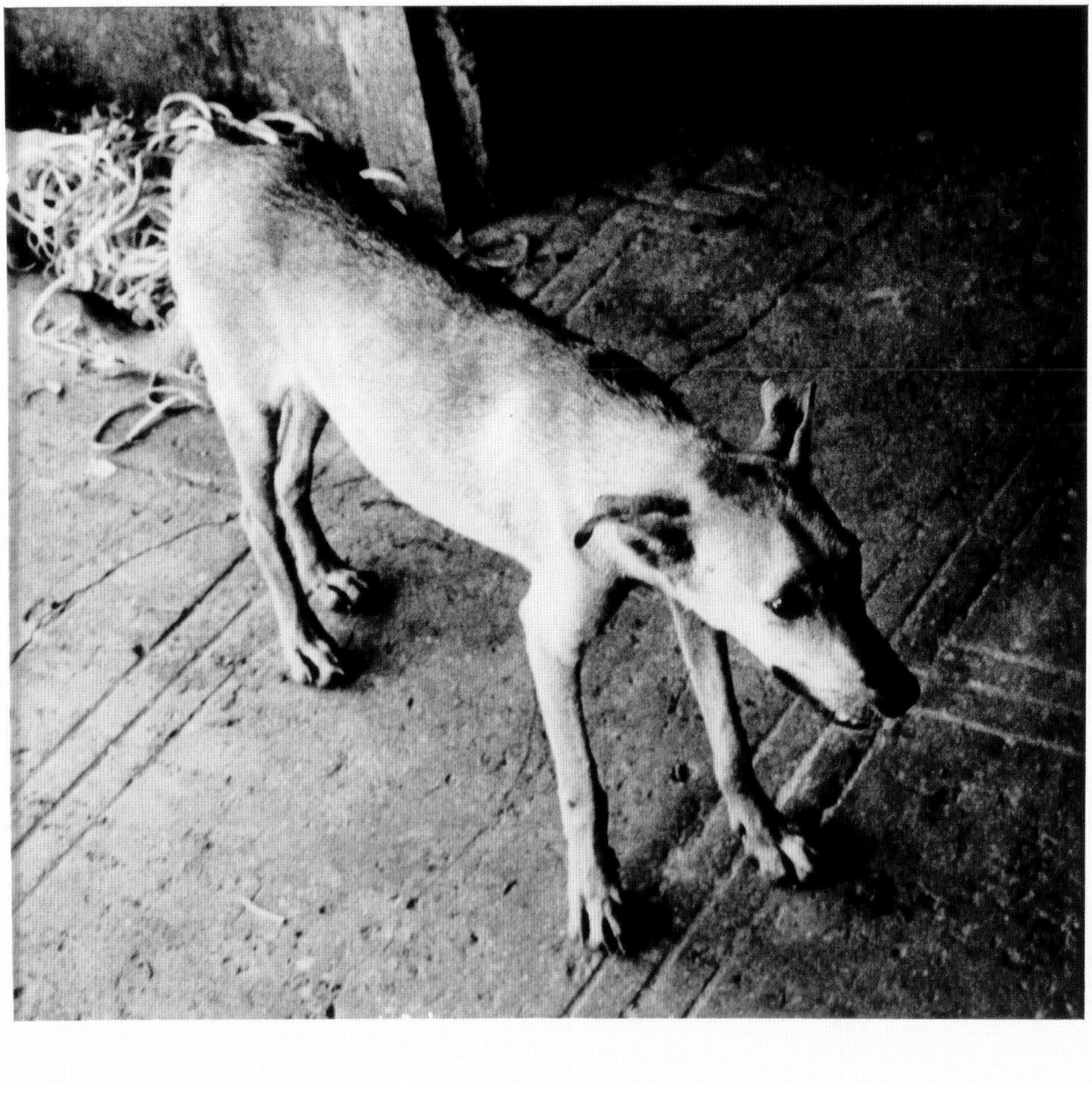

Pacatula has been born. Disasters surround her as she plays. She will know of weeping before laughter. . . . She forgets the past; she flees the present; she awaits with eagerness the life to come."

I live between my Rome and my Jerusalem: my Ciudad Juárez and my New Orleans. Except that neither one is a holy city. And both cities are dying and both cities kill and both cities draw me toward them. And both cities have been written off and in both cities faces without names are writing the future with blood.

I have ignored God or the questions about God since I first walked into the forest and desert. The saints I spent time with in my twenties, when I inhaled drugs and for a spell thought the saints were the fellow outcasts and outlaws of their time. I swallowed whole St. Augustine and St. Jerome, also St. Anselm, St. Thomas Aquinas, Meister Eckhart, St. Teresa, St. John of the Cross. And the little flowers of St. Francis of Assisi, especially his time with the wolf. I paid no attention to Christ and Jehovah.

Now in the bright light of a new day as the killing comes down and the ground cracks underfoot, I return to these holy bones stored on dusty shelves in scorned libraries. I blow the cobwebs off, and St. Augustine tumbles down and rests in my hand again.

In an earlier time: The light falls golden, the air sags with moisture and the bayou is still, the waters green and placid. There is a war in Korea, and willing dead men leave this place to join that war. There is always a war during my time on earth, and always a ready supply of willing dead men. Bird cries shred the sky. Food floats from the kitchen: a gumbo with shrimp, *andouille*, celery, onion, bell pepper, *filé*, and a very dark roux. The blackened-iron kettle rests on the stove as my aunt stirs, a cotton wrapper clinging to her abundant body. Scents fill the air: her perfume, the gumbo, the swamp smells coming through the screen door.

The land here is flat and mainly underwater. This flatness, a land form I will later learn is called a *delta*, extends upriver almost to my birthplace in Illinois. Clay at the top, black mud at the bottom. Nasal speech in Illinois, and a mixture of Irish dock accents and rich southern vowels where the waters begin to break free and taste the salt of the sea.

I remember all the furniture in the house on the bayou is veneered with rounded corners and the mirrors are oval. The bedsteads are also veneer, the cigarettes have no filters, and the women leave the red imprint of their lips on the spent stubs. Salt, cayenne, garlic, and green scum on the water. I have always welcomed the night, that darkness rich and stuffed with hidden things. The dawn, also, and the early morning. The rest sometimes seems too bright for seeing things.

I never asked questions. My aunt in the swamps, I don't know her maiden name. She had a twin sister who died. There was no money, and my earliest memory is of her doing piecework at a sewing machine in a sweatshop. She also held a soft-shelled crab up to my eyes and then later at home pan-fried it and I held it in my child's hands and ate it like a large cookie.

There have been some questions. I will answer.

What possible link is there between the great delta of the Mississippi River and the poverty and violence of Ciudad Juárez?

Answer: The delta of the Mississippi River is the richest land on earth and for two centuries it has produced the poorest people in the United States. Ciudad Juárez was to be the model for American free-trade theories and for decades it has produced corruption, poverty, and violence.

If you ask what food and cooking has to do with all this, then you do not understand appetite and if you do not understand appetite you will be baffled by love, violence, and death.

I have always been interested in how things get done and so people tell me of their skills and trades and toils and the hazards of their work. The man I spoke of worked at killing people and burying them in Juárez. Sometimes, rotten bodies must be dug up and moved in order to preserve public order and respect for the state.

The skin blisters and the doctors try to understand. They wonder if it comes from work in the chemical industry or some other kind of intense contact. When asked, the patients pause. There is no way to discuss the matter. When a body has been underground a while, the rot advances, especially when lime accelerates decay. And then an order comes to move the bodies, sometimes without any reason. Sometimes because it is discovered that the house has been leased from a significant political figure. And for the owner to have his patio returned with corpses underneath the dirt as he sips his morning coffee and goes over the newspapers, that would be an insult. Despite the best efforts—deep holes, lime, layers of concrete—there is often a seepage of gases through sudden fissures in the soil. It might be evening, a beer cold in the hand, the patio inviting and suddenly there is the layer of odor floating and it is death. This cannot be allowed. Decorum must be observed. The owners, when they occupy their fine houses, should not have to smell death. Such an experience would upend the meaning of money and privilege.

So the bodies must be moved. There is not always time to round up the Hazmat suits. There are chemicals. And then, over time, an intolerance, maybe something called an allergy, that visit to the doctors, the question: Have you worked with chemicals?

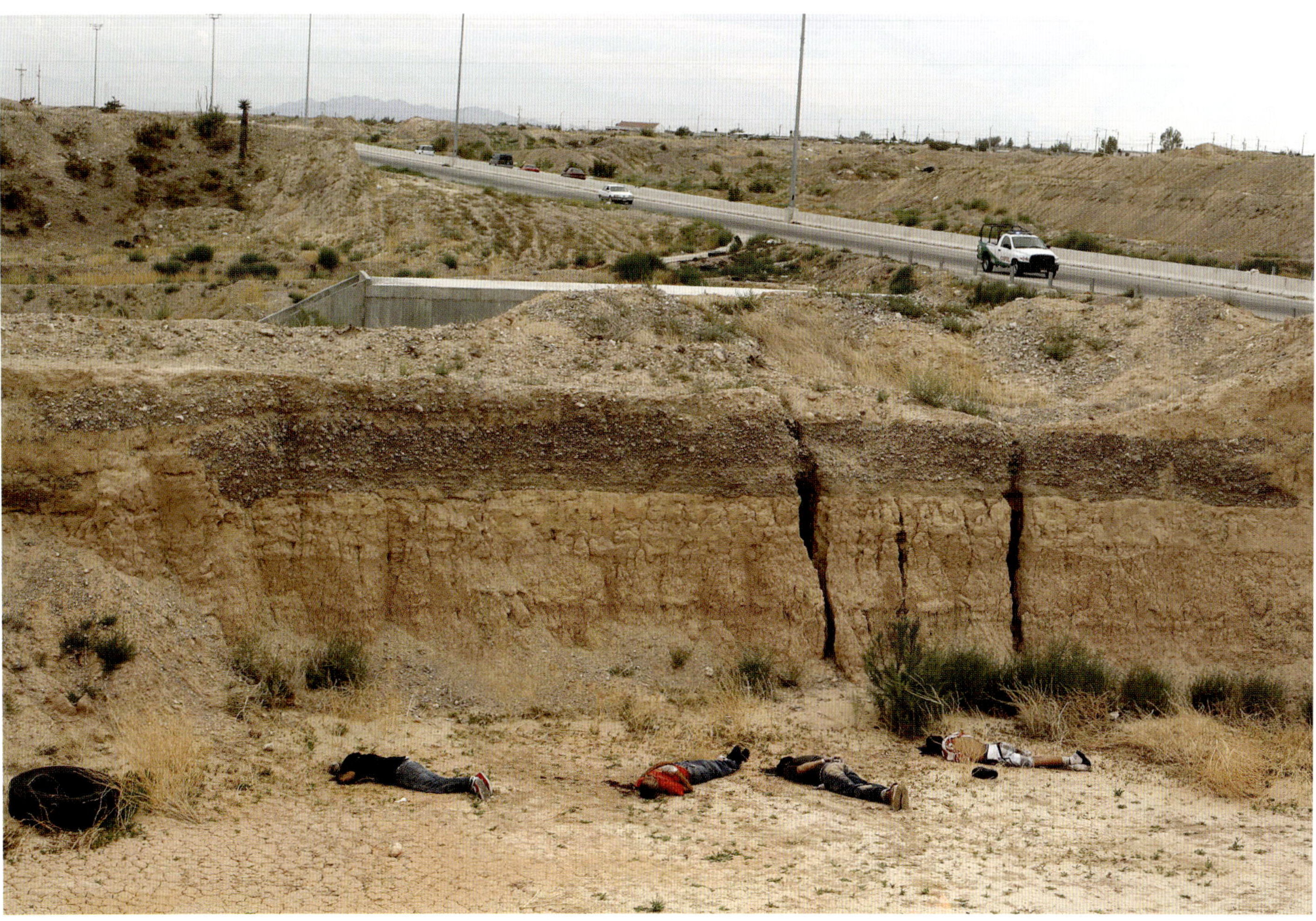

This question can be awkward.

Last night, the creek rose and the water went brown with runoff from the hills. Drops fell softly from leaves, the clouds parted after the storm and a waning moon wandered among the stars. The bats hunted insects and came close to my face.

I was twenty miles from the border in Arizona at that exact moment. I felt I was going to where I belonged.

This afternoon, during a brief break in the storm, the sun streamed down on the sunflowers, some yellow, some red and bronze, and the dirt rose up like incense. Yellow, black, and blue butterflies fluttered around and did not fear me.

These are surely signs and I must learn to read them.

St. Augustine became a Christian when he heard a child's voice singing as he sat in a garden on the edge of the Alps. He raced into the villa, opened St. Paul's Epistles and saw the line "Not in reveling and drunkenness, not in lust and wantonness, not in quarrels and rivalries. Rather, arm yourself with the Lord Jesus Christ, spend no more thought on nature and nature's appetites."

I would not wish his fate on a dog. I cannot imagine what is like to spurn nature and nature's appetites.

A young bobcat lives in the bamboo, kills doves in the yard and is willing to look into my face.

In the light rain, a javelina crosses the road in front of me.

Two buck deer emerge from the tall grass by the lane.

The great blue heron fishes the waters and pays me no mind.

Spiders now live over the stove and hang down when I make coffee.

I can sit in public cafés and not be noticed.

When I shop in the market, no one calls the police.

A black bear and cub scavenge the abandoned apple orchard in the bottomland.

There are fireflies after the night falls down.

All the saints seem to see the world as a barrier to their spiritual lives and personal salvation. They find personal salvation more important than the world itself. And they find women to be a menace to their souls.

This is clearly the best case that can be made for seeking damnation. Heaven and hell do not concern me, nor does the state

Julio César Aguilar Fuentes, Four men were murdered at the side of the Camino Real road. The discovery of the bodies was reported at 10 A.M. August 15, 2010. They were found five hours later by the federal police.

©/courtesy Julio César Aguilar Fuentes

of my soul. Scorning the world is beyond my understanding. Why be here then?

A faint shower last evening brings up the raw scent of the grass come morning. The sun rises as a disk of gold, the hummingbirds descend with lust in their hearts, acorn woodpeckers pillage the feeders and a vulture sits high in the cottonwood across the wash and basks in the early light. A great blue heron flaps across the sky.

I am always puzzled when I am told life is meaningless.

I am always puzzled when I am told the meaning of life.

I have decided to take all the theories of violence, snap them across my knee and toss the fragments away. All this because my hands are rank with the strong scent of tomato leaves and the sunflowers have seared golden circles into my eyes. The hummingbirds let me stand two feet from the feeder and pay me no never mind.

I have decided to learn from appetites. I will slobber and drool and chew and inhale. I am done with dainty feeding. The quick and the dead share one thing: appetites. They both want to consume things. The theories assume there is a normal world where violence is absent. I see a world of appetites where the thing called violence answers yet one more hunger. Maybe it is the new fast food for those who do not have time for fine dining.

I have decided to drink cold water, eat black pepper, and listen to the stars on black nights.

I have decided.

I am not a camera.

I am not a theory.

I am a hunger.

St. Augustine says: "Some people, in order to discover God, read books. But there is a great book: the very appearance of created things. Look above you! Look below you! Read it. God, whom you want to discover, never wrote that book with ink. Instead, He set before your eyes the things that He had made. Can you ask for a louder voice than that?"

The saints must keep up appearances.

I have decided. ❹

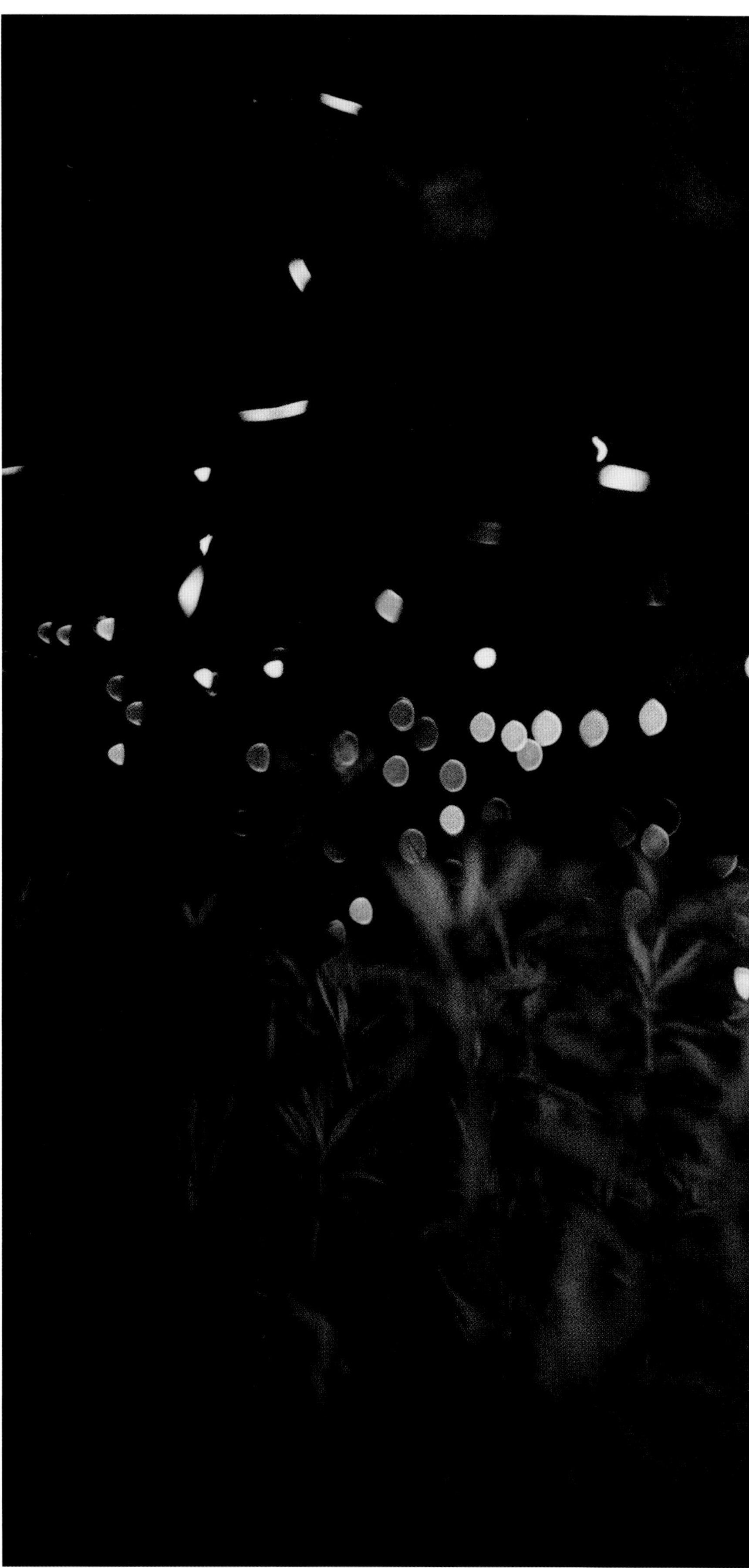

Gregory Crewdson, *Untitled*, 1996.

Courtesy the artist and Luhring Augustine

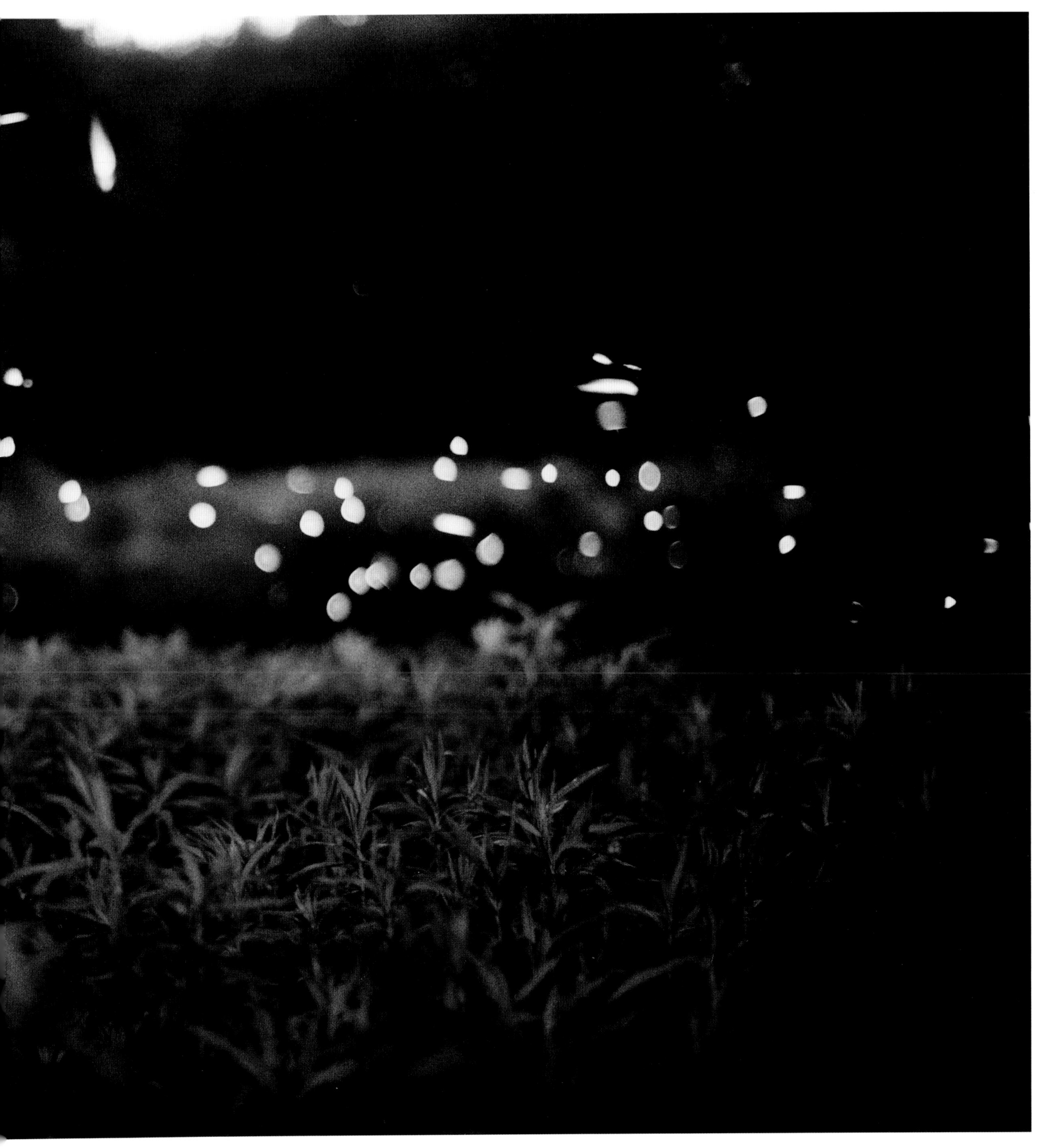

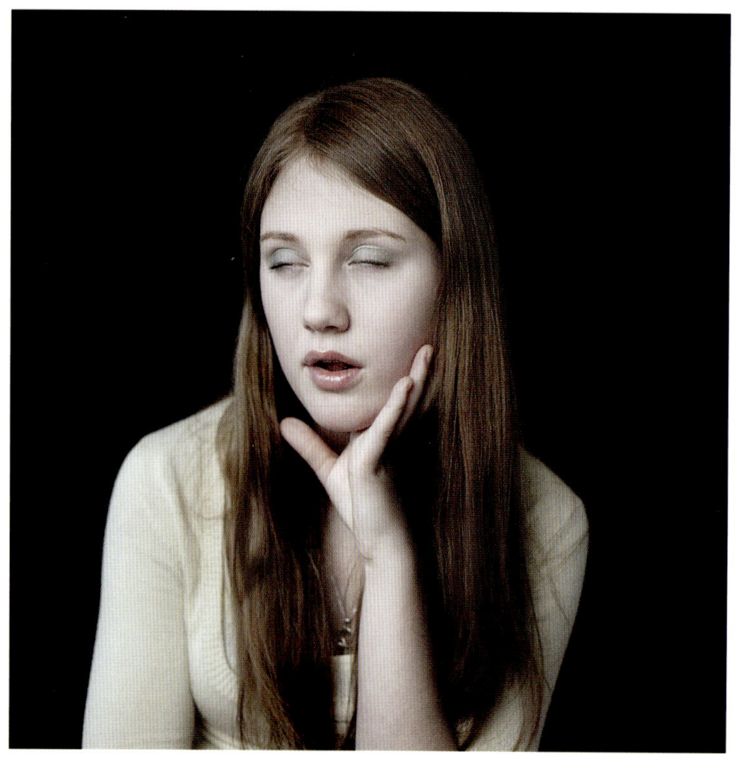

TEEN SPIRIT

Each image in Swedish photographer Julia Peirone's recent series More Than Violet *is the result of culling through hundreds of exposures made during a session with a female teenage model. Instead of seeking an ideal of teenage beauty, in her editing process Peirone seeks out the most vulnerable movements and expressions that, taken together, reveal a lexicon of gesture specific to this moment between childhood and womanhood. Fingers twirl and tug at thick shocks of hair; bubble gum inflates and deflates; eyes roll backward with sleepiness or disaffection or, in certain images, what seems to be something like spirit possession.*

The teenage girl as entity, as concept, has been created in part by images—she is variously mystified, manipulated, distorted, sexualized, idealized, and sometimes rendered with as much honesty as photography can engage. Among the photographic precedents for Peirone's studies are the black-and-white images of dreamy young subjects by Julia Margaret Cameron, and the coolly formal portraits of girls by contemporary Dutch photographer Hellen van Meene. Like these photographers and others, Peirone examines this liminal, ephemeral age with intensity; her photographs evince both puzzlement and amusement.

Peirone's images maybe discomfiting, but they playfully point to a matrix of relations surrounding images, young girls, and the expectations of the viewer.

—The Editors

PHOTOGRAPHS BY JULIA PEIRONE

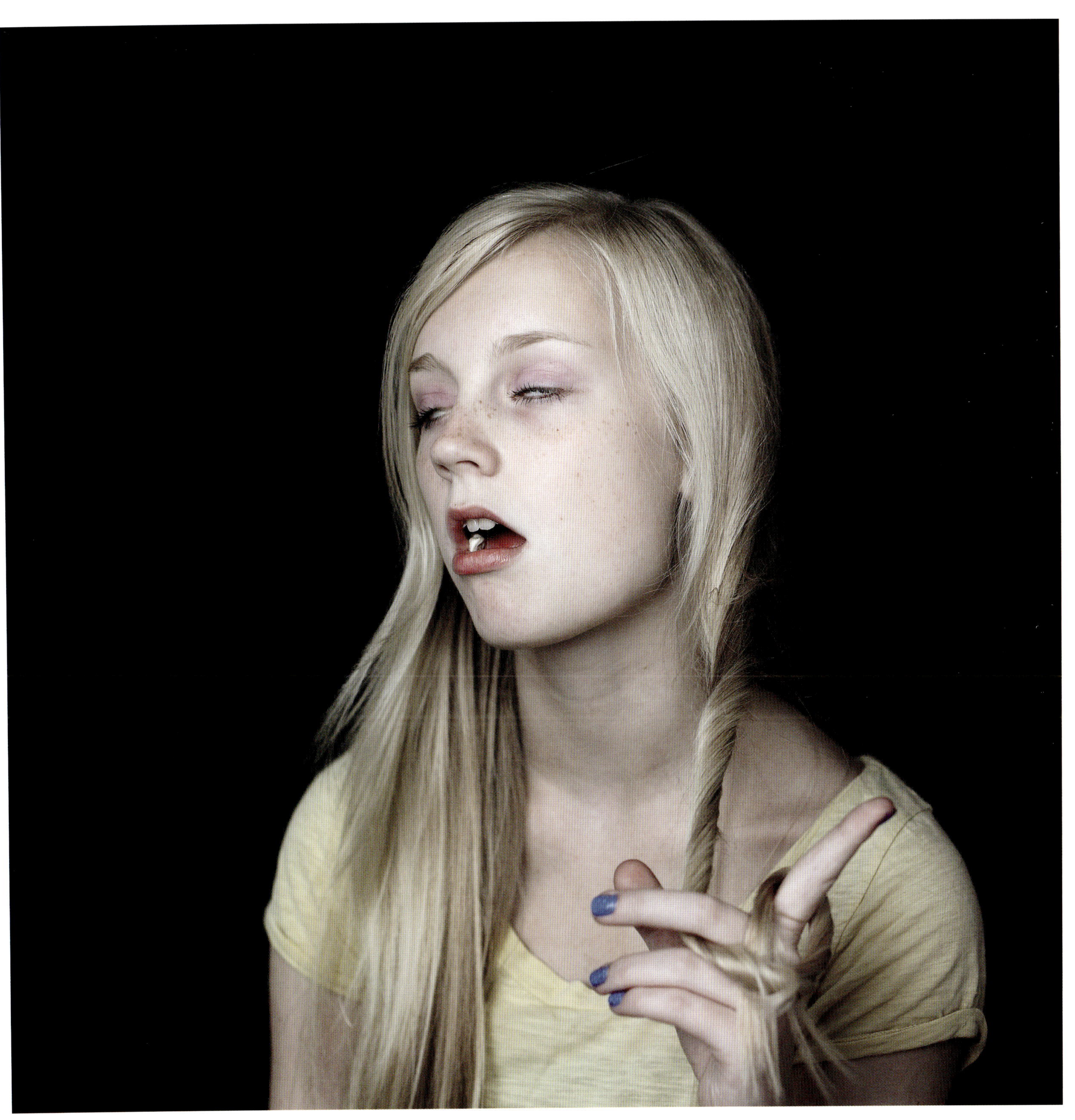

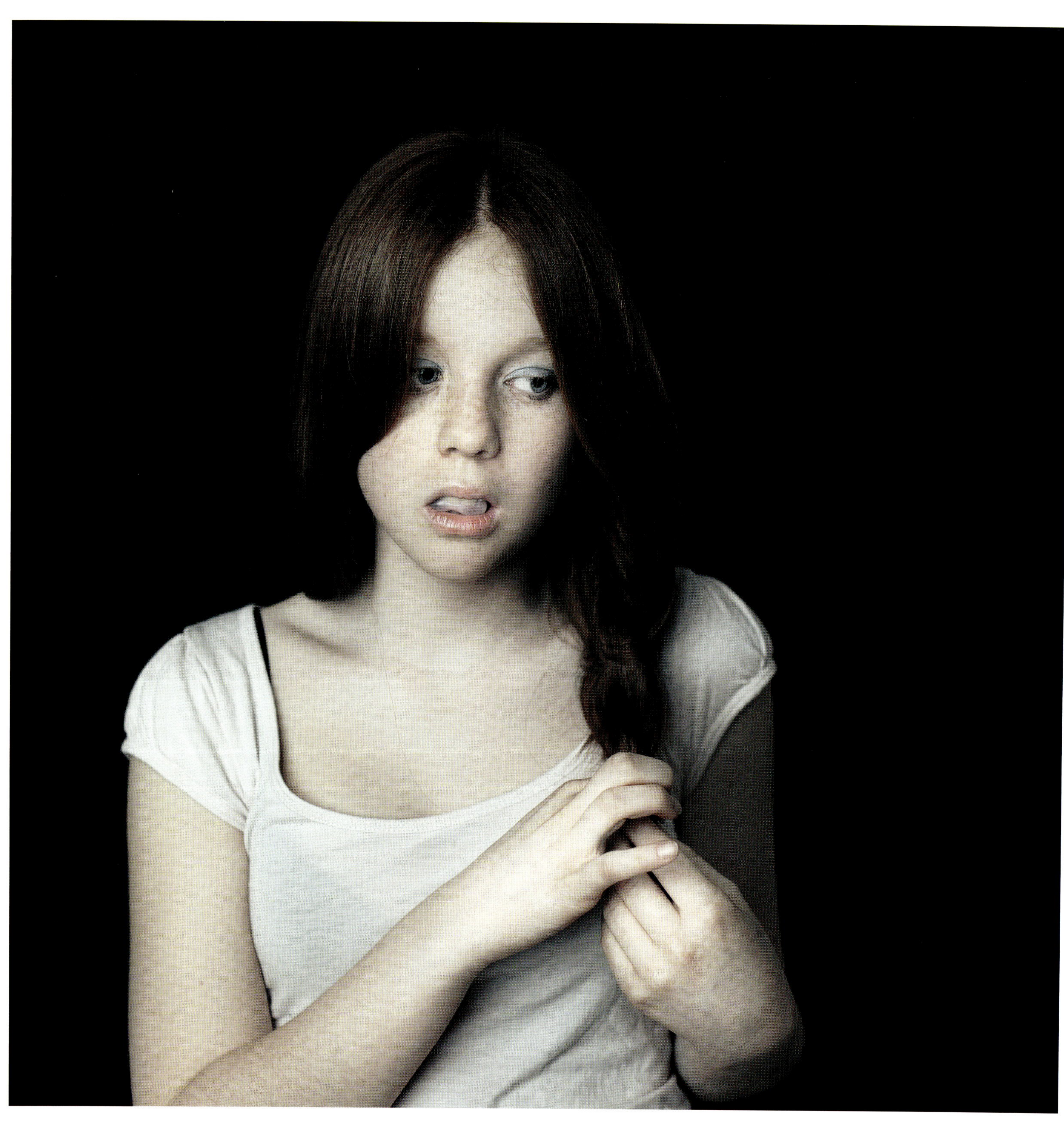

All photographs from the series *More Than Violet*.
PAGE 58: *Susanna*, 2011; PAGE 59: *Nike*, 2010;
THIS PAGE: *Sophie*, 2011.

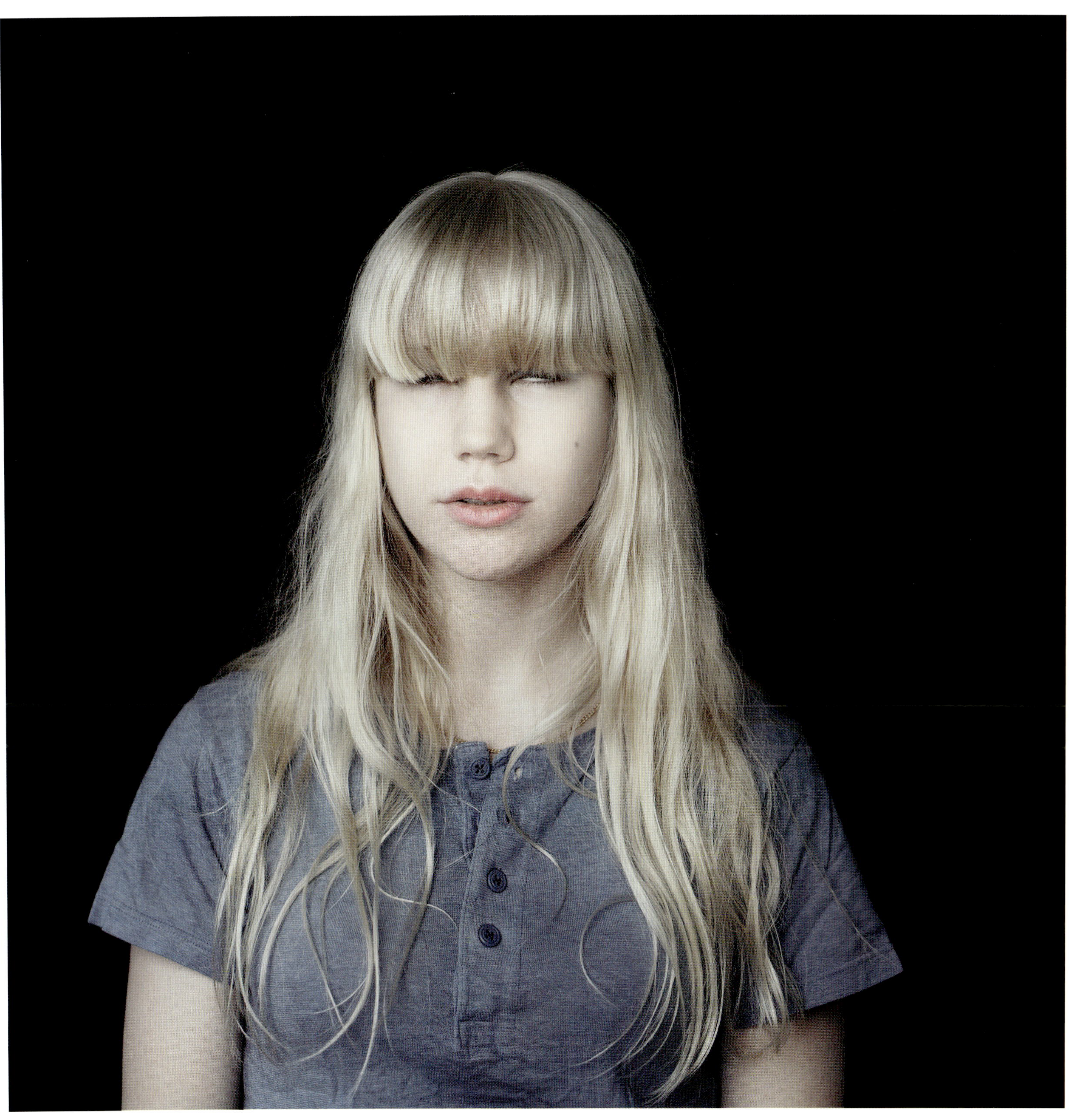

Maja, 2011.

All photographs courtesy the artist

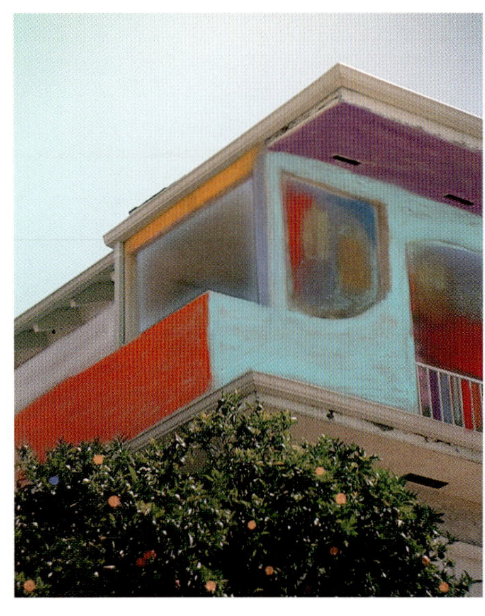

SAM FALLS
HYPER-CONSCIOUS

BY LESLEY A. MARTIN

Sam Falls's eclectic output includes writing, photography, painting, videos, collaborative curatorial efforts, and extraordinarily prolific bookmaking. (He has produced and self-published ten books in small editions of fifty to five hundred copies; in the second half of 2011 alone, he has released three new volumes with independent publishers.) His books frequently serve to contain and unify the diversity of his production.

Dipping into his work of the past five years, one finds large-format black-and-white photographs made (using expired film stock) at the American Wing of the Metropolitan Museum of Art; closely observed nature studies, subtly manipulated in hue; wildly colored semidigital abstractions; portraits, paintings, and other pictures (some found, some created by Falls) staged and rephotographed; as well as images that are layered with Photoshop "brushwork" in addition to actual paint. Sifting through this widely ranging material can be vertiginous; ultimately it is greatly rewarding.

If the ethos of contemporary art photography could be summarized in a bullet-point list, it might include the following ideas (each accompanied by an image by Falls): *The Non-Series Series*, in which the notion that a photographic exploration should express itself as a thematically and aesthetically coherent set of similarly constructed images is patently rejected; *The Neo-Dada Still Life*, in which the whimsical juxtaposition of commonplace objects suggests a rethinking of our relationship to the physical world and its portrayal via images; and *The Blurring of Facture Boundaries*, in which photography is pursued as a remix of sculpture, painting, and other media, putting to the test traditional strictures on photographic genres. There would be other ideas on the list, including *The Return of the Romantic*, characterized in part by a brightly saturated palette and an earnest interest in graphic patterning—driven to some degree by nostalgia, but also by the infinite variations of color easily controlled and available in the digital-imaging space. And most pervasive of all: *The Hyper-Conscious Image*, defined by a heightened awareness of the history and practical uses of photography, as well as of the impact of changing technologies on this history. (And this entire list might be filed under the heading *Sons and Daughters of the Pictures Generation*.)

There is no such checklist, of course, that can capture the visceral impact of ideas put sharply, beguilingly into visual forms, which is what Falls excels at. When it works (and it works more often than not), it works brilliantly—resulting in images that are conceptual yet personal. This is a body of photographs driven by an idiosyncratic and poetic instinct; it also leaves one to imagine a finely tuned image-making machine, somewhere deep in the heart of Brooklyn, thrown into overdrive and firing on all cylinders to create a joyously undifferentiated shuffle of the seriously theoretical, the unironically pop, and the unapologetically gorgeous.◉

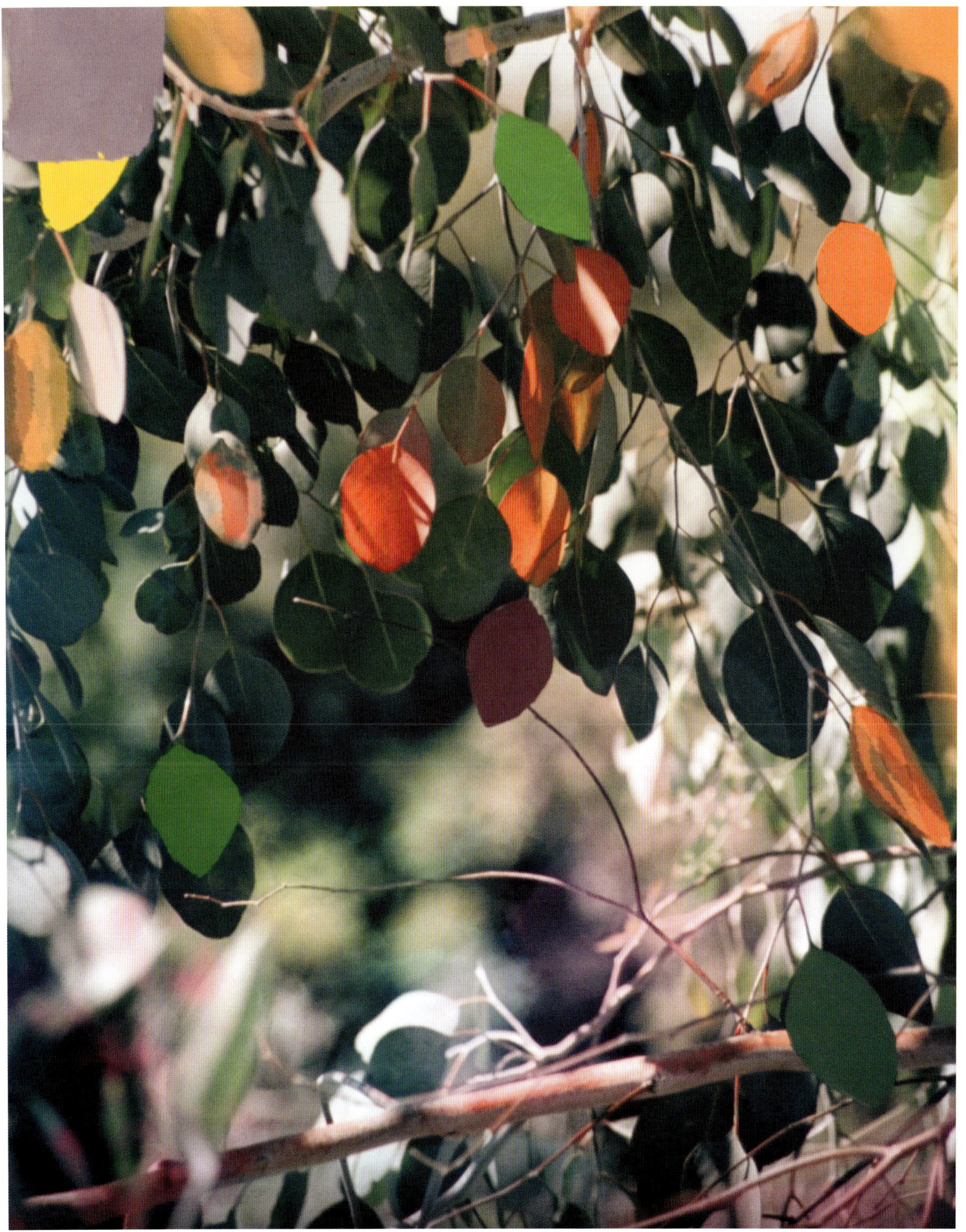

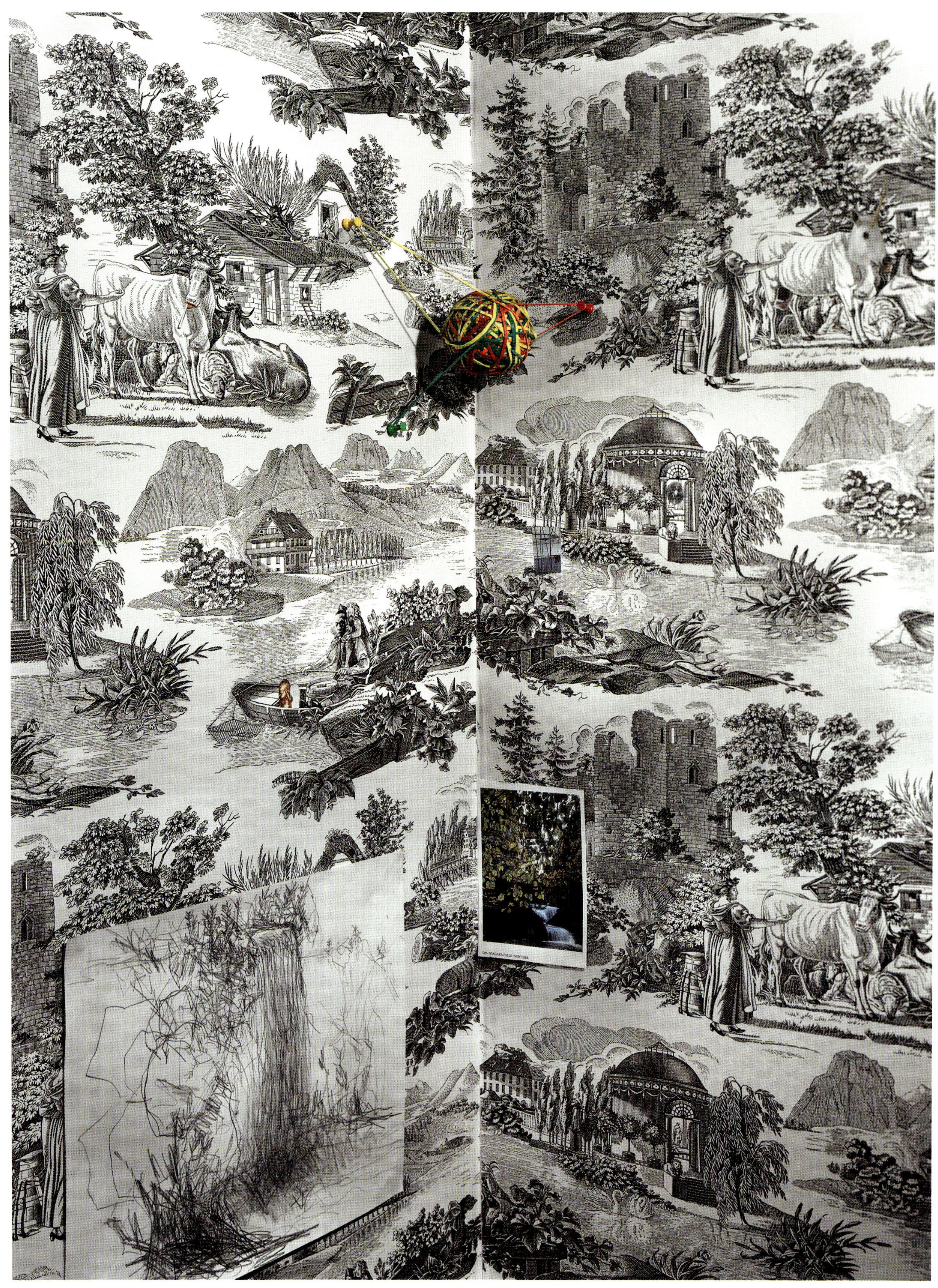

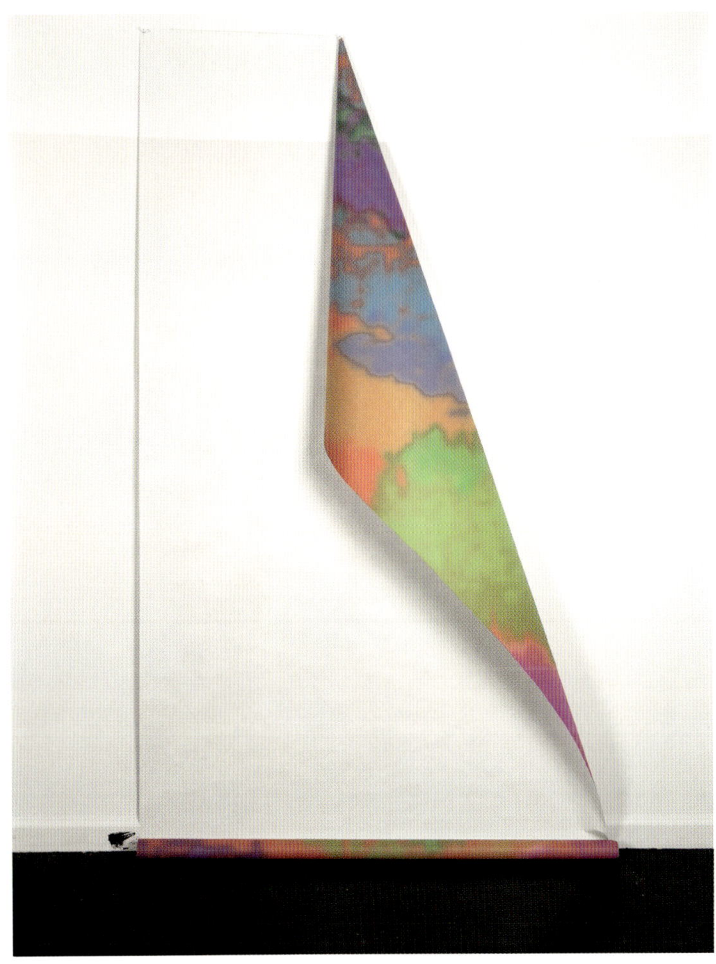 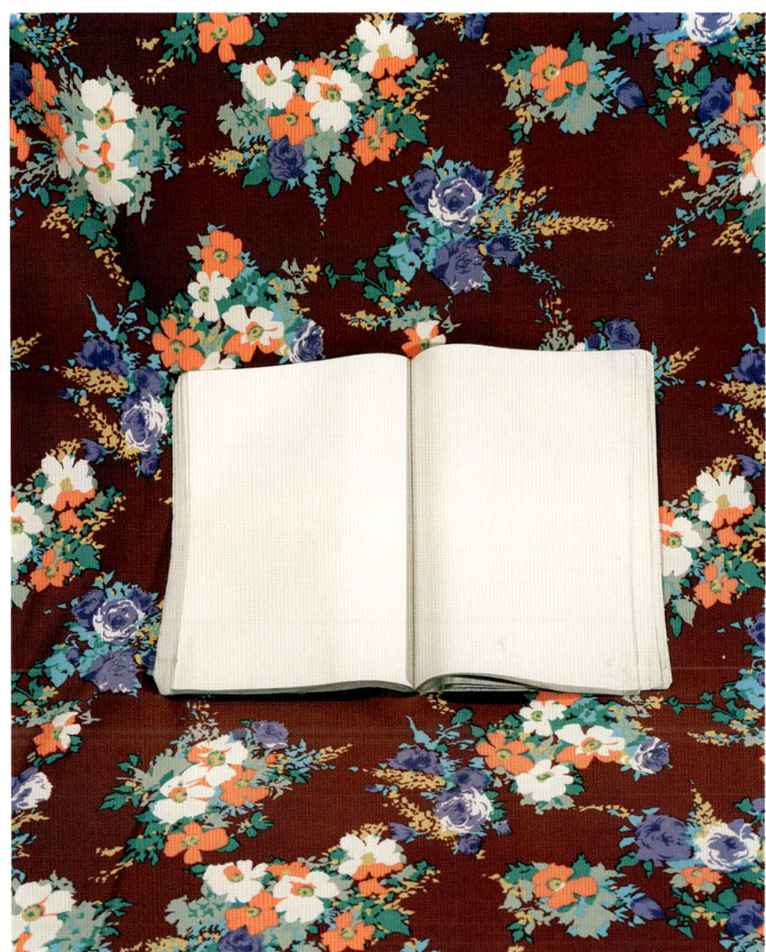

PAGE 62: *Orange County House*, 2010; PAGE 63: *Red Box Foliage*, 2010;
OPPOSITE: *Untitled (corner)*, 2009; THIS PAGE, LEFT: *Painted Seamless (back)*, 2010; RIGHT: *Open Book in Flowers*, 2009.

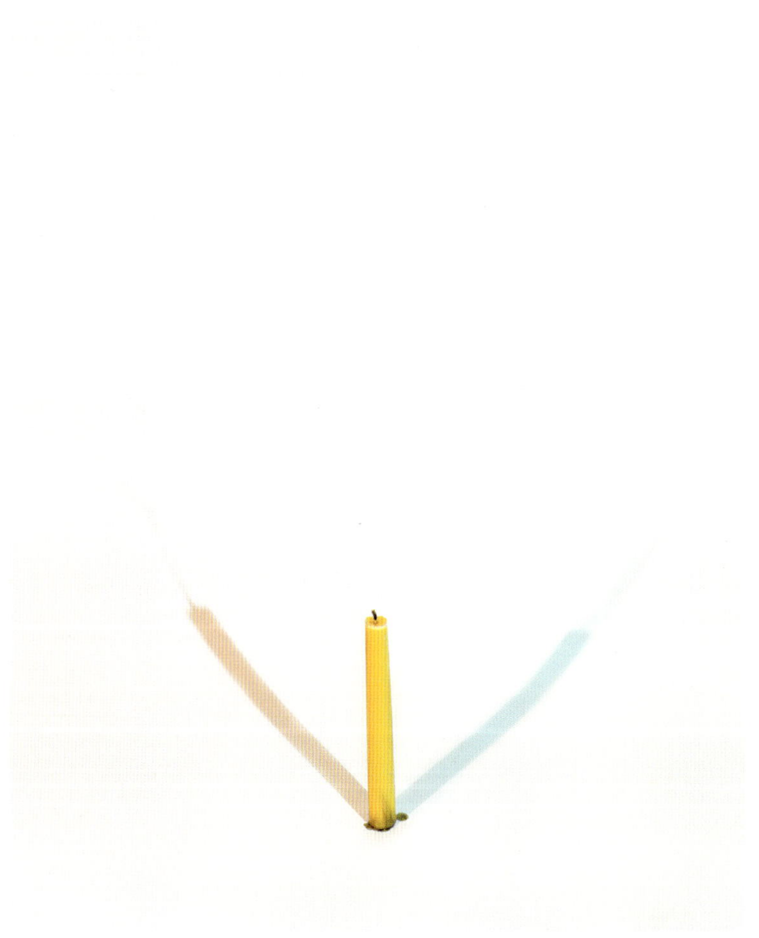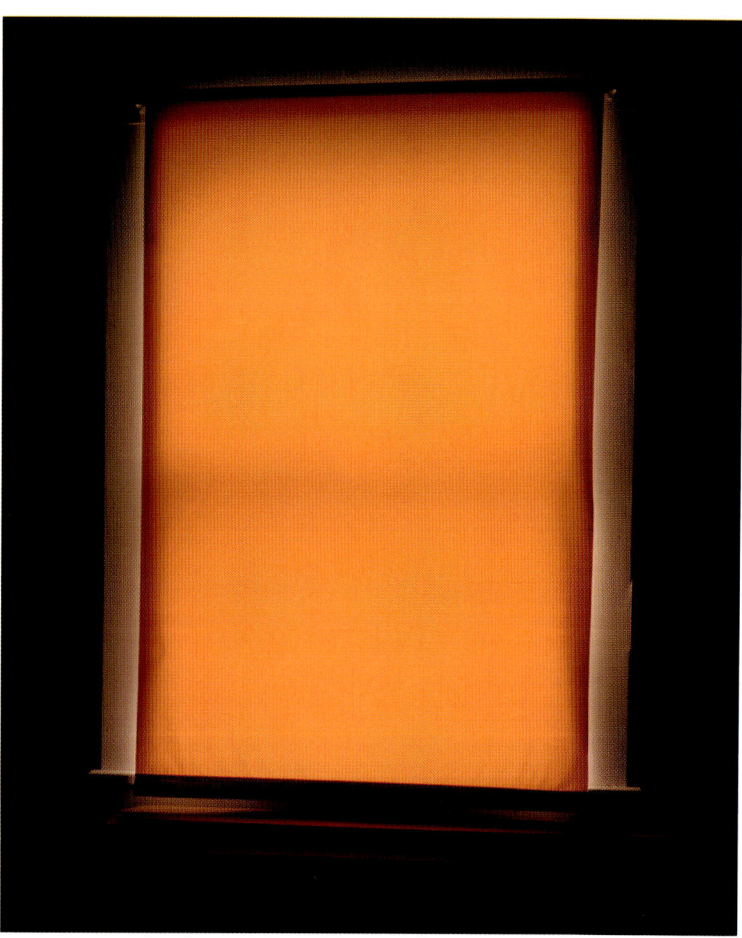

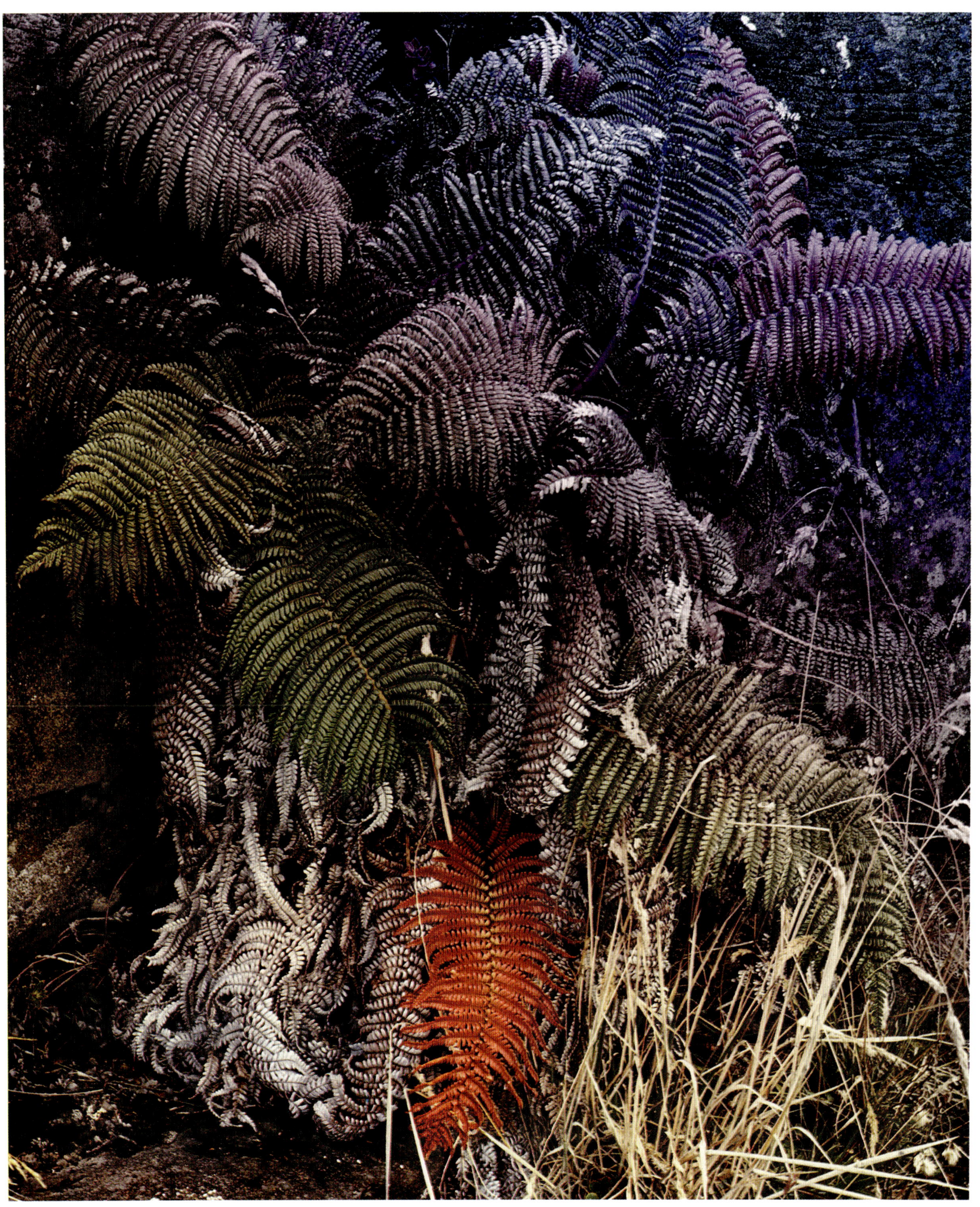

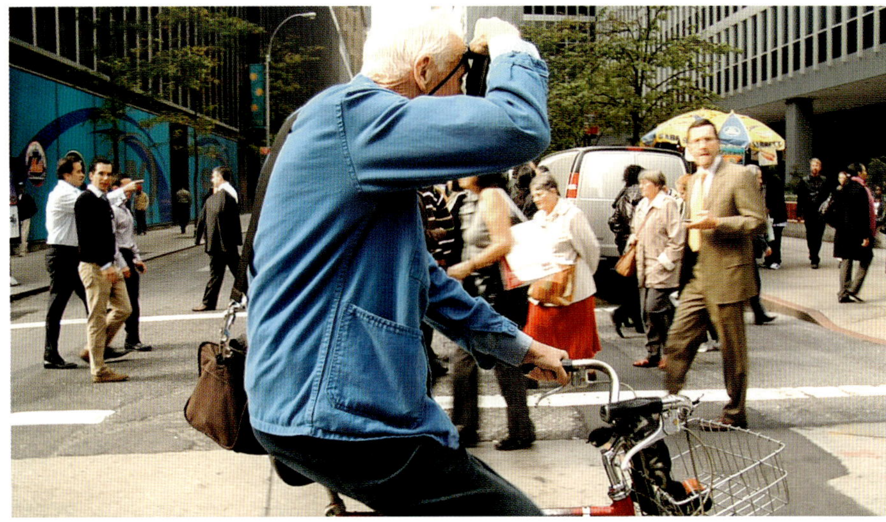

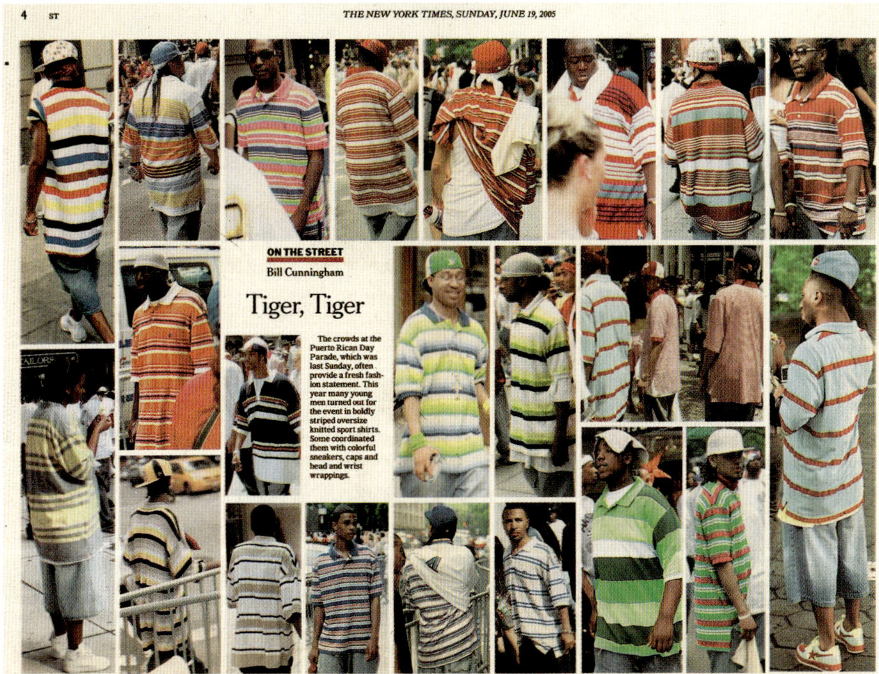
THE NEW YORK TIMES, SUNDAY, JUNE 19, 2005
ON THE STREET
Bill Cunningham
Tiger, Tiger
The crowds at the Puerto Rican Day Parade, which was last Sunday, often provide a fresh fashion statement. This year many young men turned out for the event in boldly striped oversize knitted sport shirts. Some coordinated them with colorful sneakers, caps and head and wrist wrappings.

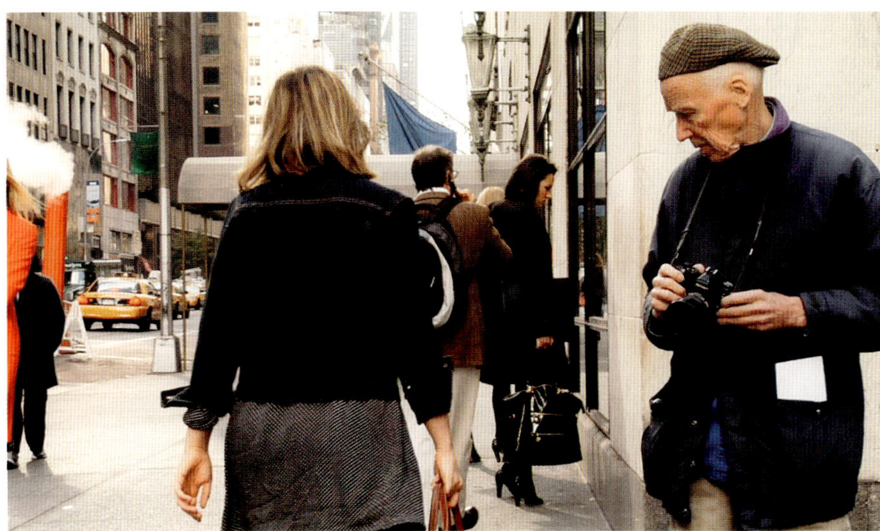

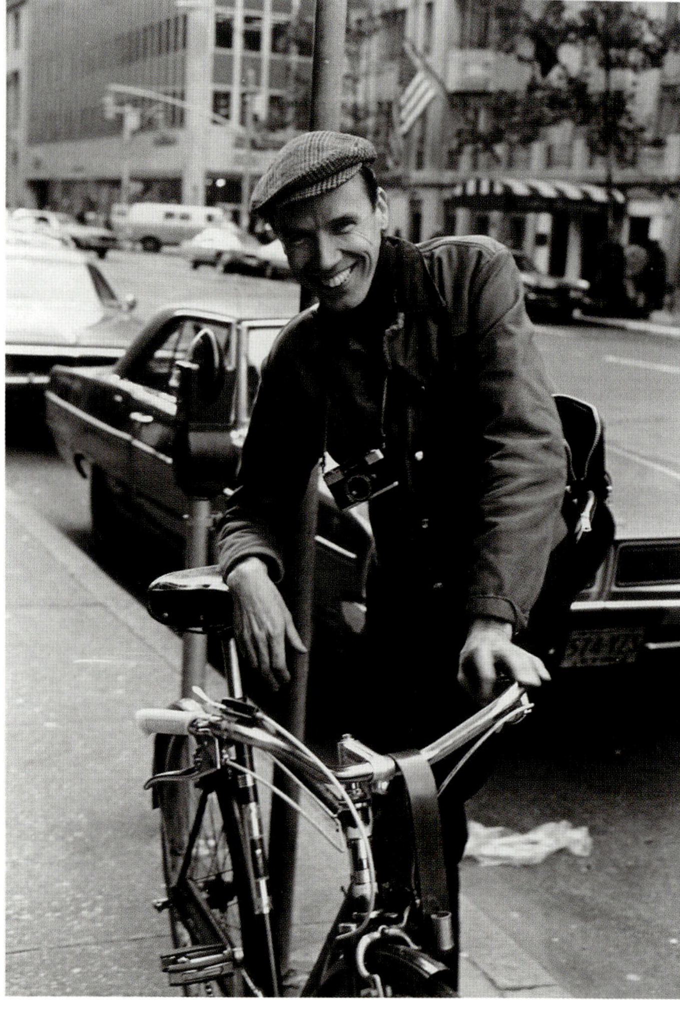

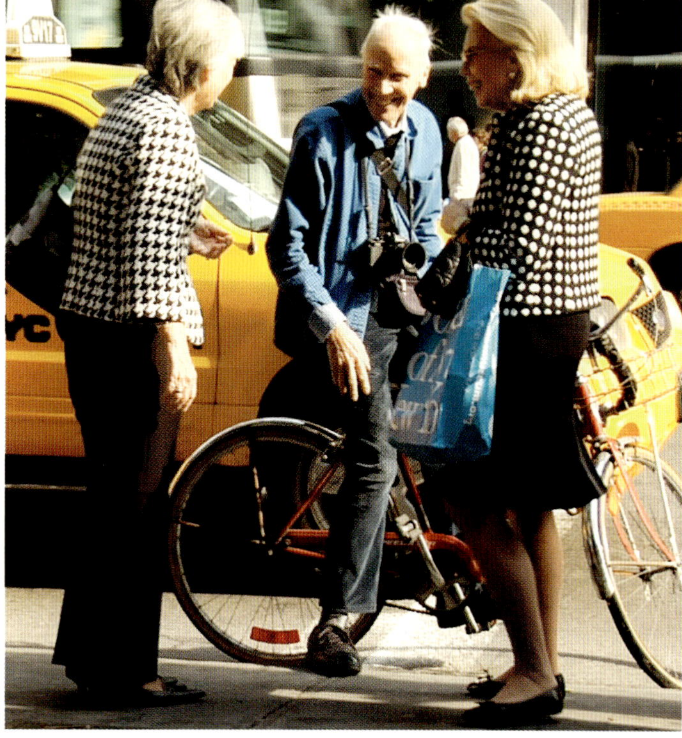

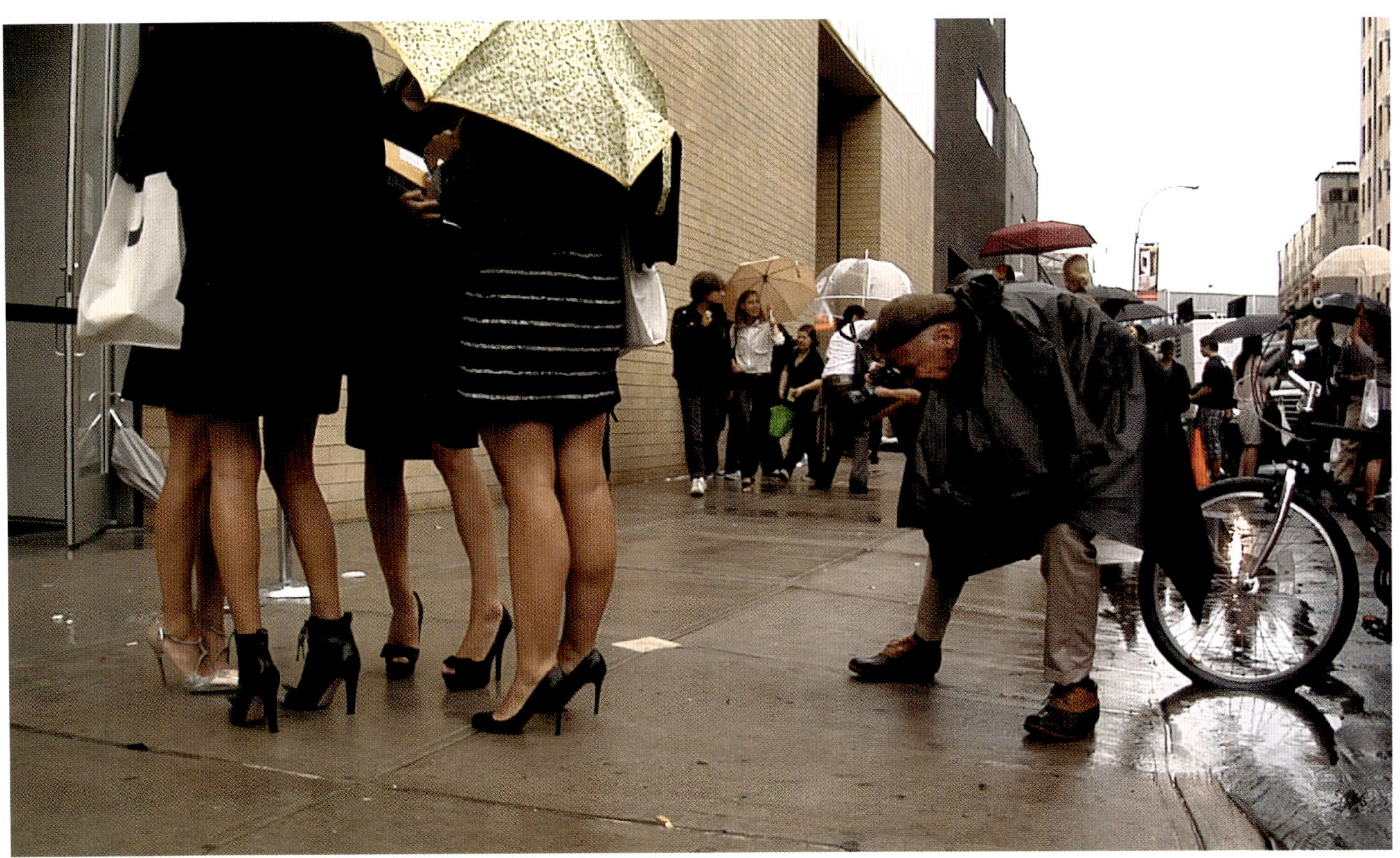

BILL CUNNINGHAM NEW YORK

Although the subject of Richard Press's 2010 film *Bill Cunningham New York* is rarely off the screen, he remains tantalizingly elusive. Cunningham, the photographer whose weekly "On the Street" feature for the *New York Times* has made him a legend and a cult figure in fashion circles, says he prefers to work "discreetly and quietly. *Invisible* is the word." New Yorkers will recognize him as the lean, alert man in the utilitarian blue coat (the same one Parisian street sweepers wear) and backward newsboy's cap who waits at the corner of Fifth Avenue and 57th Street for someone to catch his eye. Famously, maddeningly self-effacing, he deflects compliments, shies away from other cameras, and has always refused exhibitions, publications, and any kind of attention from the press. He participated in the film reluctantly and only after years of patient cajoling by his former *Times* colleague, critic Philip Gefter, Press's partner and the producer of the film, as well as Cunningham's unseen interviewer. Cunningham, who turned eighty in the course of the filming, is a cheerful but intensely focused presence—an uncompromising, no-nonsense charmer who remains a mystery to some of his fondest friends. Occasionally, Gefter probes into areas Cunningham is clearly uncomfortable discussing, but when it comes to his work, he's voluble and happy to chat.

"The best fashion is in the street," Cunningham says early in the film. "It always has been and always will be." His career in photography has included runway and behind-the-scenes shots from fashion shows (the most memorable of which were published as extensive portfolios in *Details* in the late 1980s) and party pictures for the "Evening Hours" feature in the Sunday *Times*, but his images of creatively dressed people seen in passing are his most distinctive and important work. Published regularly in the *Times* since 1989, they're a history of contemporary attire and attitude—encyclopedic in range and rigorously egalitarian. (His coverage was diverse and multicultural long before those words entered the conversation.) Cunningham has little interest

BY VINCE ALETTI

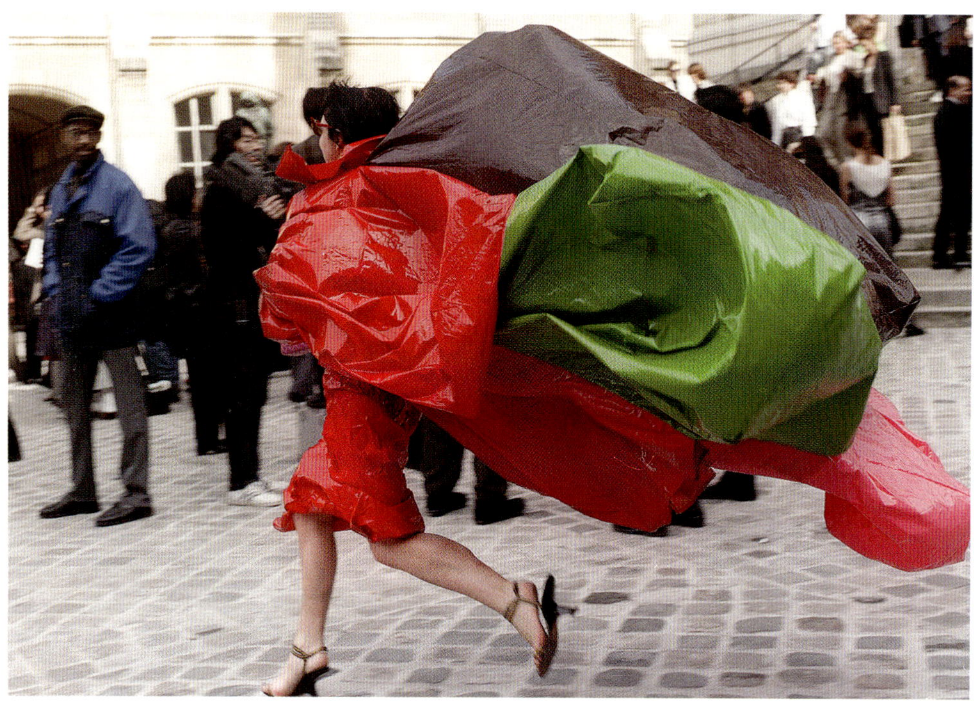

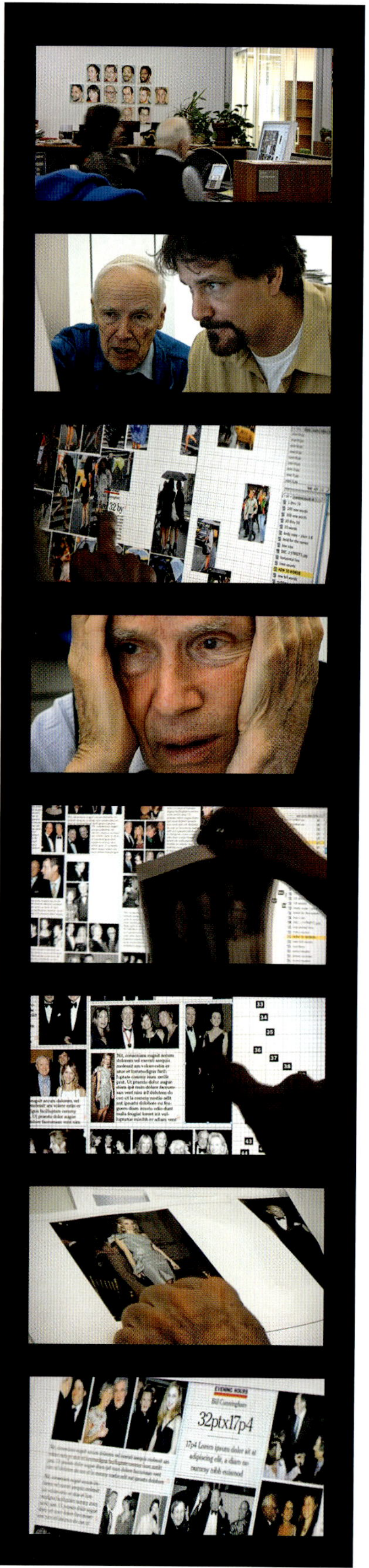

in celebrities (since he doesn't go to the movies or own a television, he claims not to know who they are) and no fondness for conventional good taste. "A lot of people have taste," he says, "but they don't have the daring to be creative." A dedicated fan and early supporter of the fashion avant-garde—including Azzedine Alaïa, Rei Kawakubo, and Issey Miyake—he also recognizes dash and daring wherever it crops up, whether it's the Puerto Rican Day Parade, an opening night at the Museum of Modern Art, or Wigstock. Cunningham has a historian's recall for fashion past (and has infuriated designers by printing pictures of their copies and vintage originals side-by-side) and a sociologist's eye for the ever-changing scene, so he's often the first to take note of fads (oversize T-shirts, visible underwear), trends (bright colors, leggings), and revivals (madras). "It's not really what I *think*," he tells Gefter. "It's what I *see*. I let the street speak to me."

Kim Hastreiter, the *Paper* editor who is one of the film's several savvy talking heads, says Cunningham is "like a war photographer—he'll do anything to get the shot." Manhattan is not exactly a combat zone, but we do see the intrepid photographer biking around town on a second-hand Schwinn, then darting off on foot, mid-conversation, whenever a "stunner" comes into view. Cunningham's routine—the film's prime concern—is repetitive: riding, waiting, shooting, bantering, setting up party shots, and laying out his *Times* pages with the help of a Mac-wise assistant who sometimes runs out to pick up film from a same-day processor nearby. (Cunningham has decidedly not gone digital.) When he stops for a meal, it's a meager, hand-held one in a coffee shop—"the cheaper the better," he announces. "I like very simple, down-to-earth things. I don't like anything fancy." His life is not without pleasure—face-to-face with exceptional, unconventional beauty, he glows with a childlike joy—but, on the evidence here, it's driven by a punishingly monastic level of self-denial. One of the film's narrative threads involves Cunningham's imminent eviction from a studio apartment above Carnegie Hall that looks more like an office-supply storage space. Metal file cabinets filled with prints

t I see. I let the street speak to me."

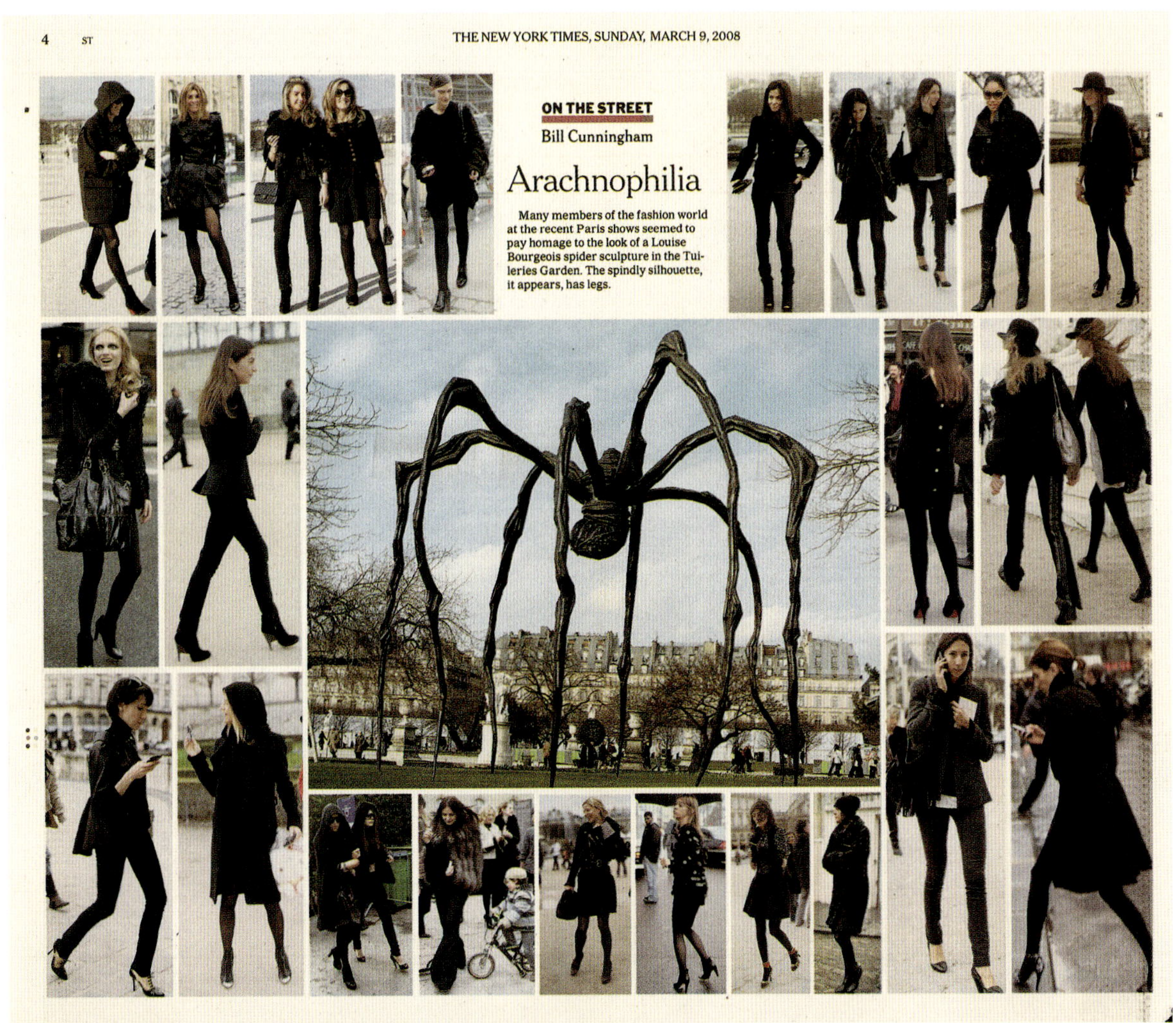

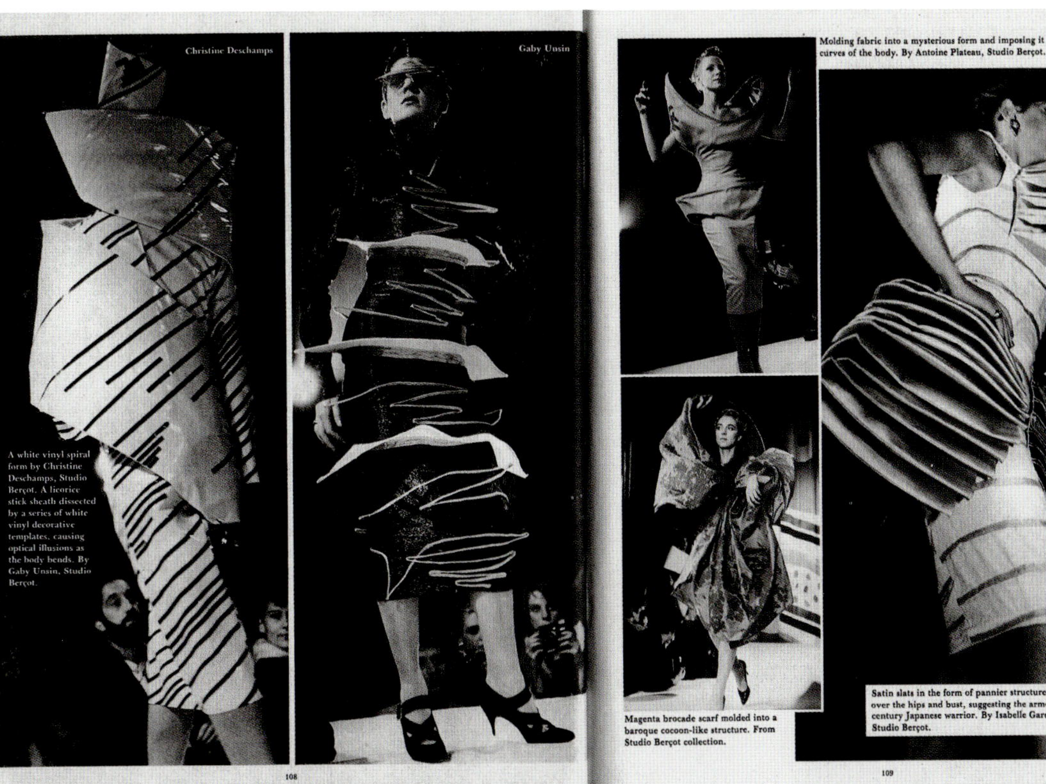

PAGE 68: TOP LEFT, BOTTOM LEFT, AND BOTTOM RIGHT: Film stills from *Bill Cunningham New York* (Richard Press, 2010); TOP RIGHT: Nicholas Vreeland, *Bill Cunningham in New York City*, ca. 1980; CENTER LEFT: Cunningham's "On the Street" column in the *New York Times*, June 19, 2005; PAGE 69: Film still from *Bill Cunningham New York*; OPPOSITE, TOP LEFT: Bill Cunningham, *Isabella Blow in Paris*, 1999; LEFT: Film stills from *Bill Cunningham New York*; THIS PAGE, TOP: Cunningham's "On the Street" column in the *New York Times*, March 9, 2008; BOTTOM: A layout from one of Cunningham's features published in *Details* magazine in the 1980s.

Film stills: courtesy First Thought Films and Zeitgeist Films; Vreeland: ©/courtesy Nicholas Vreeland; Cunningham: courtesy the artist

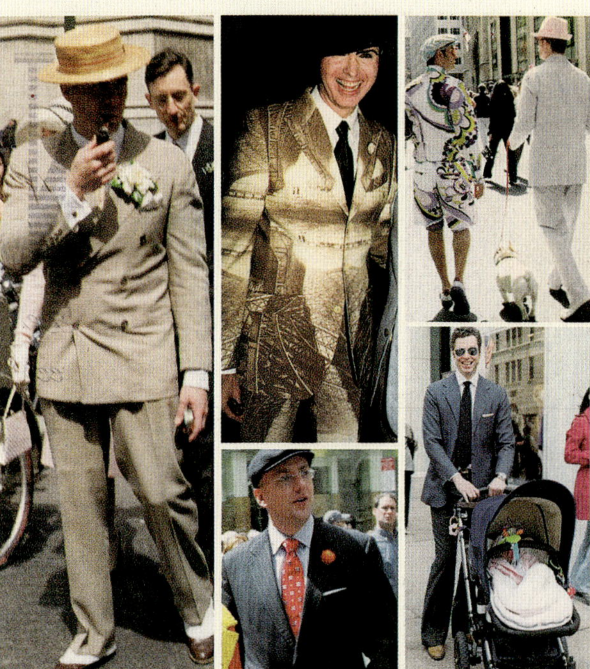
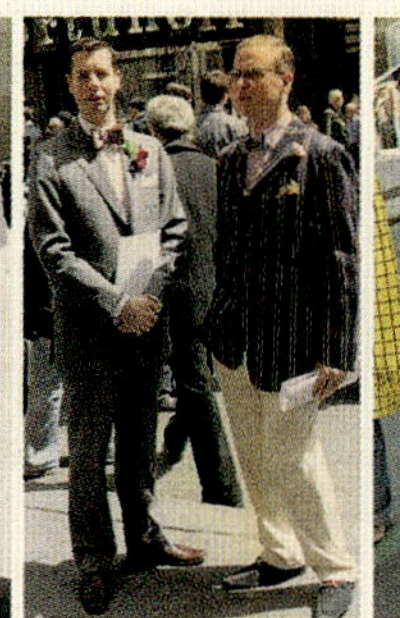
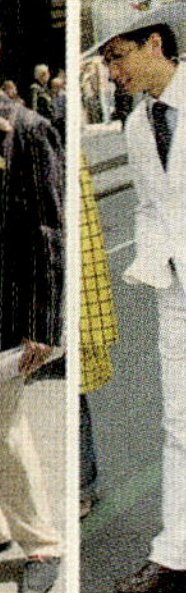
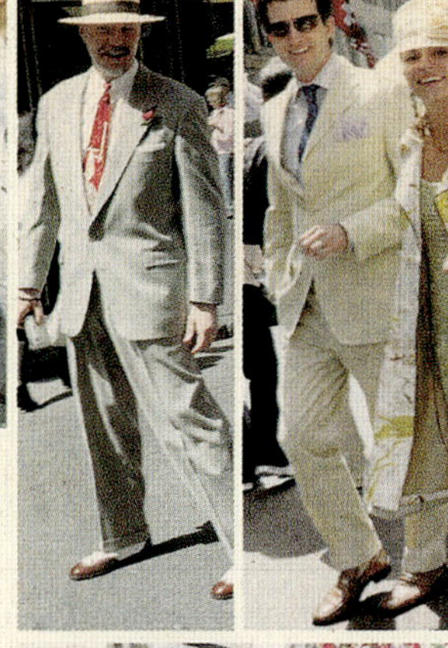
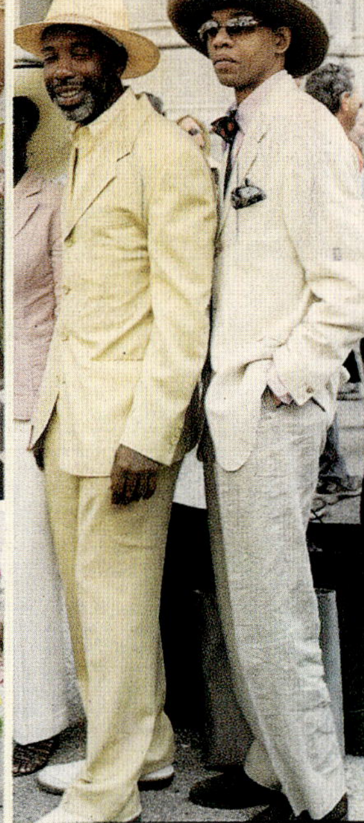
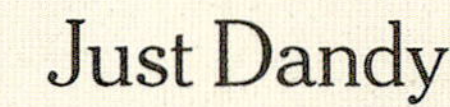

THE NEW YORK TIMES, SUNDAY, APRIL 23, 2006

ON THE STREET

Bill Cunningham

Just Dandy

In spite of everything — teenagers, hip-hop, casual Fridays — the suit survives. Traditionalists button up the tried and true, maybe wearing a rakish hat or two-tone shoes for special occasions. But free-spirited guys have more fun. Patrick McDonald, top, second from left, bought his suit at the recent Elton John charity auction; and Shail Upadhya, bottom row, outfits himself with the assistance of a tailor in Queens. Observed over a 10-day period, Mr. Upadhya mixes plaids to a fare-thee-well.

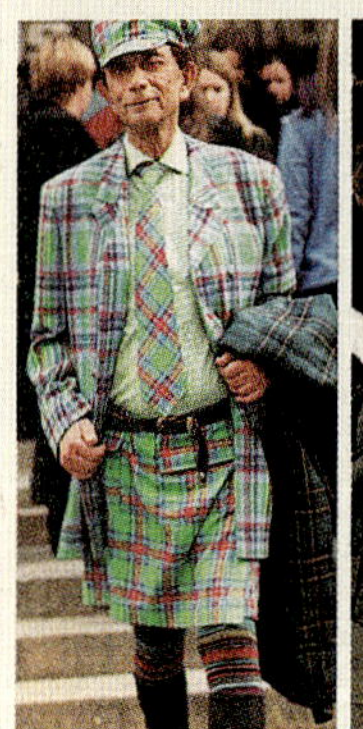
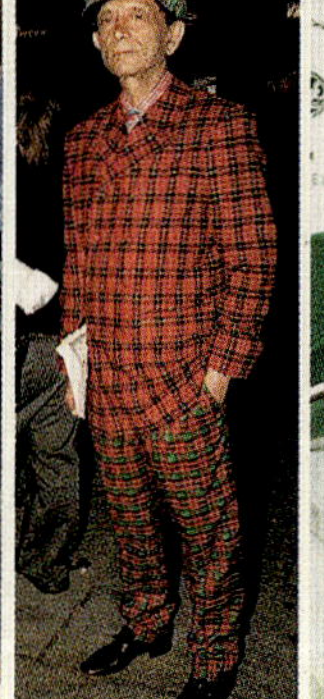
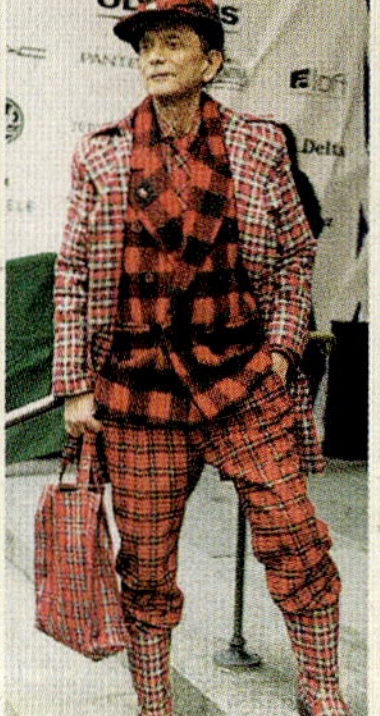
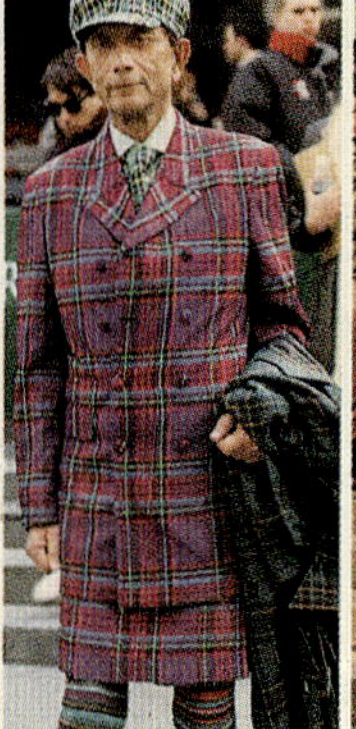
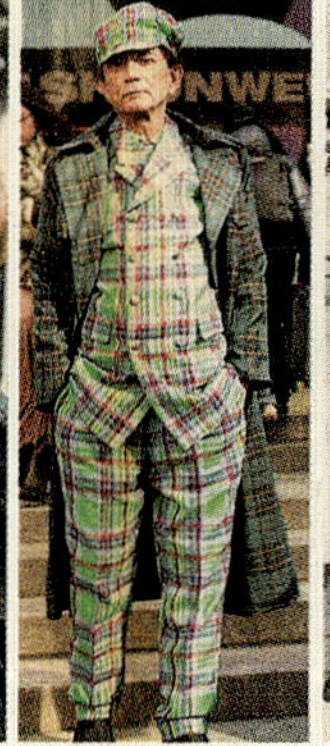
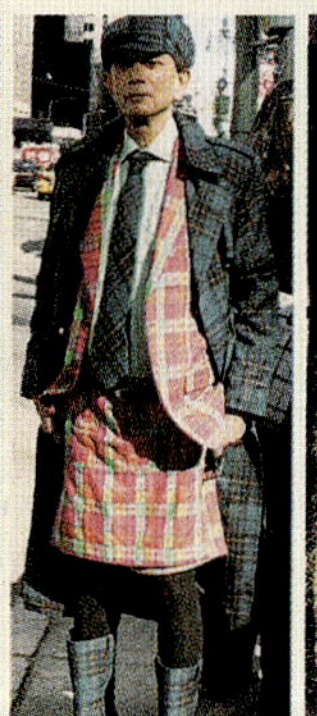
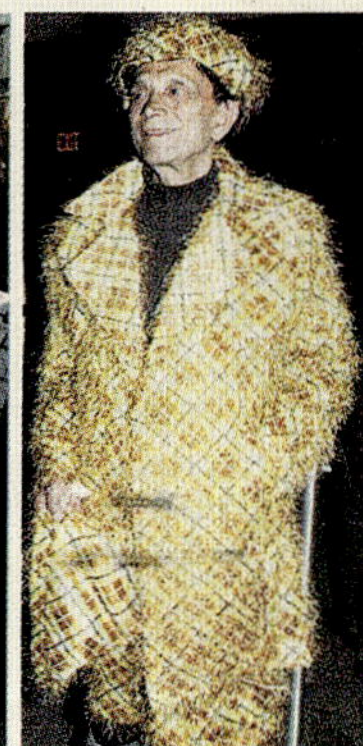
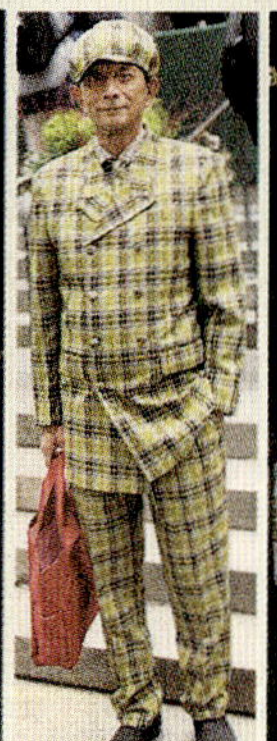
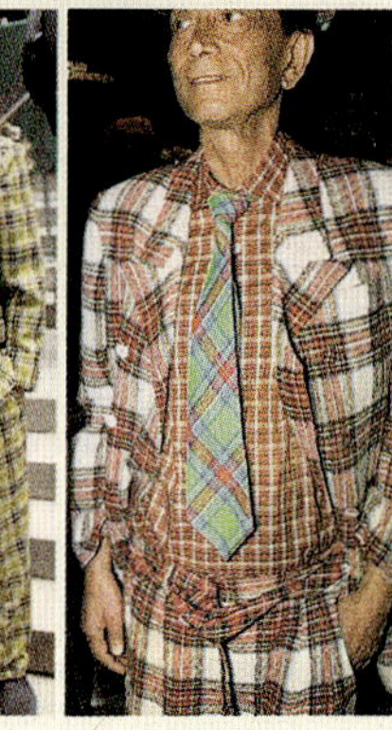

and negatives line every wall; books, magazines, and cardboard boxes of archive material are stacked on top. The bed is a narrow mattress just off the floor; the bathroom is down the hall. Shown a new apartment nearby with a wall of windows overlooking Central Park—the one he eventually relocates to—he wonders: "Who the hell needs a kitchen and a bathroom?" Before he moves in, he has the landlord remove all the kitchen fixtures so he can fill it with file cabinets. Friends guess that he comes from money because only the eccentric rich could live so poorly.

In fact, it seems, his background in Catholic, suburban Boston was solidly middle-class. But somewhere along the line he came to regard money as compromising, if not corrupting, and he often refuses to accept it. He tore up the checks he received from *Details*, still pays his own way to the Paris shows, and won't take even a glass of water at the charity balls and banquets he covers. "If you don't take money," he says, "they can't tell you what to do. That's the key to the whole thing: *don't touch money.*" His credo: "Money is the cheapest thing. Liberty, freedom, is the most expensive." Cunningham's old-school principles about filthy lucre are admirable (if self-righteous), but his quasi-puritanical refusal doesn't stop there. Toward the end of the film, Gefter broaches a delicate subject: has this self-sufficient loner ever had a romantic relationship? Cunningham laughs at the question but stalls by asking: "Do you want to know if I'm gay?" Having raised the question Gefter may have been leading up to, he bats it aside and goes back to the original one. Romance "never occurred to me," he says. "I guess I was just interested in clothes." Asked if he regrets that, he insists he does not—"I wouldn't even think about it. There

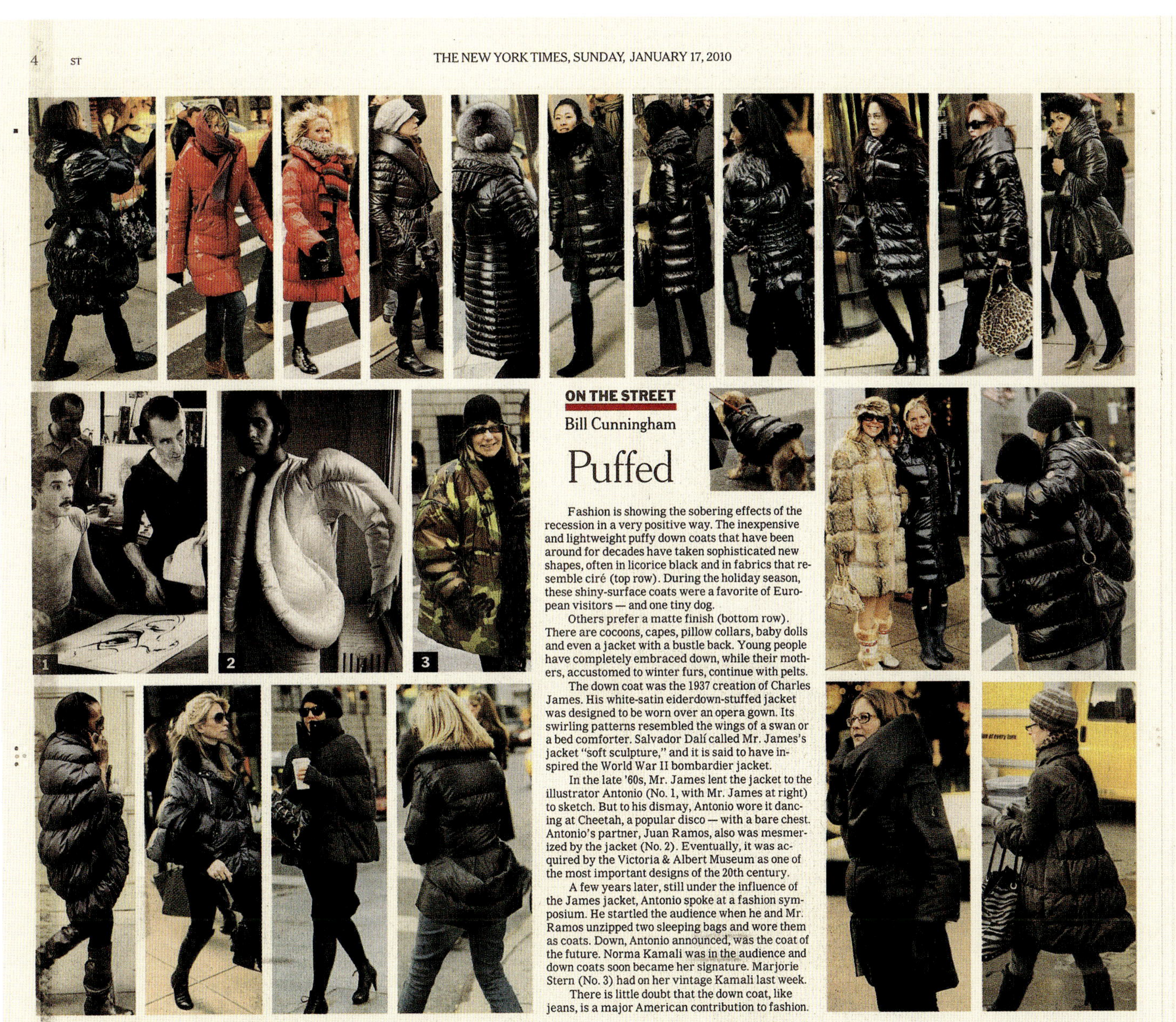

ON THE STREET

Bill Cunningham

Puffed

Fashion is showing the sobering effects of the recession in a very positive way. The inexpensive and lightweight puffy down coats that have been around for decades have taken sophisticated new shapes, often in licorice black and in fabrics that resemble ciré (top row). During the holiday season, these shiny-surface coats were a favorite of European visitors — and one tiny dog.

Others prefer a matte finish (bottom row). There are cocoons, capes, pillow collars, baby dolls and even a jacket with a bustle back. Young people have completely embraced down, while their mothers, accustomed to winter furs, continue with pelts.

The down coat was the 1937 creation of Charles James. His white-satin eiderdown-stuffed jacket was designed to be worn over an opera gown. Its swirling patterns resembled the wings of a swan or a bed comforter. Salvador Dalí called Mr. James's jacket "soft sculpture," and it is said to have inspired the World War II bombardier jacket.

In the late '60s, Mr. James lent the jacket to the illustrator Antonio (No. 1, with Mr. James at right) to sketch. But to his dismay, Antonio wore it dancing at Cheetah, a popular disco — with a bare chest. Antonio's partner, Juan Ramos, also was mesmerized by the jacket (No. 2). Eventually, it was acquired by the Victoria & Albert Museum as one of the most important designs of the 20th century.

A few years later, still under the influence of the James jacket, Antonio spoke at a fashion symposium. He startled the audience when he and Mr. Ramos unzipped two sleeping bags and wore them as coats. Down, Antonio announced, was the coat of the future. Norma Kamali was in the audience and down coats soon became her signature. Marjorie Stern (No. 3) had on her vintage Kamali last week.

There is little doubt that the down coat, like jeans, is a major American contribution to fashion.

---

was no time. I was working night and day"—but then hedges, admitting to "body urges" that "you control . . . as best you can."

This is sad and a bit embarrassing—all the more so when Gefter follows up Cunningham's earlier aside about going to church every Sunday with a question about the importance of religion in his life. Bowing his head, Cunningham pauses for a long time and sounds choked up when he finally says something about finding "good guidance" in the church. Gefter doesn't press the issue and Cunningham brightens, returning to a less fraught subject. "As a kid," he says, "I went to church and all I looked at was women's hats."

For its most dedicated followers, fashion is not unlike religion. It inspires, comforts, and offers occasional, fleeting visions of the sublime. His private pleasures may be seriously circumscribed, but Cunningham finds flashes of sheer ecstasy out on the street—and

he preserves them for us. The best thing about *Bill Cunningham New York* is the heightened illusion of seeing through his eyes. For those of us already addicted to Cunningham's weekly "On the Street" video feature on NYTimes.com, narrated with his "maahvelous," gravel-voiced pronouncements, the film lets us imagine that work in progress. As the wiry photographer bobs and weaves among the passing throngs, his images click across the screen. "It's not photography," he insists at one point. "Any real photographer would say: 'He's a fraud.' Well, they're right. I'm just about capturing what I see and documenting what I see." And who could ask for anything more? ◬

OPPOSITE AND THIS PAGE: Examples of Cunningham's "On the Street" columns in the *New York Times*, April 23, 2006 and January 17, 2010.

A MESSAGE TO MARY ELLEN MARK FROM LOURDES SANCHEZ

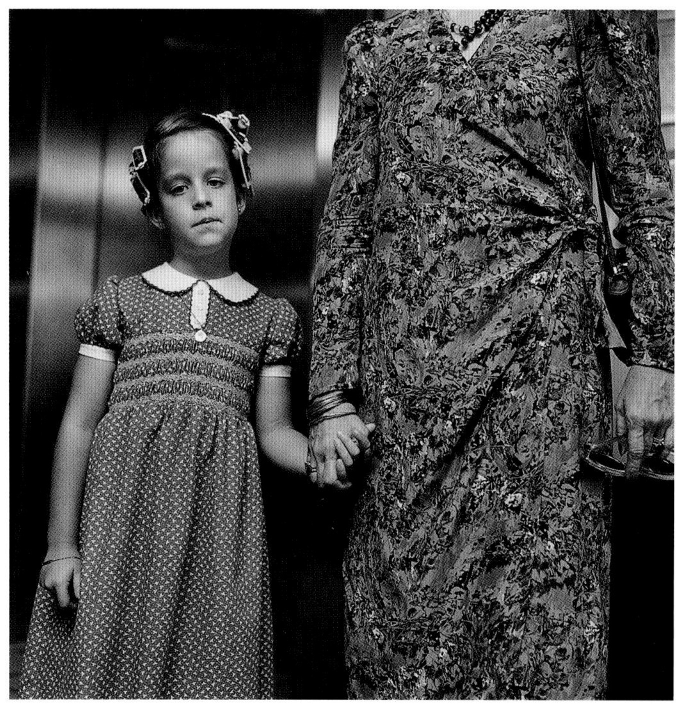

Monday, April 18, 2011

Mary Ellen,

I have to tell you how much respect I have for you as a photographer and artist. I honestly didn't know who you were or anything about this picture until one day I decided to look myself up on Google and see what would come up. I Googled my maiden name first. I instantly saw a little girl in curlers and thought: Wow that's weird, I was always in curlers. Then I zoomed in and recognized that it was me.

I want to express to you just how much that picture encompasses the feelings I had as a child—and more, now as an adult. That picture tells so much of my childhood and my relationship to my mother. You caught my soul in that picture.

I'm a daughter of a narcissistic mother and have suffered in confusion for many years. Finally at the age of thirty, after having three children of my own, I've come to realize how my feelings of confusion came to be. I guess what people have experienced with their own mothers comes out when they themselves become mothers.

I was an accessory to my mother. The way she is clutching my hand in the picture, and my face of sadness at being forced to perform at some children's fashion show full of lights and people clapping—I was terrified, and that is apparent in my expression. *Just smile, then she will be happy*, is what I was thinking. That day, it seems, I couldn't even crack a smile.

I did fashion shows for her all the time. I hated them. I felt sick, nauseous, and shaky on the rides to the fancy hotels she took me to, thrown in the leather back seat of her Jaguars or Cadillacs or

whatever they were, hoping not to vomit on my new dresses. She would disappear to go sit at tables with her friends while I changed clothes and got my hair twisted and pulled in some dark backroom full of strangers and pinchy shoes.

I learned to comfort myself.

She was never the type of mother to hold me, hug me, kiss me, tell me she loved me. She wasn't concerned about how sad I was, how bored at Neiman Marcus and Saks. Instead of playing at the park or with friends, I mingled with salespeople while she was in dressing rooms. I talked to them about my day at school, about my grades, about how I hated my math teacher. My mother never listened, but the salesgirl did—she knew she'd better if she wanted to earn her commission for the day. I talked, they listened. I was happy.

My mother wanted me to look good. I was a reflection of how great a mother she was because I looked nice from the outside. Something wasn't nice until she looked at the tag for the designer— if it was a recognizable one, to her the item was nice. If not, it was crap. (For some reason, I've always preferred the crap. . . .)

I was an unplanned pregnancy. My two brothers were sixteen when my mother found out she was pregnant again. I don't know what must have occurred that day she told my dad they would have to start all over again, but I can only think it wasn't good.

I don't know what it feels like to have an unwanted child. I myself had a homebirth with my son because I wanted to *feel* the birth, I wanted to connect. She never got it. She lied and told her friends I gave birth at South Miami Hospital—so I never got the flowers they sent.

She could never understand it. She never connected to any of us.

My mother is all about handbags and dresses. They know her by name at Carolina Herrera. She visits the salespeople at the stores more often then she does my children and me. On the other hand, she buys my kids broken toys from Goodwill, and stained clothing—that's what narcissists do, I guess. Once I outgrew the phase when she dressed me and was ready to shop for my own clothes, I can't remember ever buying an outfit at a real store. She always took me to Goodwill—I thought it was the only place I was allowed to buy clothes. While she spent $800 on a jacket I had to be OK with one costing $8. I never understood it but was afraid to question it.

A friend's mom took me to Sears for my first bra. I wore hand-me-downs for my communion dress and *quinceañera* dress.

My mother would send me away on long vacations with my godmother. Rosy was her name. She was the one who mothered me and comforted me when I was sick. She was the first person to hug me. I'll never forget it: I had pink eye, and she just got into the bed and put a little Kleenex over my eye with some medicine in it and hugged me for what felt like hours.

Rosy was proud of me. She showed me off to people at stores and laughed and said yes when they asked if I was her daughter. As much as she wanted me to be her daughter, I wished she had been my mother. We both had blue eyes, which was cool to me since both my parents had brown eyes. She was one of the mothers in my pre-K class who took a liking to me—I would go over to her house and I would pretend I lived with them: it was a big family, full of love and affection. It felt like family. It's funny, because at my own house I felt like the guest.

I named my third child after her. Sienna Rose.

My mother never liked my straight hair; it was always in curlers. My face was always too pale and blush was constantly applied. She never liked my sense of style or taste and she always made sure to tell me. She never let me just be who I was—a little girl who liked getting into the dirt, planting stuff, and playing kickball. She wished I was unlike myself and more of something she wanted me to be. She always put me into itchy embroidered dresses and doused me in gold jewelry, just like her.

I hated it all—it was so fake. But I performed for her. I wore what she wanted me to and smiled for the cameras. No one else ever came to my shows or saw what I was doing—not my brothers, not my father. But I did it, and I did it *well*. I always stole the show. I was the one who came out with the designer and walked down the catwalk at the end of the fashion show. And everyone stood up from their chairs for me and my mother was a hero. Everyone came to her and congratulated her on how well I'd done. Then she would take me out for a Happy Meal. I had made her day; she was the mother with the cutest kid. The saddest kid.

I found a copy of this picture in a small box I always carried with me as a child. I had forgotten I even had it, and I had no idea how meaningful it would be for me looking at it as a mother myself. I guess a mother has a keen awareness, an instinct, looking into a child's eyes . . . I always look for sadness in my children's eyes, hoping that joy is all I find. So I looked into my own eyes and as soon as I did, I saw sadness. I recognized it.

The picture captures that weird, strained relationship between mother and daughter. How we as daughters sometimes become the aspiring dreams of what our mothers wish they themselves were or could've been. It's as if time stands still and we *are* them. We become their puppets. Their Chanel purses. I was like my mother's purse: I was an accessory.

SELECTED BOOKS

EXCERPTS

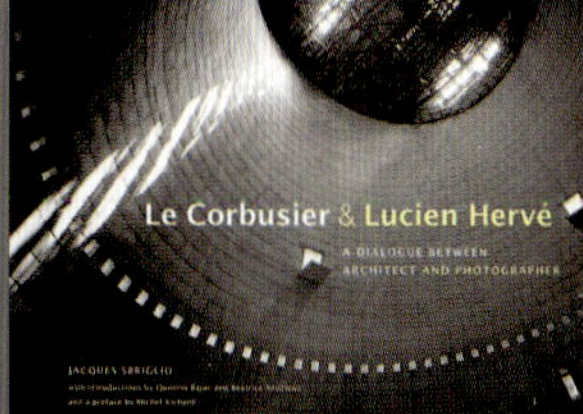

Le Corbusier was quick to appreciate the photographs Hervé took during a single day on the work site of the Cité d'habitation in Marseille at the end of 1949. "For forty years," he enthused, "I've been looking for a photographer able to express architecture": to express—that is, to translate *in signs*—every existing thing by extracting its meaning.

Hervé differed both in his working methods and in his photographic culture from the practitioners that Le Corbusier had theretofore been employing. Self-taught, steeped in avant-garde photographic culture, in tune with Bauhaus ideas . . . Hervé perfectly incarnated the "modern sensibility," which he shared fully with Le Corbusier.
—from Quentin Bajac's Introduction, "Expressing Architecture"

LE CORBUSIER & LUCIEN HERVÉ: A DIALOGUE BETWEEN ARCHITECT AND PHOTOGRAPHER
Los Angeles: Getty Publications, 2011

Hervé was by no means the first photographer to work for Le Corbusier. . . . An amateur photographer himself (at least in the early years), a compulsive user of images of diverse origins and kinds to illustrate his theoretical contributions to the period between the two world wars, Le Corbusier was a member of that generation of artists and thinkers who became increasingly aware, particularly during the 1920s, of the important influence of mechanical reproduction processes on the perception and definition of works of art, most notably in the plastic realm of three-dimensional works. . . .

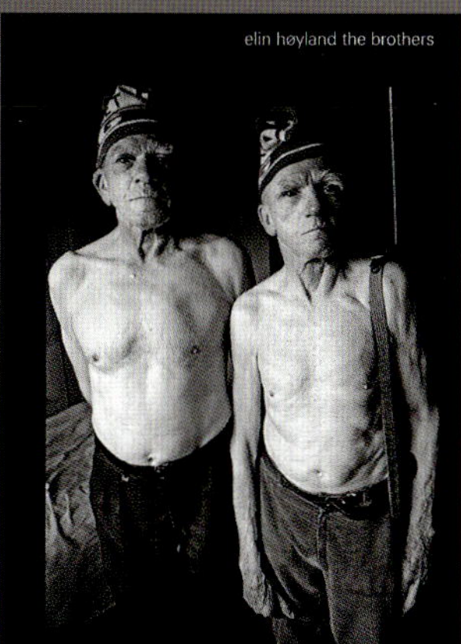

Elin Høyland's THE BROTHERS
Stockport, U.K.: Dewi Lewis, 2011

Although digital media are beginning to change this, a photobook is the closest still photography gets to the film—a thought which seems pertinent in relation to Elin Høyland's poignant photoessay, *The Brothers*. . . .

(continued on next page)

Høyland also taps into another aspect of contemporary photographic practice, one in which Scandinavian photographers have been prominent. In their rush to interpret the cutting edge of contemporary life, photographers have been drawn inevitably to the modern metropolis, with all its thrills and terrors. A sizeable minority, however, have been attracted by rural life. To the consternation of some commentators, photography does nostalgia very well, so is ideal for documenting the anti-urban syndrome, the desire on the behalf of urbanites to escape the metropolitan rat-race and return to a "simpler," more "basic" way of life, to the "gentle," traditional values lost in the dog-eat-dog milieu of the city.

But Elin Høyland's vision is rooted in a strain of Scandinavian rural photography that firmly resists this nostalgia and the notion that country life is a bed of roses—as we see in the more sentimental brands of landscape photography. There may be a sense, as there is in Høyland, that a certain tradition and way of life is fast disappearing, but whether that should occasion regret is another matter. And while there is a clear flavour of the diaristic about regarding the minutiae of lived lives, the tenor of many of these investigations of Scandinavian rural life is sociological, almost anthropological, even if the photographers are closely related to both place and subjects. . . .

What is important is what Høyland does not tell us. In a very real sense, it is the gaps between the photographs, if you like, that makes the sequence so effective, and effecting.

—from Gerry Badger's essay "Pregnant Silences: Elin Høyland's 'The Brothers'"

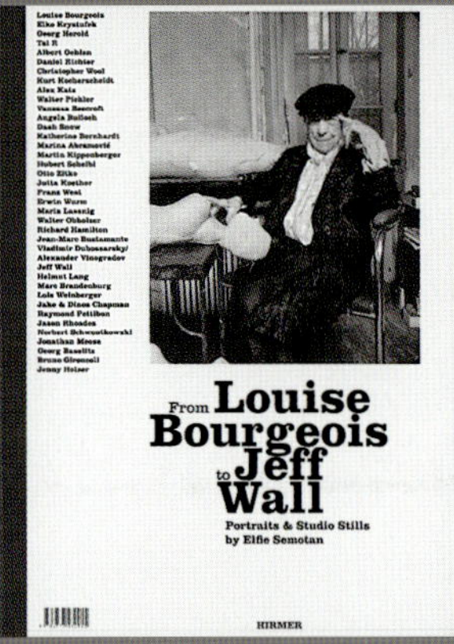

Elfie Semotan
FROM LOUISE BOURGEOIS TO JEFF WALL: PORTRAITS & STUDIO STILLS
Munich: Hirmer, 2010

Since the first use of photographic techniques, around the mid-19th century, the genre of "artist photography" has been one of the fields of application for the new technology. The way thinkers, inventors, scientists and writers blended in with the given canon of bourgeois portrait photography is surprising and only understandable in the context of the new, heightened social standing of the art profession within the intellectual life of this era of change. . . .

Stability, security, and serenity are not criteria that exist in the world of Semotan's photography; her portraits show their subjects in the condition of their temporal existence. Like momentary sculptures, they are peeled out of their background, but not without being re-integrated into its atmospheric setting and staginess; light and perspective virtually recreate the person's figure, crystallize it and furnish it with three-dimensional qualities. . . . The sculptural bodies round out and are embedded in an attributively inhabited room.

—from Margrit Zuckriegl's essay

Mary Ellen, this picture says so many things to me. It's priceless how straight my mother is standing—thinking she's the star—but it says to me that all that mattered to you, the photographer, was me. You saw me in my curlers, and liked me. Her head is out of the frame: that accessory she held by the hand was what mattered to your camera lens. Me, with curlers, not fancy curly sprayed hair, no Dippity-Do, just me. And that decked-out mother in her Oscar de la Renta dress and diamonds just got her head cut off, because she didn't matter. I mattered.

I have three children of my own and am married to an unbelievable man, and I'm living a life I never thought possible. Although we don't have much, I am happy, truly happy. My mother continues her extravagant lifestyle, buying things that cost more than my monthly rent, and comes by once or twice a month to say hi with her Goodwill bag for my kids. . . . But I matter. My husband thinks I'm a goddess. My two-year-old son tells me he loves me constantly; my five-year-old daughter thinks I'm all-knowing and a glorious cook; and my youngest daughter—eleven months old— kicks her feet with joy when she sees me from the highchair . . . and that gives me all the joy and love and affection I need. I matter to them and that's all that matters to me.

Mary Ellen, this email is longer than I intended it to be, as so many memories flooded into me. I appreciate your reading it. Thank you for making me tap into that time in my life, thank you for making me a better mother, thank you for making me matter enough to you to want to take my picture.

—Lourdes Sanchez ◬

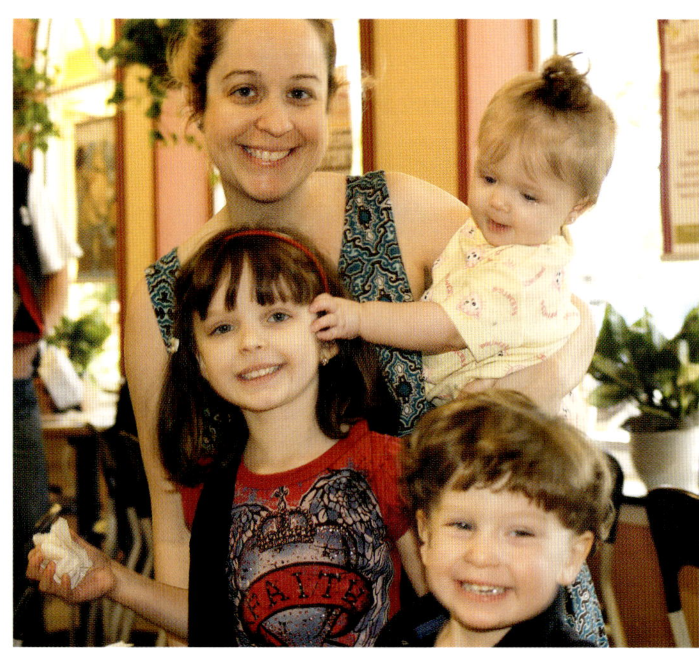

DEBORAH LUSTER'S *TOOTH FOR AN EYE: A CHOROGRAPHY OF VIOLENCE IN ORLEANS PARISH*

Violence and loss have been consistent themes in Deborah Luster's photographic practice since she began working with a camera in 1988, after her mother was shot to death by a hired killer. Acknowledging the murder as a key motivating factor, Luster has said: "When you've experienced a loss in your life, you keep telling the story over and over. That's what's happened in my work."

Luster indirectly dealt with that brutal family tragedy through her portraits of inmates in Louisiana state prisons, published in her monograph *One Big Self: Prisoners of Louisiana* (Twin Palms, 2003), and she approaches it from a different angle in her latest book. Here the emphasis is on victims rather than convicted perpetrators, and the subjects are places rather than people. *Tooth for an Eye: A Chorography of Violence in Orleans Parish* (Twin Palms, 2011) is an outsized volume centering on twenty-nine tondo photographs of homicide sites in and around Luster's adopted home city, New Orleans—the murder capital of the United States and one of the world's deadliest cities. She made them with an 8-by-10-inch Deardorff field camera, and they represent about one-sixth of the series's original prints. In exhibitions Luster displays the full corpus, bound into six large-format ledgers, on a custom-built table and augments them with two oval-framed color videos, both portraying victims' family members and friends in silent sequences that fade from one to another.

Images of the victims in Luster's book are relegated to collages on the inside front and back covers. These vertical excerpts show them during apparently happy times—smiling confidently in student-yearbook portraits, informally posed in snapshots, and in one case mugging in a photo-booth strip. The contrast between these upbeat images and Luster's bleak photographs of the crime scenes effectively highlights the fact that these individuals have been rendered nonexistent. So has everyone else, it almost seems. The only living soul we see in any of Luster's published images is a woman with her back turned toward us as she sits on a folding chair on a motel balcony in the

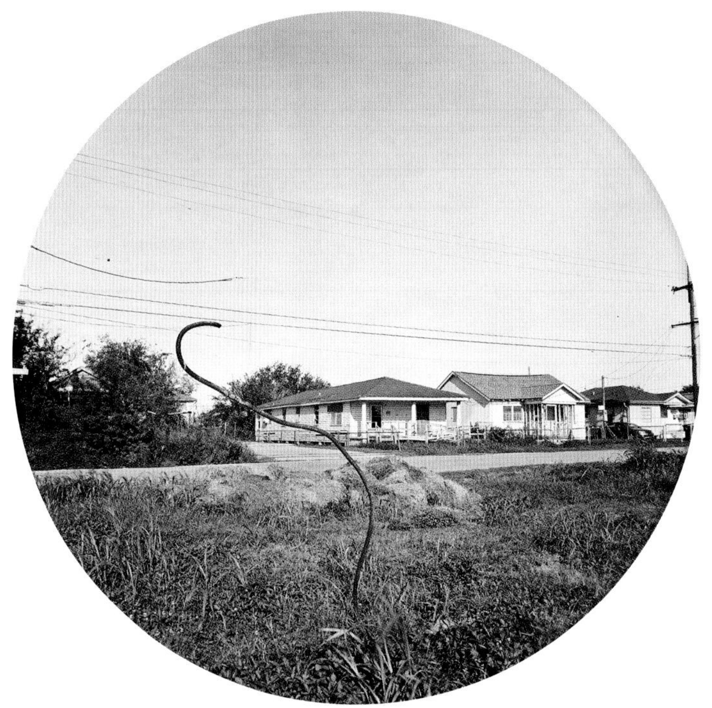

middle distance of one photograph. The overwhelming emphasis is on absence rather than presence—or on absence as itself a kind of lingering presence. Luster conjures a ghost-town atmosphere, giving the impression that the entire city has been all but abandoned. The images foreground the loneliness of death, and particularly of unanticipated, violent death. In each case we're struck by the fact that we may be looking at the last thing the victim saw before permanently losing consciousness.

In the book's first photograph a pair of metal-framed glass doors is detailed in tight close-up from the inside of a meat market. The view of the Hollygrove community outside—as seen through a patchwork of advertising decals, neon signs, and placards that forbid smoking and loitering—is overexposed, seemingly on the verge of fading into oblivion. Seventeen-year-old Brandon Aggison died here after being used as a human shield in a drive-by shooting at 9:25 P.M. on January 8, 2002, according to handwriting reproduced on the facing page.

The latter information is entered on a form Luster devised for presenting the facts of each murder she documented. In addition to the locations, murder dates, and victims' names, these forms include spaces for additional notes and for two-part, rubber-stamped numerical coordinates corresponding to the previously mentioned ledgers and their image sequences. The term "disarchive" printed

LEFT: *Tooth for an Eye*, disarchive #01–16; Location: 700 block of Burgundy Street (French Quarter); Date(s): September 1978; Name(s): John M. Workman (34); Notes: Stabbing. **ABOVE:** *Tooth for an Eye*, disarchive #05–11; Location: 1500 Alabo Street (Lower 9th Ward); Date(s): October 13, 1994, 11 P.M.; Name(s): Kim Marie Groves (32); Date(s): January 17, 2004, 1 P.M.; Name(s): Donald James (64); Notes: Gunshot to head. N.O.P.D. Officer Len Davis ordered Paul "Cool" Hardy, a drug dealer, to murder Grimes in retaliation for her filing a complaint of brutality against Davis and his partner.

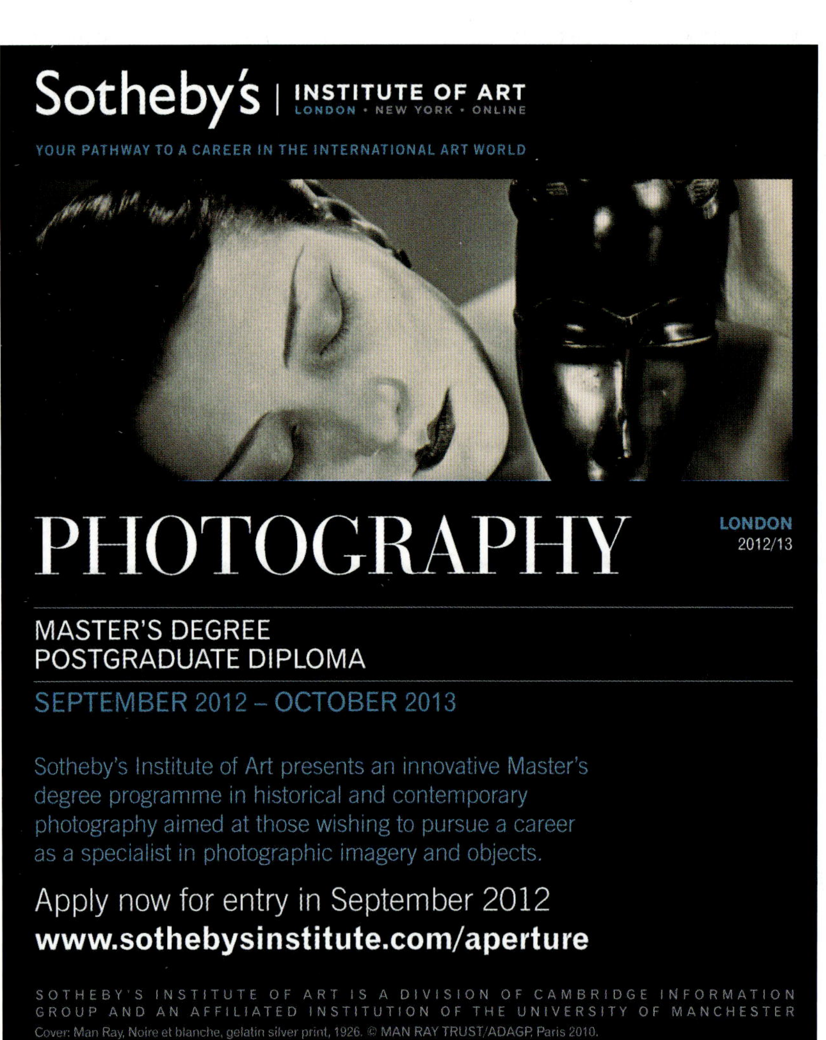

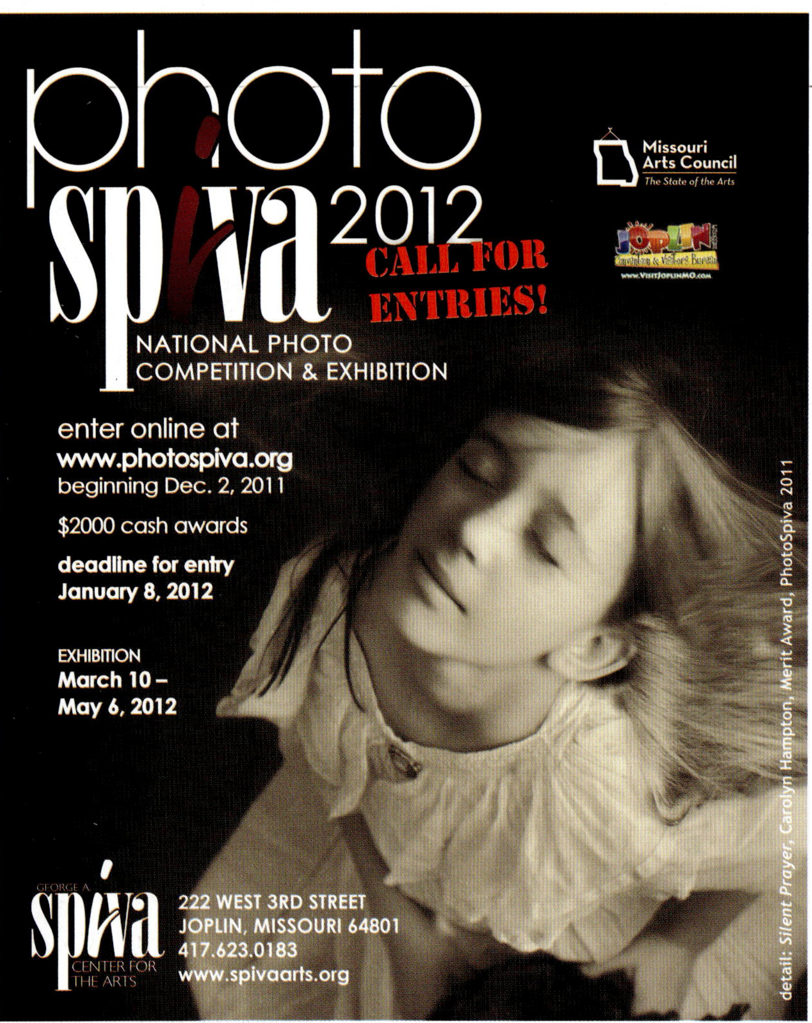

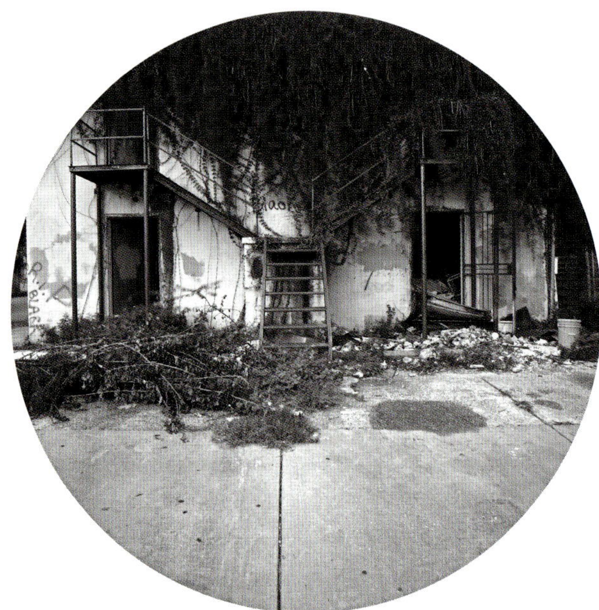

on these forms is her way of acknowledging their unofficial nature, while also paying homage to reclusive portrait photographer Michael Disfarmer, whose self-adopted name reflected his disavowal of the farm family into which he was born in rural Arkansas, where Luster was also raised.

A vacant lot in New Orleans's Lower Ninth Ward—the low-income neighborhood famously devastated in Hurricane Katrina—occupies the foreground of one of Luster's most effective images. Implanted in the grass at its center is a sinuously bent length of steel rebar that suggests a reversed question mark or a snake frozen in midstrike. The facing page's disarchive form indicates that this was the site of two murders spaced over about ten years. The accompanying note indicates that the earlier victim was murdered by a drug dealer on the order of a police officer previously targeted by the victim in a brutality complaint—not the only reference in the book to deadly crimes perpetrated by members of the city's notoriously corrupt police force.

In an afterword, Luster quotes writer Julia Reed's comment that living in New Orleans is "not unlike living in the Old Testament." That comparison is starkly emblemized in another photograph from the Lower Ninth Ward, the most prominent feature of which is a crudely painted mural on the damaged aluminum siding of a storefront church's exterior. Alongside its image of a man triumphantly posed over the collapsed figure of his victim is a hand-lettered text referencing the biblical account of the original deadly violent act: "Today Cain is still killing his brother with a rock . . . KILLING

THIS PAGE: *Tooth for an Eye*, disarchive # 05–15; Location: 1200 block Luro Street (7th Ward); Date(s): September 12, 1996; Name(s): Artiero Alvear (55), Note(s): Hit in head with tire iron; Date(s): November 27, 2003, 6:30 A.M.; Name(s): Leonard Mitchell (49); Note(s): Gunshot to torso. Lying on sidewalk. OPPOSITE: *Tooth for an Eye*, disarchive #02–04; Location: North Rampart and Forstall (Holy Cross-L9); Date(s): July 24, 1994; Name(s): Doretta Sylve; Note(s): Murdered by her son.

All images © Deborah Luster/courtesy Twin Palms Publishers, www.twinpalms.com

AGAIN." The facing page informs us that this is the site where, on July 24, 1994, Doretta Sylve was murdered by her son.

Most of the locations Luster photographed for the project lack such aptly distinguishing features and reflect the randomness of street violence. Despite their nondescript character, Luster manages to poetically convey the haunted aspect of these scenes, as well as the overwhelming sadness and horror of what they've silently witnessed.

The book's main title calls to mind the often-cited biblical passages referencing the ancient Babylonian proscription for enacting justice—"an eye for an eye, and a tooth for a tooth." But it also alludes to tooth in eye surgery, a procedure for curing blindness due to severe corneal and ocular surface damage. (A tissue lamina cut from an extracted tooth is drilled and the resultant hole fitted with optics, then the lamina is grown in the patient's cheek for several months before being implanted on the eye.) In commenting on the title, Luster notes that she used to collect extracted teeth and glass eyes. As for the subtitle, *chorography* is a somewhat obscure geographical term that refers to a detailed description, analysis, or map of a particular region.

The last victim commemorated in the book, twenty-two-year-old Brian Christopher Smith, suffered multiple gunshot wounds and was left lying face-up, according to information opposite the final photograph—a view of white, cloudless sky that sets off tightly strung power lines on which thirteen birds are perched like heralds of bad luck. ⓐ

—Tom Patterson

Tom Patterson is a freelance art writer, an independent curator, and the author of several books on contemporary outsider art. His writings have appeared in *Artnews*, *Art Papers*, *Bomb*, and *Raw Vision*, among other art magazines. He lives in Winston-Salem, North Carolina.

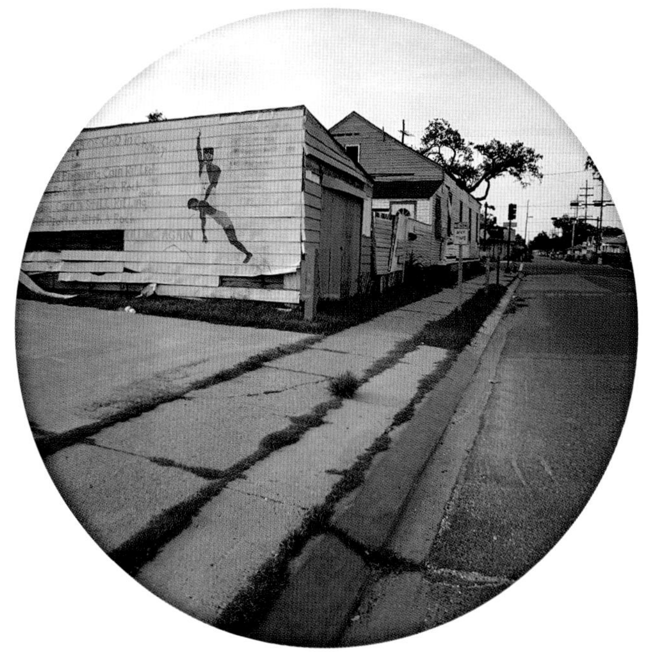

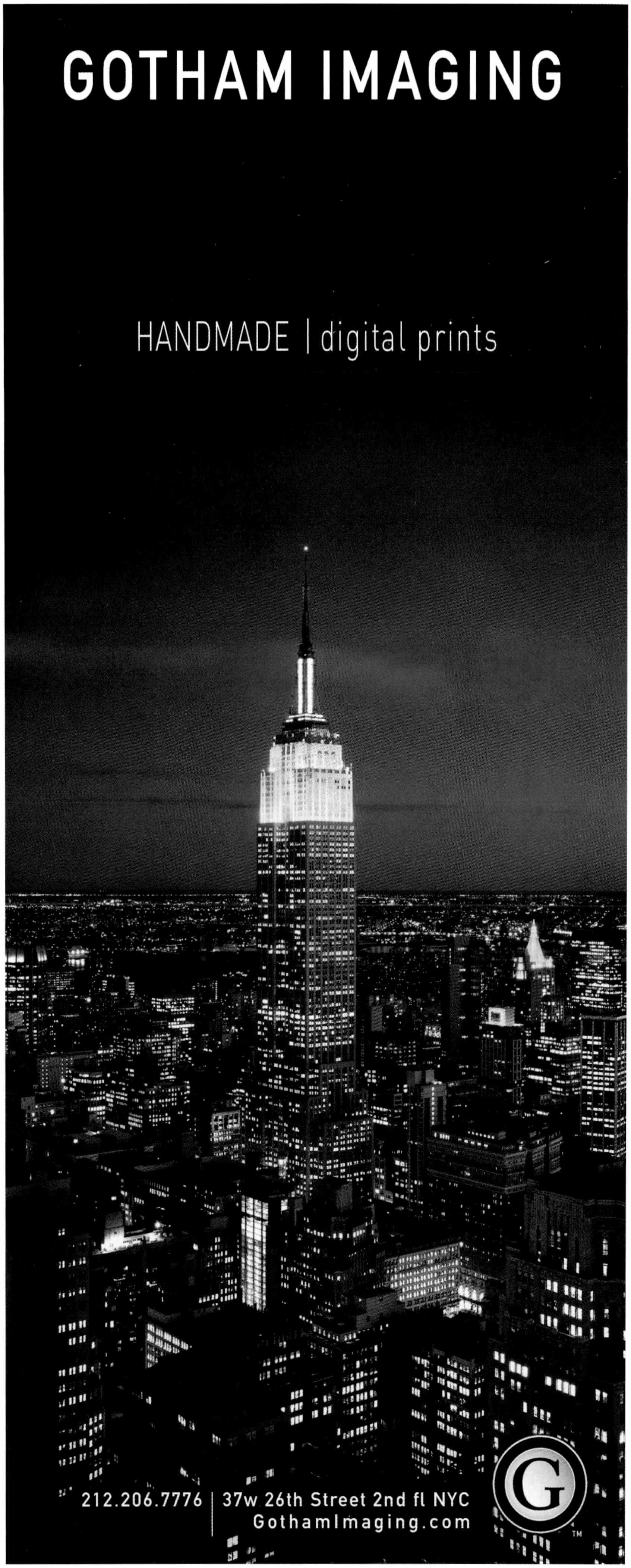

NEIL LaBUTE
ON RUTH ORKIN'S *AN AMERICAN GIRL IN ITALY*, 1951

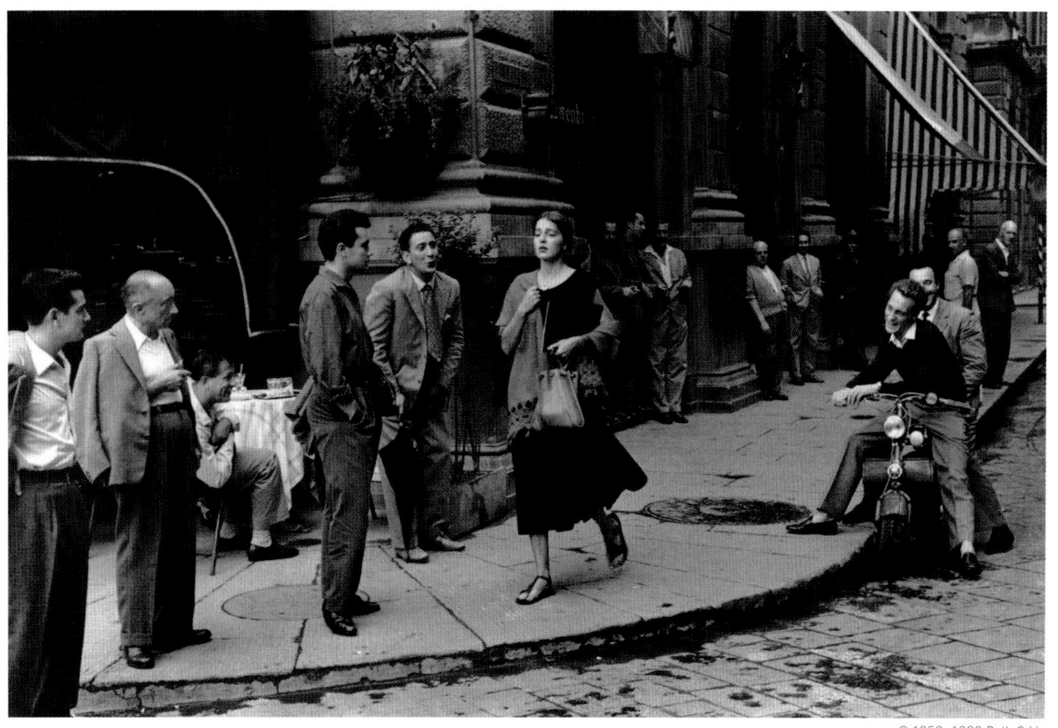

© 1952, 1980 Ruth Orkin

Look at her face.

You've probably seen Ruth Orkin's seminal photograph a dozen or more times in your life, but have you stopped to really look at the young woman's face in the picture? Study the silent anguish etched on her features as she clutches her bag and sketchpad in one hand and pulls her sweater around herself in vain while walking the human gauntlet before her. The fear almost literally leaps off the page. *An American Girl in Italy* is a truly remarkable piece of work and a complete story in itself—if a picture is honestly worth a thousand words, Ms. Orkin managed to capture about fifty thousand words on film that day. It wouldn't take a Raymond Carver to write a collection of short stories from every person's perspective on that street, but you could imagine him doing it and even he might not be able to give full voice to the human spectacle that graced Ms. Orkin's lens in 1951. Like all great art, it appears to be as much a mistake as a planned masterpiece. A millisecond later and from a slightly different angle and this would be the travel shot it was intended to be. As luck would have it, however, one chapter from the history of men and women was forever illustrated by Ruth Orkin on a piece of Kodak photo-paper that day (or whatever she used in the developing process).

I go back to this image time and again just to stare at the drama that Ms. Orkin captured there. I won't waste your time with too many details (the picture was originally part of a series titled *Don't Be Afraid to Travel Alone*, her model was the young art student Jinx Allen, it was shot at the Piazza della Repubblica in Florence, and it appeared first in *Cosmopolitan*) because it just doesn't matter. What matters are those amazing faces—not just the girl but the veritable gallery of rogues who make up the whistling, gawking, staring, challenging men within the frame. It's like the cast of Fellini's *I Vitelloni* got together with their brothers and fathers and uncles and decided to gang up on an innocent girl in broad daylight (a film that this picture predates by two years). It almost makes you a little embarrassed to witness it. Almost. It's also almost impossible to look away. That's the trick of a real classic, no matter the medium—the viewer is forever suspended somewhere between fascination and revulsion.

I actually referred to this picture many times for inspiration when I was making my first film, *In the Company of Men*, in 1997; I knew that I would never be able to capture a moment as pure and complex as this in a fictional film, but the photograph became a kind of touchstone for me. I felt that if I could even come close to creating the kind of anxiety that Ms. Orkin's picture generates in a viewer then I'd have done something worth watching. The success or failure of my own attempt is up to each respective audience, but from this viewer's opinion, Ms. Orkin's work is a complete and resounding success.

An American Girl in Italy makes me feel, makes me think, and makes me gasp. I can ask for nothing more. ◗